新时代智库出版的领跑者

国家智库报告 2022（44）
National Think Tank
国际

发展与合作：中国与阿根廷的视角

王镭 主编　廖凡 徐琼 副主编

DEVELOPMENT AND COOPERATION: PERSPECTIVES OF CHINA AND ARGENTINA

中国社会科学出版社

图书在版编目(CIP)数据

发展与合作：中国与阿根廷的视角／王镭主编 . —北京：中国社会科学出版社，2022.12

（国家智库报告）

ISBN 978 - 7 - 5203 - 8163 - 5

Ⅰ.①发… Ⅱ.①王… Ⅲ.①中外关系—友好往来—研究报告—阿根廷 Ⅳ.①D822.278.3

中国版本图书馆 CIP 数据核字（2021）第 055069 号

出 版 人	赵剑英
项目统筹	王 茵　喻 苗
责任编辑	范晨星　侯聪睿
责任校对	刘 娟
责任印制	李寡寡

出　　版	中国社会科学出版社
社　　址	北京鼓楼西大街甲 158 号
邮　　编	100720
网　　址	http://www.csspw.cn
发 行 部	010 - 84083685
门 市 部	010 - 84029450
经　　销	新华书店及其他书店

印刷装订	北京君升印刷有限公司
版　　次	2022 年 12 月第 1 版
印　　次	2022 年 12 月第 1 次印刷

开　　本	787×1092　1/16
印　　张	15.75
插　　页	2
字　　数	205 千字
定　　价	89.00 元

凡购买中国社会科学出版社图书，如有质量问题请与本社营销中心联系调换
电话：010 - 84083683
版权所有　侵权必究

序　言

1972年，中国与阿根廷建交。建交以来，双边关系发展顺利，各领域互利合作日益深化，两国在国际事务中保持着良好合作。2014年，习近平主席对阿根廷进行国事访问，中阿宣布建立全面战略伙伴关系。2022年2月，习近平主席会见来华出席北京2022年冬奥会开幕式的阿根廷总统费尔南德斯，双方发表《中华人民共和国和阿根廷共和国关于深化中阿全面战略伙伴关系的联合声明》，并签署"一带一路"谅解备忘录等一系列合作文件。

2018年11月底，习近平主席对阿根廷进行国事访问期间，中国社会科学院与阿根廷科技创新部签署《关于设立中国—阿根廷社会科学虚拟中心的协议》并纳入访问成果。

"中国—阿根廷社会科学虚拟中心"作为中阿学术交流合作高端平台，旨在支持中国社会科学院研究人员与阿根廷专家学者就对两国发展与合作具有重要意义的选题开展学术对话，增进相互理解，共同产出成果，为推动中阿全面战略伙伴关系持续深入发展提供智力支持。

中国社会科学院会同阿根廷科技创新部，以"中国—阿根廷社会科学虚拟中心"为平台，组织双方多领域专家围绕社会科学在经济社会发展中的作用、人口转型与城镇化、迈向高质量发展的工业化进程、新冠肺炎疫情后经济社会发展、环境保护与中阿合作机遇、经济全球化、共建"一带一路"等共同关注的问题开展研讨交流,提出中阿在相关领域开展合作的建议。

2022年是中阿建交50周年,双边合作迎来新的契机。值此重要时间节点,中国社会科学院和阿根廷科技创新部合作,将双方专家前期交流主要成果进行梳理形成本书,以期促进两国学术交流互鉴,推动双边关系行稳致远。

Preface

China and Argentina established diplomatic relations in 1972 and the bilateral relations between the two countries have developed smoothly since then. Mutually beneficial cooperation in various fields has deepened, and the two countries have maintained good cooperation in international affairs. Chinese President Xi Jinping paid a state visit to Argentina in 2014, and during the visit, China and Argentina announced the establishment of the comprehensive strategic partnership. In February 2022, Argentine President Alberto Fernandez came to China to attend the opening ceremony of the Beijing 2022 Winter Olympics, and met with Chinese President Xi Jinping. China and Argentina issued a Joint Statement on Deepening China-Argentina Comprehensive Strategic Partnership and signed a Memorandum of Understanding on the Belt and Road Initiative and a series of other cooperation documents.

The Chinese Academy of Social Sciences and the Ministry of Science, Technology and Innovation of the Argentine Republic signed the Agreement on the Creation of the Argentine-Chinese Virtual Center in Social Sciences (hereinafter referred to as the "Virtual Center") when President Xi Jinping paid a state visit to Argentina at the end of November 2018. This agreement was one of the outcomes of the visit.

As a high-level platform for Argentina-China academic exchange and cooperation, the Virtual Center aims to support experts and scholars from the Chinese Academy of Social Sciences and Argentina to conduct academic dialogue on topics of significance for the development and cooperation of the two countries, to enhance mutual understanding, to produce joint research results and to provide intellectual support for promoting sustained and in-depth development of China-Argentina comprehensive strategic partnership.

Under the framework of the Virtual Center, the Chinese Academy of Social Sciences and the Argentine Ministry of Science, Technology and Innovation organized experts of the two countries from various disciplinary backgrounds to carry out exchanges on issues of common concern including the role of social sciences in economic and social development, demographic transition and urbanization, industrialization process towards high-quality development, post-epidemic economic and social development, environmental protection and opportunities for China-Argentina cooperation, economic globalization and Belt and Road cooperation, and put forward suggestions for China-Argentina cooperation in related fields.

The year 2022 marks the 50th anniversary of the establishment of diplomatic relations between China and Argentina, which is a new opportunity for bilateral cooperation. On this important occasion, the Chinese Academy of Social Sciences and the Argentine Ministry of Science, Technology and Innovation have worked jointly to produce this book on the basis of the main results of previous exchanges between experts of the two sides, with a view to promote academic exchanges, mutual learning and long-term and steady bilateral relations between the two countries.

摘要： 阿根廷是拉美第二大国，工业门类较齐全，农牧业发达。中国与阿根廷是全面战略伙伴。建交50年来，中阿双方相互尊重、平等相待，在涉及彼此核心利益和重大关切的问题上相互支持，两国关系经受住了国际风云变幻考验，始终健康稳定发展。两国务实合作顺利推进，传统友谊在团结抗疫中得到升华。双方均坚持多边主义，反对干涉他国内政，维护国际社会公平正义和发展中国家共同利益。目前阿根廷是中国在拉美第六大贸易伙伴，中国是阿根廷全球第二大贸易伙伴。中阿在投融资、能矿、电力、科技、教育、人文等各领域的合作不断深化、前景广阔。

社会科学研究揭示经济社会发展规律，在促进国家发展繁荣、增进人民福祉方面发挥重要作用。面对逆全球化和新冠肺炎疫情冲击等挑战，亟待社会科学研究和回答一系列重大问题。中国和阿根廷有着良好合作基础，有条件也有必要在社会科学领域加强机制性交流，增进共识，促进两国共同发展。

本书梳理分析中国和阿根廷社会科学的演进，围绕重要议题阐析两国发展状况，并在此基础上对加强双方合作提出建议。2022年是中国和阿根廷建交50周年，在社会科学领域进一步开展互学互鉴，将有力促进两国发展战略对接，推动中阿全面战略伙伴关系迈向更高水平。

关键词： 中阿合作；社会科学；经济社会发展；全球化；"一带一路"

Abstract: Argentina is the second largest country in Latin America with relatively complete industrial sectors and developed agriculture and animal husbandry. China and Argentina are comprehensive strategic partners. Over the past 50 years since the establishment of diplomatic relations, China and Argentina have respected each other, treated each other as equals, supported each other on issues of their core interests and major concerns, and the relations between the two countries have withstood the test of international vicissitudes and witnessed healthy and steady development. Practical cooperation between the two countries has been smoothly promoted, and traditional friendship has been sublimated through solidarity to fight against COVID-19. Both sides adhere to multilateralism, oppose interference in the internal affairs of other countries, and safeguard the fairness and justice of the international community and the common interests of developing countries. At present, Argentina is China's sixth largest trading partner in Latin America, and China is Argentina's second largest trading partner in the world. The cooperation between China and Argentina in various fields such as investment and financing, energy and mining, electricity, science and technology, education and people-to-people exchange is constantly deepening with a promising future.

Social science research reveals the law of economic and social development and plays a significant role in promoting a country's development and prosperity and the well-being of the people. Faced with challenges such as de-globalization and the impact of COVID-19, social science research is urgently required to study and answer a series of important questions. With a good foundation of cooperation, China and Argentina have the condition and necessity to strengthen institutional exchanges in the field of social sciences so as to enhance consensus and advance the common development of both countries.

This book reviews the evolution of social sciences in China and Argentina, analyzes the development status of both countries around important issues, and makes suggestions for strengthening bilateral cooperation. 2022 marks the 50th anniversary of diplomatic relations between China and Argentina, and mutual learning in the field of social sciences will actively create synergy between the development strategies of the two countries and promote the China-Argentina comprehensive strategic partnership to a higher level.

Key Words: China-Argentina Cooperation; Social Sciences; Economic and Social Development; Globalization; Belt and Road

目 录

社会科学：在中国经济社会发展中发挥重要作用 ………… （1）

中国的人口转型、城镇化与家庭小型化 ………………… （14）

中国环境保护基本经验及中国—阿根廷合作机遇 ………… （23）

中阿携手共建"一带一路" ………………………………… （35）

工业化进程：迈向高质量发展 ……………………………… （43）

在经济全球化中育新机、开新局 …………………………… （55）

疫情后经济社会发展 ………………………………………… （64）

社会科学研究及其作用：阿根廷的视角 …………………… （72）

中国崛起和"一带一路"倡议下的阿根廷和拉美：
　　建设性融合的相关挑战及建议 ……………………… （88）

Contents

Social Sciences: Play a Significant Role in China's
　　Economic and Social Development ………………… (97)
Demographic Transition, Urbanization and the Trend
　　Towards Smaller Household Size in China ……………… (112)
China's Basic Experience on Environmental Protection and
　　China-Argentina Cooperation Opportunities ……………… (124)
China-Argentina Cooperation under Belt and Road
　　Initiative …………………………………………………… (143)
Industrialization Process: Toward High-Quality
　　Development ………………………………………………… (155)
Economic Globalization: Seeking for New
　　Opportunities and Prospects ……………………………… (173)
Economic and Social Development in the Post
　　COVID-19 Pandemic Era ………………………………… (186)
Social Science Research and Its Role: A Perspective
　　of Argentina ………………………………………………… (200)
Argentina and Latin America under the Rise of China
　　and the Belt and Road Initiative: Challenges
　　and Proposals for a Constructive Integration ……………… (225)

社会科学：在中国经济社会
发展中发挥重要作用[*]

科学研究是人类实现认识世界、改造世界的重要途径。社会科学研究揭示经济社会发展规律，以其研究成果服务于经济社会发展，增进人民福祉。中国的社会科学与中国发展的伟大实践相伴，紧密结合中国实际，在与时俱进的研究探索中，为中国发展提供智力支撑。

一 中国社会科学研究的认识论基础与特质

马克思创立的历史唯物主义和辩证唯物主义为中国社会科学研究提供了科学的世界观和方法论，构成了中国社会科学研究认识论的底层逻辑。

物质与意识是世界的两大基本现象。辩证唯物主义指出，"物质是世界的本质和基础，意识是对物质的能动反映，世界统一于物质；物质决定意识，意识对物质具有反作用"[①]。物质这个概念，在认识论上指的是"不依赖于人的意识而存在并为人

---

[*] 王镭，中国社会科学院国际合作局局长。
[①] 杨河主编：《马克思主义哲学纲要》，北京大学出版社2005年版，第40页。

的意识所反映的客观实在"①。

社会科学的科学性，根本地体现于坚持按照客观世界的本来面目认识世界，一切以事实为依据，实现人的意识对客观实在的正确反映，反对本本主义，排斥主观臆想。

实践是辩证唯物主义、历史唯物主义中的一个核心范畴。其哲学含义是指改造社会和自然的有意识的活动。人类是通过实践去把握物质世界的。中国的社会科学研究与中国发展实践密切相连，并在与中国发展实践的紧密结合中，实现自身的科学性，进而有效发挥其承载的促进经济社会发展的功能。中国的社会科学研究突出体现着以实践为中心的特质。

（一）来自于实践

植根中国实践，理论联系实际，是中国社会科学研究的鲜明特色。在研究选题上，中国的社会科学以研究中国经济社会发展面临的重大理论问题、现实问题为主攻方向，回答时代之问、发展之问。在研究方法上，以实事求是为原则，注重调查研究，紧密结合而不是脱离国情、世情，反对闭门造车，不搞玄空学问。在理论学说上，不以西方教科书为金科玉律，反对机械移植，不搞照搬照抄，积极构建中国特色、中国风格、中国气派的社会科学学科体系、学术体系、话语体系。

（二）服务于实践

经世致用是中国学术的优良传统。服务于国家发展实践是中国社会科学研究的根本出发点和落脚点。社会各界和政府部门构成社会科学研究的需求方。社会科学研究机构为社会提供咨询服务，为各领域政策制订提出建议，对政策实施成效做出

---

① 杨河主编：《马克思主义哲学纲要》，北京大学出版社 2005 年版，第 44 页。

评估。社会科学研究基于学理和科学方法对经验材料进行科学分析，凝结出服务实践的功用价值。

（三）在实践中创新

实践是检验真理的唯一标准，是中国社会科学研究遵循的信条。客观世界和人们的实践活动始终处于运动变化中。社会科学研究不能墨守成规，要不断探究新情况，解决新问题，突破原有局限，修正、拓展、丰富理论和研究方法。实践、认识、再实践、再认识，循环往复，以至无穷，这是人类认识发展的辩证法，也是社会科学创新发展的必由之路。理论只能来自于人的实践活动，理论反过来又指导人的实践，并在经历实践检验的基础上不断完善和发展。

以实践为中心的中国社会科学研究，走出了有自身特色的发展道路，并凭借其以实践为中心的认识论特色和理论特色，在世界社会科学的百花园中绽放光彩。

二 改革开放以来社会科学对中国经济社会发展做出重要贡献

秉承以实践为中心的特质，中国社会科学深深植根于中国实现现代化的发展实践中。1949年中华人民共和国成立后不久，新中国第一代领导人就提出了建设社会主义现代化国家的宏伟目标。1978年召开的中国共产党十一届三中全会作出把党和国家工作重点转移到社会主义现代化建设上来的战略决策，确定以经济建设为中心、实行改革开放。40多年来，中国社会科学为走出一条适合中国国情的发展道路孜孜以求，不懈探索中国现代化建设规律，为丰富和发展中国特色社会主义理论做出了应有贡献。其贡献突出体现在如何处理好如下几方面重大关系上，有效发挥了推动中国经济社会发展的功能。

（一）政府与市场

改革开放以来，中国实现了从传统的计划经济体制到前无古人的社会主义市场经济体制的深刻变革。这其中坚持的根本方向是，在走中国特色社会主义道路前提下，充分发挥市场在资源配置中的决定性作用，更好发挥政府作用。中国社会科学研究积极借鉴国际成熟市场经济制度经验，强调在建设中国特色社会主义市场经济中处理好政府与市场的关系。这包括，一方面尊重市场经济一般规律，最大限度减少政府对市场资源的直接配置和对微观经济活动的直接干预，激发各类市场主体活力，促进生产力发展；另一方面，重视发挥好政府"看得见的手"的作用，有效弥补市场失灵。政府在引入和完善市场竞争机制、营造有序的市场运行环境、为市场构建有力的基础设施条件、发挥再分配调节作用、打造市场经济需要依托的社会安全网等方面，需要做出卓有成效的努力。围绕处理好市场作用与政府作用辩证关系，中国经济运行的体制机制不断改进和完善，推动实现中国经济快速、健康发展。

（二）国有与民营

实行改革开放40多年来，中国实现了从单一公有制到公有制为主体、多种所有制经济共同发展的深刻变革。公有制为主体、多种所有制经济共同发展确立为中国的基本经济制度。围绕国有经济与民营经济关系，中国社会科学界深入研究一系列重大问题，包括公有制经济、非公有制经济财产权的保护；实现各种所有制经济权利平等、机会平等、规则平等；优化国有经济布局，做强做优做大国有资本；同时，非国有资本参与国有企业改革，更好激发非公有制经济活力和创造力等。改革开放以来，中国的非公有制经济在国家政策引导下发展起来，民营经济贡献了中国经济60%以上的GDP。在中国经济构成中，国有经济和民营经济并非相互对立，而是发挥各自比较优势，相互合作，共同驱动着中国经济成长。

（三）城市与农村

1949年中华人民共和国成立后，中国依靠农业农村支持，在一穷二白的农业社会基础上推动工业化、城镇化。特别是改革开放40多年来，依靠农村劳动力、土地、资金等要素支撑，快速推进工业化、城镇化，中国的城市面貌发生翻天覆地的变化。着眼长期以来城乡发展不平衡这一中国基本国情，中国社会科学界始终将如何调整城乡关系、工农关系作为重大研究方向，深入农村、城镇调研，针对城市支持农村、优先发展农业、推进农业农村现代化、走城乡融合发展之路等提出重要政策建议，为加快农业农村发展、推进经济社会现代化转型提供有力智力支撑。1978年中国常住人口城镇化率为17.9%，到2019年，已提升到60.6%，其间数以亿计的农民进入城镇。2021年，中国如期打赢脱贫攻坚战，7亿多农村贫困人口彻底摆脱绝对贫困。到2021年从中国经济三次产业结构看，已经从1981年的33.4∶44.8∶21.8，转变为2019年的7.1∶39.0∶53.9，实现了从传统农业社会向现代工业社会的跃升。[①] 中国成为世界上唯一拥有联合国产业分类中全部工业门类的国家，建立了全世界最完整的现代工业体系，成为世界制造业第一大国，成功走出了一条快速推进工业化的道路，用几十年时间走完了发达国家几百年走过的工业化进程。

（四）公平与效率

中国共产党作为执政党高度重视不断加强和改善国家治

[①] 谢伏瞻：《全面建成小康社会的理论与实践》，《中国社会科学》2020年第12期。

理，实现了同时创造经济快速发展和社会长期稳定两个奇迹。既做大蛋糕、又分好蛋糕，处理好公平与效率的关系，是同时创造"两个奇迹"的根本原由。中国社会科学界从实现共同富裕这一中国特色社会主义制度本质要求出发，始终关注如何解决收入差距、城乡差距、地区差距等问题，深入研究收入分配制度改革、基本公共服务均等化、构建社会保障体系、加强法治建设、健全民主制度等重大课题，提出相关发展与改革方案。中国作为有 14 亿多人口的大国，已经建成了包括养老、医疗、低保、住房在内的世界最大的社会保障体系，人民获得感、幸福感、安全感不断增强。面对突如其来的新冠肺炎疫情，秉持人民至上、生命至上，国家采取最坚决、最彻底的防控措施，有效遏制疫情蔓延，科学医治病患，最大限度的保护了人民生命安全和身体健康，同时有序实现复工复产，经济发展稳定转好，中国的组织、治理体系经受住了疫情带来的世纪大考，展现出特有的韧性和优势。以中国特色社会主义制度为根基，在不断促进社会公平正义基础上，中国实现了经济社会健康持续发展。

（五）国内与国际

中国改革开放 40 多年的一条基本启示是，"开放带来进步，封闭必然落后"①。中国将对外开放确立为基本国策，为中国发展拓展了空间，也为世界发展带来机遇。中国社会科学界深入研究如何在积极主动参与经济全球化进程中统筹用好国内国际两个市场两种资源；如何有效引入境外直接投资，带来中国发展所需的资金、技术、管理经验；如何实现中国出口贸易持续增长，创造中国发展所需的就业、外汇等；如

---

① 习近平：《论坚持全面深化改革》，中央文献出版社 2019 年版，第 519 页。

何增加进口,更好满足国内市场对高质量产品的需求,促进国际经贸平衡可持续发展;如何在中国企业"走出去"中发挥好自身优势,塑造对外投资国际竞争力等。经过40多年改革开放,中国实现了由封闭半封闭到全方位开放的历史转变。中国与世界经济已经深度融合,成为货物贸易第一大国,外资流入第二大国,外汇储备连续多年位居世界第一,多年来对世界经济增长的贡献率超过30%。

以上这些重大关系,也是许多发展中国家在寻求经济社会发展中共同面临的重大课题。基于中国改革开放实践,中国社会科学界在深入研究、探索中,为处理好这些重大关系建言献策,为成功走出中国式现代化道路贡献了智慧。

三 面向未来 30 年:社会科学在中国发展新时代担当新使命

2021年是中国现代化进程中具有标志性的一年,中国如期实现全面建成小康社会目标,也是中国"十四五"开局之年。按照《中华人民共和国国民经济和社会发展第十四个五年规划和2035年远景目标纲要》(简称"十四五"规划和2035年远景目标纲要),到2035年中国将基本实现社会主义现代化,到本世纪中叶建成富强民主文明和谐美丽的社会主义现代化强国。未来30年,将是中国实现建设社会主义现代化国家目标的新发展阶段。

习近平主席深刻指出,"理念是行动的先导,一定的发展实践都是由一定的发展理念来引领的。发展理念是否对头,从根本上决定着发展成效乃至成败"。[①] 面对新发展阶段,中国提出

[①] 习近平:《论把握新发展阶段、贯彻新发展理念、构建新发展格局》,中央文献出版社2021年版,第475页。

贯彻创新、协调、绿色、开放、共享的发展理念，统称为新发展理念。新发展理念回答了在新发展阶段实现什么样的发展、怎样实现发展这个重大问题。新发展理念是一个系统的理论体系，回答了关于发展的目的、动力、方式、路径等一系列理论和实践问题。未来30年，中国的社会科学研究将在新发展理念这个系统的理论体系引领下展开，结合新发展阶段中国发展面临的突出挑战，捕捉新问题，给出新解答。

（一）科技进步挑战

科学技术是第一生产力。经过改革开放40多年的努力，中国实现了科技实力显著提升，一些领域从跟跑向领跑转变，彻底改变了科技水平全面落后的局面，为经济社会发展铸就了强大引擎。自2013年起，中国已成为世界第二大研发经费投入国[1]，研发人员总量稳居世界第一[2]。专利申请数和授权数居于世界首位。同时，中国的科技创新能力总体上还不适应高质量发展要求，一些产业发展和国家安全的关键核心技术受制于人，原始创新能力不强。只有进一步壮大国家科技实力，才能催生新发展动能，赢得竞争和发展的主动权。在新发展阶段，中国科技发展的奋斗目标是，创新能力显著提升，到2035年科技实力将大幅跃升，关键核心技术实现重大突破，进入创新型国家前列[3]；到2050年建成世界科技强国[4]。为此，

---

[1] 陆雅楠：《我国研发经费投入强度创新高》，《人民日报》2019年9月1日第1版。

[2] 国家统计局：《科技发展大跨越 创新引领谱新篇》，国家统计局网站，2019年7月23日。

[3] 王志刚：《担当科技自立自强使命 加快建设科技强国步伐》，《科技日报》2020年11月30日第1版。

[4] 王志刚：《中国到2050年要成为世界科技强国》，中国新闻网，2019年3月11日。

围绕有效提升科技自主创新能力这一关键命题，中国社会科学界亟待研究如何通过改进制度安排，使政府力量和市场力量协同发力，用好多方资源，攻克重大科技难题；如何有效强化企业创新主体地位，加强对企业科技创新活动的激励；如何深化高水平大学教育和基础研究领域改革，持续加大基础研究，解决在部分关键技术领域面临的"卡脖子"难题；如何增强产学研用有机结合，建立创新联合体，协同突破产业技术瓶颈；如何发挥中国超大规模市场和完备产业体系优势，创造有利于科技成果产业化应用和迭代升级的有利环境，加速科技成果向现实生产力转化；如何完善资本市场建设，拓宽直接融资渠道，为科技创新提供有力金融支持；如何进一步加强知识产权保护，营造公平竞争市场环境，使创新投入得到合理回报等。此外，以数字化、智能化为特征的第四次工业革命浪潮带动社会生产力解放和生活水平提升的同时，也带来科技应用的道德和伦理风险、数字鸿沟、贫富分化、市场垄断等挑战，迫切需要社会科学研究提出相应的规制和约束方案。

（二）人口变化挑战

中国人口变化呈现的基本趋势是人口自然增长率持续走低，人均预期寿命延长，老龄化程度快速提升。按照国际标准，65岁以上老年人口占比超过7%就步入老龄化社会。2019年，中国65岁以上的人口占比为12.57%。[1] 一方面，人口抚养比下降的时期已经结束，人口红利削减，社会养老负担加重。另一方面，2004年开始中国人口结构出现刘易斯拐点，农村富余劳动力向非农产业转移达到瓶颈状态；自2012年，中国16—59岁

---

[1] 韩保江主编：《"十四五"〈纲要〉新概念》，人民出版社2021年版，第194页。

劳动年龄人口数量和占总人口比重出现下降[①]。随着新增劳动力减少，劳动力成本上升，劳动力供给开始出现结构性短缺。伴随劳动力等要素供给状况变化，制造业在经济中占比总体出现下降，在服务业整体层次不高的状况下，拖累经济总体劳动生产率的增长；老龄社会中消费率相对下降，经济增长需求动力相对减弱。面对人口老龄化带来的多重问题，迫切需要社会科学界结合中国实际寻求破解之道，主要包括，如何通过发展教育和提升劳动力素质，形成新的人口红利；如何加快科技进步、结构调整等提升全要素生产率和潜在增长率；如何改革户籍制度，优化劳动力城乡间配置效率；如何提升社会保障水平，为经济转型提供社会安全网，又统筹考虑需要和可能，避免落入高福利负担陷阱等。

（三）生态环境挑战

自工业革命以来，人类活动大量排放二氧化碳，是导致气候变化的主要因素。气候变化对人类可持续生存发展带来了重大威胁，走低碳发展之路已成为国际社会共识。40多年来，中国实现经济快速增长，但也付出了较高的环境、资源代价。着眼可持续发展，中国实行日趋严格的生态环境保护政策。2020年9月，习近平主席在联合国大会上宣布，中国力争于2030年前实现二氧化碳排放达到峰值，2060年前实现碳中和。从发达国家的经历看，从二氧化碳达峰到实现碳中和，要经历40—70年，中国目标用30年时间实现此过程，将完成全球最高碳排放降幅。减排降碳将成为中国促进经济社会发展全面绿色转型的总抓手，是一场深刻的社会生产生活变革。为此，中国社会科学界需深入研究如何编制实现碳达峰、碳中和行动方案，编制

---

① 李希如：《人口总量平稳增长　城镇化水平稳步提高》，国家统计局网站，2019年1月23日。

和实施好各地和各行业部门的应对气候变化和生态环境保护规划；2019 年，清洁能源占中国能源消费比重为 23.4%，煤炭消费占比为 57.7%，[①] 如何实现当前中国以煤为主的能源消耗结构，转变为以清洁、可再生能源为主的结构；如何实施能源行业的基础设施、设备的重组和改造；如何大力提升能源使用的效率，降低单位 GDP 二氧化碳排放；如何重点发展新能源汽车、低碳交通基础设施等，全面推进工业、建筑、交通、公共机构等领域的节能降耗；如何为能源结构乃至经济基础的转型提供足够的资金支持；如何提升全社会低碳发展意识，改变片面追求 GDP 增长的陈旧发展观念、消费观念，实现经济发展、改善环境、提高生活水平相辅相成，互为促进；如何加强排放和环境保护监督检查等。

（四）逆全球化挑战

突如其来的新冠肺炎疫情肆虐全球，全球产业链供应链运行受阻，贸易和投资活动持续低迷，2008 年国际金融危机以来就已遭遇逆流的经济全球化正经历更大挫折。然而，经济全球化是社会生产力发展的客观要求和科技进步的必然结果，从长期看经济全球化的历史潮流不可逆转。中国始终支持经济全球化，反对单边主义、保护主义，反对利用疫情搞"去全球化"、搞封闭脱钩。面对来自逆全球化以及外部环境的诸多新变化，中国提出加快构建以国内大循环为主体、国内国际双循环相互促进的新发展格局。新发展格局强调立足自身，把国内大循环畅通起来，有效应对外部逆全球化的风潮，确保中国经济始终保持内生活力。同时，构建新发展格局不是关门，不是封闭的国内循环，而是更加开放的国内国际双循环，强调实施更大范

[①] 国务院新闻办公室：《〈新时代的中国能源发展〉白皮书》，2020 年 12 月 21 日。

围、更宽领域、更深层次对外开放，着力建设更高水平开放型经济新体制。畅通国内国际双循环，是新阶段中国实现发展目标的基本路径，也是中国社会科学界着力研究的重大主题。为此，要深入探讨相对于以往以外需为主的发展路径如何转化为以扩大内需为战略基点、内需主导、内生增长的新发展模式，打造稳固的经济基本盘；如何把实施扩大内需战略同深化供给侧结构性改革有机结合起来，优化升级产业结构，提升供给质量，形成需求牵引供给、供给创造需求的更高水平经济动态平衡；如何实行更加积极主动的开放战略，推动由商品和要素流动型开放向规则等制度型开放转变，全面对接国际高标准市场规则体系；如何在更多领域允许外资控股或独资经营，促进内外资企业公平竞争，打造市场化、法治化、国际化的营商环境；如何在扩大金融开放条件下，有效防范国际金融风险；如何加快在国内设立的自由贸易试验区、自由贸易港建设，将其在扩大开放、推进贸易投资自由化、便利化方面取得的改革经验，在更大范围复制推广；如何推进贸易高质量发展，拓展对外贸易多元化，提高一般贸易出口产品附加值，推动加工贸易产业链升级和服务贸易创新发展；如何维护完善多边贸易体制，加快国际自由贸易区建设，积极依托多边和区域次区域合作机制，构建全球互联互通伙伴关系；如何有效促进国际宏观经济政策沟通协调及全球经济治理体系改革和建设，更好实现中国与世界的合作共赢；如何健全促进对外投资政策和服务体系，同时应对好对中国企业的围堵打压，保障中国企业对外投资安全利益；如何践行好共商共建共享原则，推进高质量共建"一带一路"，使之成为连接国内国际双循环的重要纽带等。

生产力的发展是经济社会形态变化的根本决定力量。上述挑战涉及科技、人口、资源、商品、资金等要素的国际流动与配置，是影响生产力状态、水平及其变迁的关键因素。处于新发展阶段的中国，虽然面临上述挑战，但只要积极有为地应对好挑战,就能将挑战转化为机遇,其中蕴含着巨大的发展潜力和前景。面向未来30年中国新发展阶段,中国社会科学研究将继续秉持理论联系实际、实事求是的基本原则,依托经济学、社会学、政治学、历史学等各学科专业,在应对挑战中发现问题、分析问题、解决问题,并在其中不断丰富理论和方法,提升为中国经济社会发展实践服务的能力和水平。

四 结语

自工业革命以来,人类社会在现代化这一历史变革中前行。第二次世界大战后,古典现代化理论、依附理论、世界体系理论、后现代理论、再现代化理论等相继出现,国际学术界对现代化过程的认识逐步拓展深化。中国同广大发展中国家和新兴经济体一样,都进行着现代化道路的艰辛探索。中国依据自身国情,坚定走中国特色社会主义道路,以此作为其现代化道路的根本选择。1978年中国实行改革开放以来,围绕建设什么样的中国特色社会主义,怎样建设中国特色社会主义这一基本主题,中国社会科学工作者深入实际,客观认识中国发展实践,探索中国现代化建设规律,回答经济社会发展面临的理论和现实问题,为走出一条适合中国国情的发展道路做出了应有贡献。

世界上不存在放之四海而皆准的现代化模式、现代化标准。各国只能依据各自国情,走符合自身特点的现代化道路。正是因为实现现代化道路的多样性,应当积极促进在各国社会科学界之间开展广泛、深入对话,相互交流、借鉴发展经验,同时发现各国发展中的利益交汇点,促进实现共同发展繁荣。

中国的人口转型、城镇化与家庭小型化[*]

一 中国人口结构的变化

从全球来看,中国作为第一人口大国,其年龄结构的变迁,不仅影响本国的劳动力市场与消费需求的变化路径,而且还对世界的产业结构布局与移民趋势发挥着重要引导作用。现在,中国已经从成年型人口转变为老龄化人口。中国的人口政策,也从计划生育时期过渡到生育政策调整时期,并很快会发展到自主生育时期。

1949 年,中国人口的平均预期寿命为 35 岁左右。伴随社会的安定与经济的发展,预期寿命逐步提高。加之婴幼儿死亡率的降低,中国的人口总量直线上升。1953 年总人口为 5.8 亿人,1964 年攀升到 6.9 亿人,1982 年改革开放之初攀升到 10.03 亿人,1990 年达到 11.3 亿人,2000 年达到 12.67 亿人,2010 年达到 13.4 亿人,2017 年年底达到 13.9 亿人左右[①],2019 年超过

---

[*] 张翼,中国社会科学院社会发展战略研究院院长。

[①] 此为国家统计局数据,而根据 2017 年《中国统计年鉴》表 2-1 的数据,1982 年的总人口是 10.16 亿人,1990 年是 11.43 亿人,2000 年是 12.67 亿人。也就是说,自 2000 年第五次人口普查之后,数据与原来公布的一致。2017 年年底的数据来自于《中华人民共和国 2017 年国民经济和社会发展统计公报》。

14亿人。

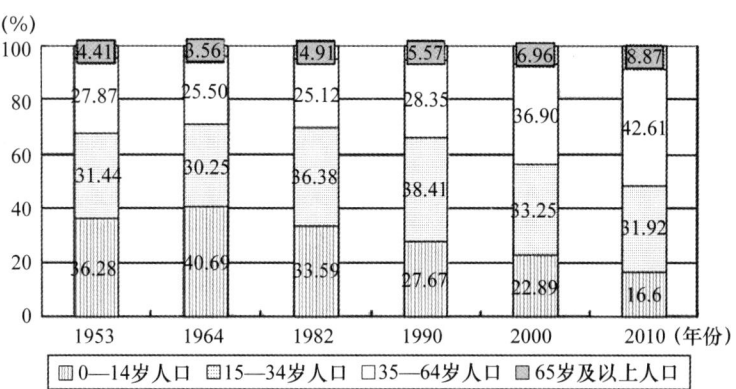

图1 中国六次人口普查分年龄段的人口结构

从年龄结构来说，在1953年第一次人口普查时，0—14岁少儿人口所占比重为36.28%，15—34岁青年人口所占比重为31.44%，35—64岁人口所占比重为27.87%，65岁及以上老年人口所占比重为4.41%。在1964年第二次人口普查时，0—14岁少儿人口所占比重为40.69%，15—34岁青年人口所占比重为30.25%，35—64岁人口所占比重为25.50%，65岁及以上老年人口所占比重为3.56%。但到2000年第五次人口普查时，0—14岁少儿人口所占比重就降低到22.89%，15—34岁青年人口所占比重下降为33.25%，35—64岁人口所占比重上升为36.90%，65岁及以上老年人口所占比重上升为6.96%。大体来说，学术界认为2000年左右中国进入老龄化行列。

2019年年底，0—15岁（含不满16周岁）人口所占比重为17.8%，16—59岁人口所占比重为64.0%，60岁及以上老年人口所占比重增长到18.1%，65岁及以上老年人口占总人口的比重上升到12.6%。按照学术界的预测，中国65岁及以上老年人口占总人口的比重可能会在2022年左右上升到14%左右。

表1　　　　　　　　　　2019年中国人口结构

指标	年末数（万人）	比重（%）
全国总人口	140005	100.0
其中：城镇	84843	60.6
乡村	55162	39.4
其中：男性	71527	51.1
女性	68478	48.9
其中：0—15岁（含不满16周岁）	24977	17.8
16—59岁（含不满60周岁）	89640	64.0
60岁及以上	25388	18.1
其中：65岁及以上	17603	12.6

在国际上，如果65岁及以上人口占总人口的比重达到14%，则这个国家会进入老龄型国家的行列。从这里可以看出，中国从老龄化时期进入老龄型时期，可能只用20—22年的时间。在人口大国中，中国是迄今为止老龄化速度最快的国家。中国的发展，是压缩式的现代化发展。中国在几十年的时间走过了发达国家几百年走过的人口转型之路。这种快速转型在制造发展之人口红利的同时，也为未来的发展蕴含了极高的老龄化压力。

为什么中国在改革开放以来会保持长达40多年的快速增长，其答案可以概况为以下几点：其一是少儿人口的快速下降降低了少儿抚养比，扩大了劳动力人口的绝对供给和相对供给。其二是减轻了家庭压力，增加了家庭积累，使父母亲可以将有限的积累集中在较少的子女身上，迅速提升子女的人力资本。其三是改革开放吸引了外资，使资本与劳动力有效结合，在土地等资源的廉价供给中赢得增长机会。其四是通过户籍制度改革释放了流动红利，使劳动力通过市场的配置提升了经济效率。在其他人文环境和自然环境不变的情况下，这些变化可以对中国的长时段增长提供可信的解释。迄今为止，少儿人口（0—15

岁）在总人口当中所占比重还比较低，16—59 岁之间劳动力人口所占比重比较大，60 岁及以上老年人口所占比重虽然有所提高，但总抚养比仍然较低。这正是中国能够全面建成小康社会的根本支持力量。

从近期的观察也可以看出，中国大约在 2025 年以后（现在有不同的估计，如果以最近每年出生 1400 万名左右婴儿估计），即在 2025—2028 年左右，中国总人口会达到峰值，超过 14.2 亿人，然后开始掉头向下，进入人口缩减时期。所以说，小康社会建成以后中国社会老龄化水平会迅速攀升，到 2035 年左右，65 岁及以上老年人占总人口的比重会超过 20%。此后一直快速攀升，到 2050 年超过 30%。

为什么中国人口的老龄化速度如此之快呢？可能的回答是：

其一，中国的人口老化，是双重因素影响的人口老化，即在计划生育政策和经济社会发展两个因素的影响下，迅速发生从成年型人口向老龄化人口和老龄型人口的转化。改革开放以来的 40 多年，计划生育政策历经从适度转入严控再到适度放开三个阶段。在 1980 年之后，城镇只能一对夫妇生育一个孩子，农村根据人口密集程度与少数民族总人口的数量情况，有的实行"一孩政策"，有的实行"二孩政策"，有的实行不控制生育的政策。但总体趋势是越来越严。直到 2013 年之后，才开始放松，即从"单独二孩"转变为 2016 年的"全面二孩"。但改革政策的红利有限，2016 年出生 1786 万人，2017 年出生 1723 万人，2019 年只出生了 1465 万人。这是政策设计之初未曾预料到的（按照政策预期，应该比改革前每年多出生 300 万人到 400 万人）。出生人口的下降，其直接的原因在于适婚青年人口所占比例的下降。

其二是人口流动改变了青年人口的生育意愿，中国发生了农业社会人口生育模式向工业社会人口生育模式的重大转型，接着又发生了向后工业社会人口生育模式的重大转型。在农业社会,死亡率较高,只有多生才能维持家庭的繁衍。在工业社会,死亡率迅速降低,出生率迅速上升,自然增长率迅速上升。在后工业社会,低出生率、低死亡率、低自然增长率会成为常态。正因为如此,我们才必须认识到社会转型对人口转型所造成的持续性和长期性影响,而不能仅仅将当前出生率的下降解释为生活成本的上升。

其三是人力资本、女性解放、城镇化所造成的家庭模式的重大转型。中国改革开放以来的教育平等,促进了女性人力资本的迅速提升。女性受教育年限的延长以及城镇化所带来的人口流动,将女性的初婚年龄大大推迟。改革开放之初,因为"晚婚晚育"的影响,城镇的初婚年龄一度推迟,但农村初婚年龄推迟有限。在20世纪80年代,初婚年龄一度下降。但在90年代之后,整个中国女性的初婚年龄显著提升,大约在2005年前后推迟到23—24岁左右。目前,在大城市和特大城市,女性的初婚年龄推迟到27—28岁,有些城市甚至于推迟到29—30岁左右。女性受教育年数的延长,提升了其在家庭中的社会地位。社会保障制度的广覆盖,又增加了女性独立生活的能力。现在,"自愿不婚"与"被动未婚"的人群在30岁以下人口中所占比例迅速上升,这使"青年空巢"与"老年空巢"并存。其中最显著的变化是,不仅未婚人口增加,已婚人口的离婚率也迅速上升。在改革开放之初的1985年,全年结婚对数为831.3万对,离婚对数为45.79万对;在2010年,全年结婚对数为1241万对,离婚对数为267.8万对;在2015年,全年结婚对数继续下降到1224.71万对,离婚对数上升到384.14万对;在2019年,全年结婚对数继续下降到927.33万对,离婚对数上升到470.06万对。从这里可以看出,离婚对数趋于上升,结婚对数趋于下降。

在这种情况下,中国的人口战略,必须从人口大国向人力资源强国转变,必须从劳动力人口相对占比较高的人口红利向科技创新和人力资本为主的第二次人口红利开发转变，必须从中国制造向中国创新大国转变。唯有如此，才能完成党的十九大绘制的2035年基本实现现代化和2050年实现现代化中国梦蓝图。

二 人口迁移、城镇化与家庭小型化

1949年，中国城市人口占总人口的比重只有10.64%。1978年的改革开放之初，城市人口占比为17.92%，农村人口占比为82.08%。

改革开放之后，城市化的动力主要来源于以下几个方面：其一是城市或城镇的拉动——农村人口流动到城市或城镇；其二是农村的本地城镇化——即在城市的扩张或农村本身的非农化影响下农村地区成建制地转变为城市或城镇；其三是城镇内部的人户分离与城市到城市之间的人口流动——在大城市的拉力之下，中国加速了人口的大城市化。

受此影响，如表2所示，中国的城市化率逐年提升，城市人口比重1985年达到23.71%，1990年达到26.41%，1995年达到29.04%，2000年达到36.22%，2005年达到42.99%，2010年达到49.95%，2015年达到56.10%，2019年达到60.60%。这是依据常住人口的分布状况进行的判断，即依据一个人在一个地方居住满6个月而进行的调查统计。如果以3个月为标准，则城市化率会更高。但如果以白天的时点人口计算，则中国的城市化率很可能已超过75%——这应该是发达国家完成工业化之后的城乡分布状况。

中国城乡结构的变化，不仅改变了城市与乡村之间的人口分布，而且改变了人们的生活方式，也即中国在短短的几十年之中，就成功将绝大多数人口从农业上解放出来，并使之迁居到城市或城镇居住。居住形态的改变，也在很大程度上改变了人们的生活方式，使农民从定居型社会转变为迁居型社会，使人们从熟人社会转变为陌生人社会，使人们从自给自足社会转变为市场交易社会，同时也使人们从大家庭结构转变为小家庭结构或个体化生存模式。

表2　　　　　　　　中国城乡结构的历史变化

年份	总人口（年末）	城市人口比重（%）	农村人口比重（%）	年份	总人口（年末）	城市人口比重（%）	农村人口比重（%）
1950	55196	11.18	88.82	1978	96259	17.92	82.08
1955	61465	13.48	86.52	1985	105851	23.71	76.29
1960	66207	19.75	80.25	1990	114333	26.41	73.59
1965	72538	17.98	82.02	1995	121121	29.04	70.96
1970	82992	17.38	82.62	2000	126743	36.22	63.78
1971	85229	17.26	82.74	2005	130756	42.99	57.01
1972	87177	17.13	82.87	2010	134091	49.95	50.05
1973	89211	17.20	82.80	2015	137462	56.10	43.90
1974	90859	17.16	82.84	2017	139008	58.52	41.48
1975	92420	17.34	82.66	2019	140005	60.60	39.40

注：1.1981年及以前数据为户籍统计数；1990年、2000年、2010年数据为当年人口普查数据推算数；其余年份数据为年度人口抽样调查推算数据。2. 总人口和按性别分人口中包括现役军人，按城乡分人口中现役军人计入城镇人口。

即使居住在农村的居民，也不再单纯依靠农业生活，而可能依靠非农业而生活。也就是说，中国的农村已不是传统意义的农村。现在，中国农村所形成的阶层结构表现为：农业企业主阶层、村干阶层、农村居民阶层、农民工阶层和职业农民阶层。所以说中国农民，即传统意义上的农民，在农村居民当中存在的比重已迅速下降，职业农民比重虽然在上升，但上升速度还比较慢。农业科学技术的进步与机械化水平的提升，以及农地的加速流转等，在很大程度上提高了农业生产的效率。未来，职业农民的种田能力还会迅速提升。在自动化技术被农业部门使用之后，大约3%—5%的职业农民就可以满足已经流转的土地的耕作需求。中国再也不用将主要劳动力投放在农业生产上，中国在现代化过程中完全可以以中国的地养中国的人。中国只有18亿亩耕地，如果将荒坡地和干旱地去掉，良田不足10亿亩。如果未来土地仍然如过去的几年那样流转，则用不了多长时间，农村就会转变为以居民为主的农村，而不可能继续表现为以农民为主的农村。因此，最后一代传统农民正站在现代化的十字路口，选择着未来的职业道路。

中国城市在经历四十多年的"摊大饼"式扩张后，其建成区面积有了长足的增长。但户籍制度仍然对基本公共服务起着重要配置作用。正因为如此，城市逐渐形成了户籍人口和非户籍人口的区隔居住状态。几乎在所有的大城市和特大城市，或者在所有的超大城市，都形成城市中心区人口为户籍人口，而环带人口为流动人口的格局。流动人口主要由两部分组成，其一是城市到城市的流动人口，其二是农村流动到城市的人口。城市越大，非户籍人口所占的比重就越大，户籍人口跟当地人口倒挂现象就越严重。如北京和上海，都有差不多800万—900万的非户籍人口。在深圳市，流动人口的数量大大超过了户籍人口的数量。另外，像北京、上海这样的超大城市，虽然户籍人口总人数比流动人口稍微高一点，但在流动人口群居的地方，形成了本地户籍人口少而外地流动人口多的局面，在社会形态上形成了大分居、小居住状况。于是，原来的城乡二元结构，就转变为城市内部的户籍人口与外地人口的新二元结构。

在现代化建设过程中，中国正在通过户籍人口的城镇化打破这一结构的张力，形成户籍人口与流动人口的和谐相处局面，并彻底解决基本公共服务的均等化问题。

人口流动与跨区域的迁移，形成了以农民工为主的迁移家庭。与此同时，未能迁移进城市的人口则形成留守家庭。家庭人口的城乡分割,在形成成年夫妻与未成年子女所组成的核心家庭的基础上,也增加了夫妻家庭的比重。这直接导致了中国家庭的小型化趋势。到2019年,中国的家庭户规模已经降低到只有2.92人,但北京、上海和天津的家庭户规模则分别降低到只有2.56人、2.38人和2.65人。对整个东北地区来说,家庭户规模都比较小,比如说,辽宁、吉林和黑龙江三省的家庭户规模分别下降到2.54人、2.60人和2.47人。生育率的降低与人口迁移这两个因素的影响,是家庭户规模人口长期下降的主要原因。结婚率的降低与结婚年龄的推迟,是家庭户规模最近下降的主要原因。

中国环境保护基本经验及中国—阿根廷合作机遇[*]

一 引言

中国和阿根廷是两个具有独特国情的国家。为实现现代化目标，中国和阿根廷根据自己的国情，探索了不同的发展道路。在经济发展方面，两国经济发展均取得了很大的成绩，目前正处于实现现代化的关键阶段。两国同为二十国集团（G20）成员，在世界上具有重要影响力。与此同时，两国也面临着共同的生态环境问题。1978年改革开放后，中国从一个人均GDP只有156美元的贫穷国家，成为人均GDP超过1万美元的全球第二大经济体。2020年11月，中国832个国家级贫困县全部脱贫摘帽。2021年2月，习近平总书记宣告中国脱贫攻坚战取得了全面胜利。2021年7月，习近平总书记宣告中国已在中华大地上全面建成了小康社会。但是，由于传统工业化模式下环境与发展之间存在内在冲突，中国也面临严峻的环境危机。阿根廷的地理和自然条件优越，在20世纪早期人均收入曾一度进入世界前十之列，直到20世纪中叶仍然是第十五大经济体，之后由于政局不稳、汇率等各种原因，经济出现下滑和波动。2019年，

---

[*] 张永生，中国社会科学院生态文明研究所所长。本报告参考了作者的相关研究成果（张永生，2020）和作者相关课题的讨论成果。

阿根廷人均 GDP 约为 1 万美元，2020 年因为疫情下降到 8356 美元。

在快速工业化过程中，中国出现了大量环境问题。在党的十八大之前，中国关于环境与发展之间关系的认识，经历了曲折的探索过程。中国在不同时期为解决环境问题而采取的不同政策及其经验教训，就是对环境与发展关系的认识不断加深的过程。中国在党的十八大之后提出新发展理念，并形成完整的生态文明思想，不只是源于中国发展模式面临的特殊问题，背后更是工业革命后传统发展模式不可持续的普遍问题。党的十九大报告进一步提出，中国要建设的现代化，是"人与自然和谐共生"的现代化。

这个探索过程产生的思想成果和实践经验，可以成为全人类的公共知识，对中阿双方的合作有着借鉴意义。本文旨在对中国在环境保护方面的基本做法和经验进行介绍，并揭示其对中阿合作的一般性含义，为中阿环境保护合作提供相关背景知识。至于具体的合作领域与方式，则有待深入识别和进一步研究。

二 中国环境保护的艰辛探索和实践[①]

（一）关于环境保护与发展之间关系认识的演变过程

1949 年中华人民共和国成立后很长一段时间，由于工业化水平低下，工业污染还未普遍出现，加上受经典教科书影响，人们认为只有资本主义才有环境问题，社会主义不存在环境污染问题，环境问题也就未引起人们足够重视。中国于 1972 年参加联合国人类环境大会和 1973 年召开第一次全国环境保护会

---

① 张永生：《生态文明体制改革》，载谢伏瞻主编《中国改革开放的伟大实践》，中国社会科学出版社 2020 年版。

议，具有启蒙和里程碑意义。中国开展环境保护方面的工作，大体上与国际同步，均始于1972年的联合国人类环境大会。后来虽然看到社会主义也存在环境问题，但中国当时普遍相信，社会主义的优越性可以解决发展中出现的环境问题。

1978年改革开放后，中国的工作重点转入以经济建设为中心。很长一段时期，由于经济规模不大，上述认识并没有受到真正严峻的考验。随着改革开放成效日益显现，尤其是在1992年邓小平南方谈话和2000年加入WTO后，中国经济迅猛发展，并成为"世界工厂"（见图1）。之前设定的污染物总量下降目标不仅已无法实现，而且环境问题即使下再大力气也难以遏制。鉴于这些现实和西方工业化国家的发展经验，中国开始切身体会到环境与发展之间的两难。

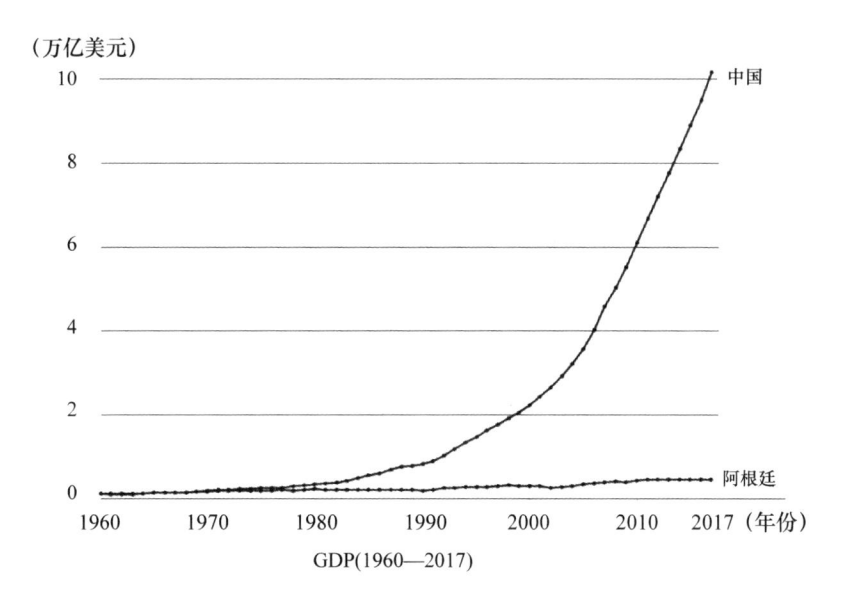

图1 中国与阿根廷的经济发展

资料来源：作者根据 https://ourworldindata.org 数据生成。

随着20世纪90年代经济全面加速带来环境问题的日益加剧，以及国际学术界、政策界关于"发展与环境难以兼得"（所谓倒U形环境库兹涅茨曲线）的认识，中国开始认识到经济发展成熟之前，很难避免环境问题。这种认识论的微妙变化，反映在国内和国际两方面的政策上。

2007年，党的十七大首次正式提出生态文明概念，将其作为全面建设小康社会的新要求之一："基本形成节约能源资源和保护生态环境的产业结构、增长方式、消费方式。……生态文明观念要在全社会牢固树立。"这意味着，虽然经济发展带来了严重的生态环境问题，但只要坚持科学发展，环境问题同经济发展是可以同时兼得的。这是中国关于环境与发展认识论的一大进步。

（二）党的十八大后发展理念和环境保护取得突破

2012年党的十八大后，生态文明概念有了新内涵，环境保护有了根本性突破。关于环境与发展关系的认识，从之前的相互兼容，进一步提升到二者可以相互促进。认识论的重大提升，带来行动上的重大变化。中国环境保护力度空前加大，并在环境和发展两方面都取得显著成效。党的十八大之后，中国开启了全面深化改革的大幕。生态文明作为"五位一体"总布局的重要内容，被提到前所未有的高度。2015年10月，习近平在党的十八届五中全会上，进一步提出了创新、协调、绿色、开放、共享的新发展理念。绿色发展成为新发展理念的核心内容。

在2018年5月18日的第八次全国生态环境保护大会上，习近平做了《推动我国生态文明建设迈上新台阶》的报告，标志着习近平生态文明思想正式确立。习近平生态文明思想的重要内容，就是"绿水青山就是金山银山"的理念，以及"人与自然和谐共生"的现代化观念。

"绿水青山就是金山银山"的理念意味着，发展背后的价值观念发生了重大转变，不再过于强调以物质财富为核心内容的GDP。环境保护和经济发展之间的关系，就从过去的对立转变为相互促进。随着发展观念或价值观念的改变，良好的自然生态环境本身，亦成为发展必不可少的内容。这就将环境保护从过去的负担，转变为新的发展机遇。

"人与自然和谐共生"，反映了新的现代化观念。在党的十九大报告中，习近平总书记从生态文明的高度，对中国要建立的现代化进行了不同于西方现代化标准的定义："我们要建设的现代化是人与自然和谐共生的现代化，既要创造更多物质财富和精神财富以满足人民日益增长的美好生活需要，也要提供更多优质生态产品以满足人民日益增长的优美生态环境需要。"这意味着，未来中国的现代化，也将不同于今日欧美在传统工业时代形成的发展内容。

三　中国关于环境保护的基本做法和经验

（一）为环境保护建立强大的制度保障

党的十八届三中全会以来，中国从宪法、党章、国家发展战略、国家治理体系和治理能力现代化、法律体系、具体机制设计等不同层面，建立了生态文明建设制度总体制度框架。

第一，中国是世界上第一个同时以宪法、执政党党章、国家发展战略（"五位一体"总体布局），为生态文明建设和环境保护提供法律制度保障的国家，也是保护环境决心最大的国家之一。生态文明的核心，是环境与发展的相互促进关系。生态文明在中国取得至高无上的法律地位，意味着中国对于通过保护环境促进经济发展有着坚定的信念和信心。

第二，生态文明制度成为国家治理体系和治理能力现代化的重要内容。党的十九届四中全会将"坚持和完善生态文明制度体系，促进人与自然和谐共生"，作为国家治理体系和治理能力必须坚持的内容进行了具体规范，包括实行最严格的生态环境保护制度、全面建立资源高效利用制度、健全生态保护和修复制度、严明生态环境保护责任制度。

第三,在实施层面建立了完备的制度体系。生态文明体制改革,主要是从自然资源资产管理、自然资源监管、生态环境保护三大领域进行制度改革与设计。总体而言,包括自然资源自然产权制度、国土开发保护制度、空间规划体系、资源总量管理和节约制度、资源有偿使用和补偿制度、环境治理体系、环境治理和生态保护的市场体系、绩效考核和责任追究制度8方面的制度。

(二)实现了一系列的改革突破

第一,环境立法思想取得突破。2014年4月,按照新的理念完成《环境保护法》修订,首次明确了环境保护法的综合法地位和"保护优先"原则。该法被称为史上最严环保法,并首次将生态保护红线写入法律,在重点生态保护区、生态环境敏感区和脆弱区等区域,划定生态保护红线,实行严格保护。

第二,在生态保护和修复制度、资源高效利用制度、生态环境治理体系改革等方面,均取得突破性进展。主要包括:自然资源资产产权制度、自然资源资产确权登记、自然生态空间用途管制改革,多规合一、红线划定、国家公园体制建设、部门机构改革,以及国家自然资源资产管理体制试点。资源有偿使用和生态补偿制度的持续推进,进一步推动了自然资源及其产品价格形成机制的逐步完善,有力地促进了自然资源资产的合理开发、高效利用、严格保护和系统修复。

第三,生态环境治理体系改革取得突破。2018年组建生态环境部,改变了多年来污染防治领域"九龙治水"的局面,从根本上实现了生态保护的统一监管执法。在管理机制方面,实行环保机构垂直管理和中央生态环保督察制度,不仅优化了组织结构,还有效地提高了行政效率和推动责任政府的建设。

第四,目标责任体系和问责机制改革取得突破。一方面,构建以污染物总量减排、环境质量改善等具体指标为导向的目标考核体系，包括"五年规划"中资源环境类约束性指标以及相关部门的专项考核。另一方面，建立在目标责任体系基础上的问责机制，包括中央生态环保督察制度、党政领导干部生态环境损害责任追究制度、领导干部自然资源资产离任审计制度等，推动长期以来积累的环境污染问题的解决。

第五，建立强制性、激励性、引导性的不同类型的制度。强制性制度包括：生态保护红线制度、自然资源资产产权制度等。激励性制度包括：推动资源税、环境税改革，推进生态补偿、用水权、用能权、排污权、林权、碳排放权的交易制度试点。

（三）大刀阔斧"向污染宣战"

随着认识论的重大转变，一直以来关于治理污染会影响经济发展的顾虑，很大程度上被消除。党的十八大之后，中央和地方采取了前所未有的环境治理和生态修复行动，包括污染防治攻坚战、水环境治理、土壤治理、农业面源污染治理、长江大保护战略、黄河流域大保护、生态红线、国家公园、清洁能源、节能减排，等等。

尤其是，党的十九大将污染防治攻坚战，同打好防范化解重大风险、精准脱贫一起，作为全面建成小康社会的三大攻坚战。2018年6月24日，中共中央、国务院发布《关于全面加强生态环境保护　坚决打好污染防治攻坚战的意见》（以下简称《意见》），明确要求着力解决一批民众反映强烈的突出生态环境问题，打好蓝天、碧水、净土三大保卫战和七大标志性战役，即打赢蓝天保卫战、打好柴油货车污染治理、水源地保护、黑臭水体治理、长江保护修复、渤海综合治理、农业农村治理攻坚战等。《意见》以2020年为时间节点，兼顾2035年和21世纪中叶，制定了污染防治攻坚战和生态环境保护的具体目标。

（四）以2060年碳中和目标引领应对气候变化和绿色转型行动

中国政府一直积极应对气候变化。在2009年哥本哈根气候变化大会之前，中国宣布了2020年碳排放强度在2005年基础上下降40%—45%的目标。在"十一五"和"十二五"时期，能耗强度、碳排放强度分别设定为下降20%、17%。在2015年中国向联合国提交的国家自主贡献承诺中，2030年碳排放强度在2005年基础上进一步下降60%—65%。

在2015年巴黎气候大会讲话中，习近平主席提出了两个"共赢"的观点。一是绿色复苏可以实现经济发展与应对气候变化之间的共赢；二是应对气候变化可以实现各国之间的共赢，各国可以做到机遇共享，而不是零和博弈。

在2020年9月22日的联合国大会上，习近平主席宣布中国"二氧化碳排放力争于2030年前达到峰值，努力争取2060年前实现碳中和"。碳中和目标的提出，根本是中国发展理念的变化。与此同时，中国对实现碳中和目标面临的艰巨挑战有清醒认识。碳中和是解决传统发展模式不可持续危机的必然选择，不是要不要的问题，而是如何实现的问题。对于碳中和的挑战，习近平主席在联合国宣布中国2060年碳中和目标时指出，"人类需要一场自我革命，加快形成绿色发展方式和生活方式，建设生态文明和美丽地球"。

中国严厉的环保行动，并没有像一些人所担心的会影响经济发展。根据国家统计局数据，在2013—2018年，中国GDP增长率分别为7.8%、7.3%、6.9%、6.7%、6.8%、6.6%。在全球新冠肺炎疫情暴发的2020年，中国成为全世界唯一实现正增长的国家，GDP增长2.3%，规模达到101万亿元人民币，人均GDP也超过11000美元。

"十四五"加大生态环境保护力度。2020年，党的十九届五中全会对"十四五"和2035年生态文明建设远景目标进行了部署,提出"构建生态文明体系,促进经济社会发展全面绿色转型,建设人与自然和谐共生的现代化"。同2015年发布的2030年国家自主贡献目标相比,中国碳排放强度下降目标从"60%—65%"提高到"65%以上",非化石能源比重目标从"20%左右"提高到"25%左右",森林蓄积量增加目标,从"45亿立方米"提高到"60亿立方米"。特别是,碳达峰时间从"2030年左右"变为"2030年前"。"十四五"时期,单位GDP能源强度将累计下降13.5%,单位GDP二氧化碳排放强度下降18%。

四 中国环境保护的基本经验

第一,新发展理念对于改革最为关键。绿色发展是发展范式的根本性转变。这种转变是一个跃变,面临着类似"鸡生蛋、蛋生鸡"的两难困境。也即,如果没有足够的绿色成功证据,则政府就不会采取有力的行动;如果不采取有力的行动,则绿色证据就不会出现。此时,领导人的远见卓识、愿景和改革勇气,就起着决定性作用。在"绿水青山就是金山银山"的理念下,生态环境保护和经济发展相互促进的愿景,就为打破这种两难冲突提供了保证。

第二,"不忘初心",以人民为中心的发展理念。发展的根本目的或初心是增进民众福祉,而不是商业利益至上。传统发展模式的一个重要后果,就是在一定程度上,发展的目的和手段本末倒置。GDP只是发展的手段,人民福祉的提高才是发展的根本目的,而良好的生态环境则是普惠的民生福祉,是"人民群众不断增长的美好生活"不可或缺的一部分。

第三,生态文明是工业文明后一种新的文明形态,不只是个别环节的修修补补,而是一个全面的系统工程,需要全面顶层设计、整体推进。绿色转型是一个典型的公共选择和协调问题,需要政府强有力地推动。政府的推动相当于提供一种转型必需的公共产品。在推动绿色转型方面，中国政府强大的动员能力，成为其独特的优势。

第四，充分发挥大国优势，通过地区竞争充分发挥各地的创新精神。"先试点、后推广"。在不同条件的地区进行各种生态文明制度试验，然后将行之有效的地区试验上升为全国性改革措施。包括以下几类试点：综合类的生态文明试点；各职能部门的专业类生态文明建设试点。这些试点的一个重要特点是，国家通常在多个地区开展同一类型的试点工作。

第五，有效的市场机制。在生态文明建设中，"市场发挥着决定性作用"。"绿水青山"转化成"金山银山"，根本上靠有效的市场机制。很多基于良好生态环境和文化的新兴产品和服务，难以用传统工业时代的商业模式和企业组织模式实现其价值，需要依靠创新型商业模式。此时，灵活且充满活力的市场机制就成为关键。

五　中—阿环境保护合作的历史机遇

目前，全球碳中和共识的形成，标志着工业革命后建立的传统工业化模式的落幕，一个新的绿色发展时代的开启。这个以绿色发展和互联网为特征的新发展时代，为中国和阿根廷开展环境保护和绿色发展合作提供了新的基础和广阔前景。一是新发展理念带来新的机遇。新的绿色发展模式，意味着新的绿色发展理念、新的绿色供给和需求、新的绿色资源。比如，基于良好的生态环境和文化可以发展新的绿色服务经济。中国和阿根廷两国生态与文化资源丰富，在这方面有广阔的合作空间。二是互联网打破了过去传统的时间和空间障碍，为克服中国和阿根廷之间遥远的地理距离提供了条件。中—阿两国之间，可以在新的绿色发展模式下，实现高水平的国际分工。

中国的经济体量远大于阿根廷，但两国人均GDP水平相当。

两国在环境保护方面有很大的合作空间。以气候变化为例，从图2可以看出，两国的温室气体排放和构成有着很大差异，反映了两国经济结构的差异。比如，阿根廷最大的排放来源是农业和土地的利用，而中国则是电力、采暖、制造和建筑。这些差异，说明两国在经贸和减排方面有着广阔的合作空间。

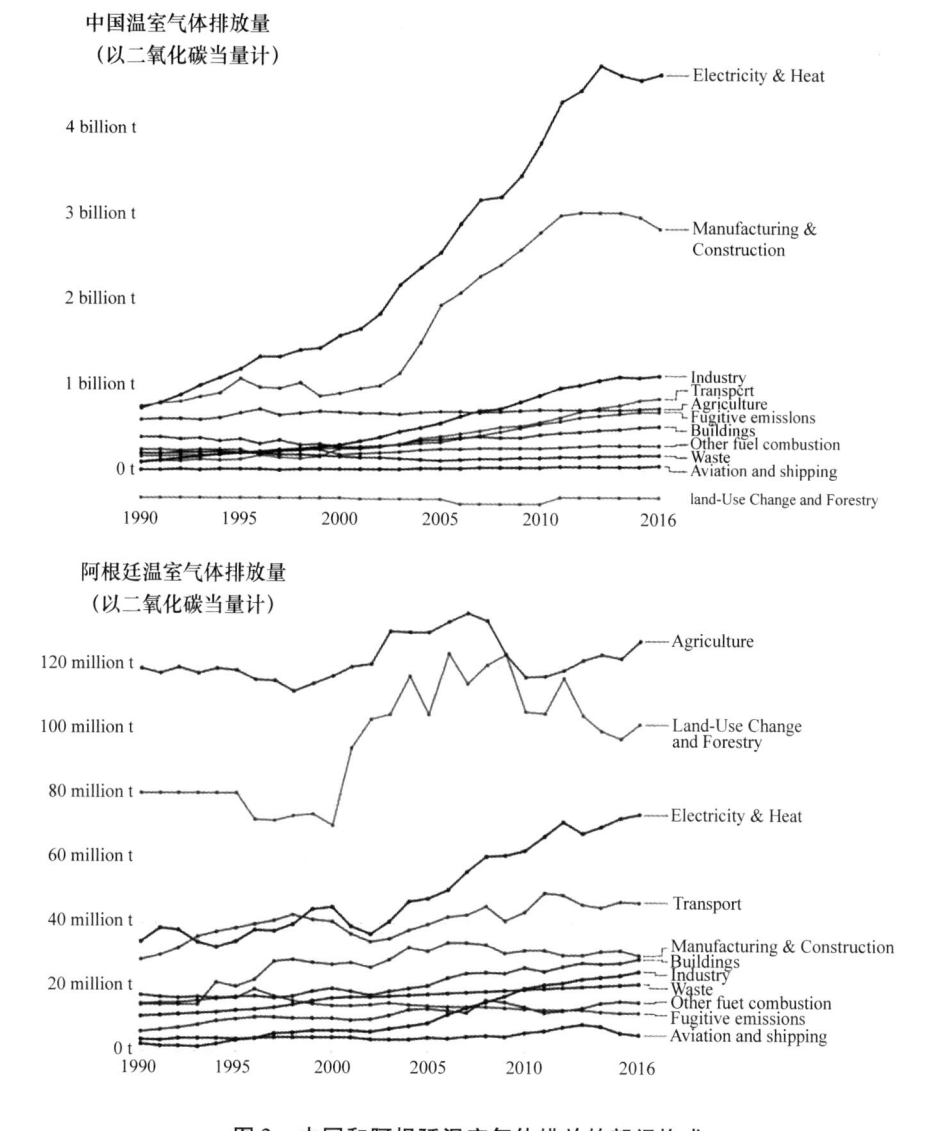

图2 中国和阿根廷温室气体排放的部门构成

资料来源：CAIT Climate Data Explorer。

具体而言，双方可以在以下方面探索合作的可能——

第一，应对全球气候变化。在技术、知识、资金方面进行合作，并推动建立公平合理有效的国际气候治理机制。

第二，环境保护方面的合作。中国和阿根廷可以共享环境保护方面的知识和最佳实践，促进环保方面的合作研究。

第三，绿色基础设施合作。中国有强大的基础设施建设能力。中国的高铁、高速公路、5G等均为世界领先。中国可以为阿根廷的各项基础设施建设提供必要的技术、资金等。

第四，开展绿色发展方面的合作。

——中国提出2060年碳中和目标，将带来百亿级的投资机会。这些机会将同阿根廷共享。

——中国在太阳能、风能、电动汽车、5G等方面，有世界领先的研发和制造能力，可以帮助阿根廷发展绿色经济。

——绿色农业合作。中国对绿色农产品有着巨大需求，而阿根廷在绿色农业方面有着很好的条件，双方可以进行大量合作。

——文化旅游体育等方面的合作。文化旅游体育等是绿色经济的重要内容。在这些方面，阿根廷有良好的优势，可以同中国开展包括足球在内的各项体育产业。

第五，海洋经济合作。中国和阿根廷同为海洋大国。中国的海洋经济占GDP近10%。阿根廷地处南半球，南极的开放利用对其具有重要战略意义，尤其是，在海洋污染和全球气候变化条件下，如何实现对海洋经济的可持续开放利用，是中国和阿根廷同时面临的重要机遇和挑战。

中阿携手共建"一带一路"*

自2013年推出以来,"一带一路"倡议逐步走入拉美地区。2018年1月,中拉论坛第二届部长级会议通过了《关于"一带一路"倡议的特别声明》等重要成果文件,认同"中国政府提出的'一带一路'倡议将为有关国家加强发展合作提供重要机遇",指明中拉优先合作领域包括对"一带一路"倡议的对接。这表明,"一带一路"已开始全面进入拉美。与之相一致,适应阿根廷的特有国情,中阿共建"一带一路"也在扎实推进,迎合双方共同的发展需求,推动双方合作迈入高质量发展的新阶段。

一 "一带一路"框架下的中阿合作

随着"一带一路"倡议的国际认同不断增强,中外共建"一带一路"国际合作快速发展,截至2022年7月,中国已与170多个国家和国际组织签署了200余份共建"一带一路"合作文件,涵盖亚洲、非洲、欧洲、拉美和南太平洋地区国家①。同期,在拉美地区24个建交国中,中国已签署21份共建"一

---

* 岳云霞,中国社会科学院拉丁美洲研究所经济研究室主任。
① "中国一带一路网",http://yidaiyilu.gov.cn [2022-08-15]。

带一路"合作文件，拉美成为中国"一带一路"国际合作不可或缺的重要参与方和现实共建方。

作为一项全球性倡议，中国对外"一带一路"合作注重世界发展的普遍需求，更着重于各个国家和地区发展的差异性需要。中拉共建"一带一路"在拉共体内获得了地区层面的认同，在双边层面则以三种形式展开：一是签署共建"一带一路"合作文件；二是官方参加"一带一路"国际合作高峰论坛，加入亚洲基础设施银行[①]，加入"一带一路"相关合作机制，或在官方文件中明确合作意向；三是实现"一带一路"精神[②]下的项目对接或规划对接。

中国与阿根廷已签署"一带一路"合作文件。2018年，习近平主席对阿根廷进行国事访问期间，中阿发表《联合声明》，明确提出，"'一带一路'倡议将为中阿合作注入动力，中阿全面战略伙伴关系可扩展至'一带一路'倡议"。2021年1月，习近平主席在与阿根廷总统阿尔贝托·费尔南德斯（Alberto Fernandez）的通信中表示，中方"愿同阿方一道努力，推进高质量共建'一带一路'合作，推动构建人类命运共同体"。2022年2月，阿根廷总统费尔南德斯出席北京冬奥会开幕式并访华期间，中阿两国政府签署"一带一路"谅解备忘录。中阿形成的"一带一路"共识促使双方务实合作不断深入，形成了"五通"领域的多项早期成果。

一是政策沟通层面，阿根廷国家元首出席了两届"一带一路"国际合作高峰论坛，阿为《"一带一路"融资指导原则》

[①] Serrano 等将此种形式视为拉美国家参与"一带一路"国际合作的具体表现。详见 Serrano, J. E., D. Telias and F. Urdinez, "Deconstructing the Belt and Road Initiative in Latin America", Emerald Insight, 2020, https://www.emerald.com/insight/2046-3162.htm。

[②] 从实际操作来看，一般认为符合"一带一路"五通建设要求的项目即为"一带一路"项目。

签署国，中阿两国政府决定在共建"一带一路"框架内加强沟通和合作，对接两国发展规划。

二是资金融通层面，阿根廷是亚洲基础设施投资银行的创始成员，而阿根廷投资外贸银行作为创始成员行，加入了"中拉开发性金融合作机制"。

三是贸易畅通和设施联通层面，阿根廷对华贸易、投资、金融与经济合作规模处于拉美地区相对领先地位。在贸易领域，中国已成为阿根廷第二大贸易伙伴，2020年中国占阿根廷总出口额的9.8%（548.84亿美元），占其进口总额的20.4%（423.56亿美元）。而在中国进口中，来自阿根廷的肉类占到了12.1%，大豆占到了7.5%，而海鲜和贝类、动物油脂、饮料、皮革等产品的比重也超过了2%，阿在中国食品及原料供应以及皮革制造业中发挥着重要作用，对相关产业供应链和生产链的稳定具有突出意义。在投资领域，中国是阿根廷主要外资来源国之一，截至2019年年底，中国在阿投资存量达到了18亿美元，涉及农业、能源、制造业等多个部门。在金融合作领域，中阿之间已经签署了五期货币互换协议，2020年8月最新一期协议的规模达到了1300亿元人民币，而同期阿根廷的人民币储备约占其外汇储备的43%，该国已成为人民币国际化的重要合作对象。在经济合作领域，中国企业已参与阿根廷多个基建和能源项目，如中国机械设备工程股份有限公司与阿方签署贝铁改造项目总承包合同，除了参与翻新改造，还提供了全线的建材、机车和车厢等设备；中国电建和上海电建联合承建阿根廷最大光伏项目——高查瑞300兆瓦光伏发电项目，现已进入商业运营；中国金风科技投资、中国电建承建阿根廷最大风电项目群——赫利俄斯风电项目群罗马布兰卡一期、三期项目已并入阿根廷国家电网系统，正式投入商业运营；而葛洲坝集团正负责位于阿根廷南部圣克鲁斯省两个水电站的建设。

四是民心相通层面，中阿两国联合录制了《魅力中国》《魅力阿中》《跨越》等纪录片，阿根廷还在中华人民共和国成立70周年之际播放"辉煌70年·中国电视月"系列节目，深化了两国民众的相互认知，促进两国民心相通。

二 "一带一路"框架下的中阿供需契合

党的十九届五中全会提出要构建"以国内大循环为主体、国内国际双循环相互促进的新发展格局"，而"一带一路"是中国新时代对外开放和对外合作的总纲领，对内则衔接新一轮改革的压力疏解和资源与市场均衡使命。在"一带一路"框架下，中阿合作能够满足双方共同发展的需要。

首先，中阿合作有助于阿根廷走出经济困境。近十年来，阿根廷经济滞后于全球新兴市场和发展中经济体的平均水平，多数时间中甚至低于发达经济体的平均增长。在2020年新冠肺炎疫情冲击下，阿根廷更是出现了有史以来最严重的经济衰退，GDP增长率为-11.78%（图1）。同期，阿根廷国家统计和普查局数据显示，其失业率超过了11%，贫困率和赤贫率达到了42%和10.5%[1]，均达到了近16年的峰值，债务压力也相对较为突出。在内生增长动力有限的情况下，对外合作是阿根廷走出危机的主要支持，中阿共建"一带一路"，有助于支持阿根廷经济增长和扩大就业，成为其摆脱困境的重要选项。

其次，阿根廷具备承接中国对外投资合作的现实能力。2014年以来，中国成为净FDI流出国；2016年以来，中国成为全球第二大对外投资国。对外投资是中国改革开放"引进来"和"走出去"战略并举下资金、技术和经验积累的自然成果，

---

[1] 央视新闻，中央电视台新闻中心新媒体官方账号。

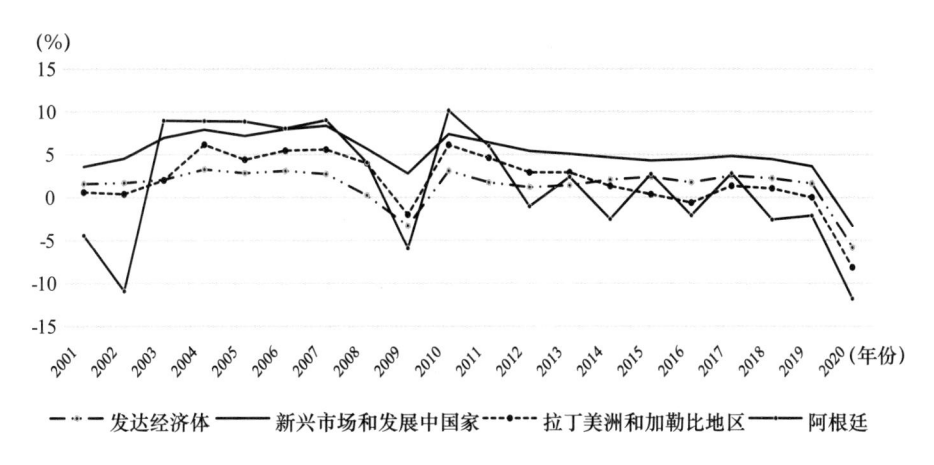

图1　世界视角下的阿根廷经济增长

数据来源：IMF，World Economic Outlook。

还承担着推动国际产能合作的重要使命。阿根廷是拉美第三大经济体，是南方共同市场的主要成员国，且工业门类较为齐全，具备为中国投资提供配套产业的能力，因此，具有承接中国投资和产能转移的动力与能力，"一带一路"框架下的中阿投资合作具有稳定扩大的基础性条件。

再次，阿根廷具有承接中国基础设施建设能力输出的强烈诉求。"一带一路"倡议的重要内容是基础设施的互联互通，中国在相关领域拥有相对成熟的技术、经验和人力优势。阿根廷则因基础设施比较落后，运输、仓储等生产性服务成本占企业生产成本比重高，压缩了制造业利润空间，抑制了工业发展。为了改善基础设施，阿根廷正在推动史上最大规模基础设施改造计划。在"一带一路"框架下，以基础设施建设投资为重点，将中国优势产能和技术引入阿根廷，能够实现中阿双赢。

最后，阿根廷具备承载人民币走出去的可行性。人民币国际化是中国新一轮对外开放的重要载体，具备在阿根廷推行的条件。目前，中国在阿根廷成功推进本币互换项目，并设有地区性清算银行，因而，具备承载人民币国际化的交易规模和操作经验，能够成为可能的试点区域。在"一带一路"框架下，中阿产能合作以及基础设施互联互通建设等，有益于形成产品流、资金流循环互动的良好局面。

三 中阿"一带一路"合作的挑战

在中阿共建"一带一路"务实合作不断扩大的同时，内外部市场环境在不断发生变化，中阿合作面临贸易领域的结构性摩擦，而双方合作还越来越多地受到外部壁垒的影响。

首先，阿根廷宏观经济与政策的波动性，对双边务实合作形成一定扰动。由于全球经济复苏乏力且内部增长失速，阿根廷近年来始终面临着高通胀、外汇短缺、汇率波动和财政失衡的困扰，被迫出台一系列外汇管制措施以防止金融市场震荡，并且对大豆、豆油等主要出口产品征收较高关税以增加收入。这些措施客观上对中国企业在阿投资与贸易形成了不利冲击。

其次，阿根廷对华贸易救济措施频繁，对双边贸易形成了一定影响。由于阿根廷国内生产的集中度较高且双方产品存在一定竞争，阿根廷是发起对华"两反一保"措施最多的国家之一。截至2020年中，阿根廷是全球仅次于印度、美国和欧盟的第四大对华反倾销诉讼国（124起），对华发起的反补贴措施继美国和加拿大之后（20起），保障措施的使用也在拉美相对领先（6起）；相比而言，中国未在WTO框架下对阿根廷发起贸易救济措施[①]。贸易摩擦在一定程度上影响了中阿之间的贸易，对两国间的贸易畅通形成负面效应。

最后，阿根廷传统基础设施建设领域和5G等新兴领域竞争激烈，利益博弈复杂。长期经济低迷加之债务压力使阿根廷政

---

① WTO trade topics, https://www.wto.org/english/tratop_e/tratop_e.htm.

府面临财政限制,难以使用公共财政资源扩大投资规模,仅能依赖外部融资实现基础设施领域投资,现已形成中、美、欧和本土竞争的局面。中国企业作为后来者,面临多重扰动因素,须适应欧美范式下的国际工程招标模式和工程标准,还须满足当地业主、同业竞争者、环保组织和社区等多层次诉求,对项目运营和管理提出较高要求。而中阿合作的快速发展,不可避免地引发传统利益集团的关注与警惕,对项目进展也形成了一定压力。

四 中阿"一带一路"合作的未来方向

"一带一路"为中阿合作提供了新平台和新动力,能够推动双方合作形成动态升级和不断突破的良好局面。中阿发展诉求有一致性,但也面临一定现实挑战,双方均应对共建"一带一路"合作能产生的风险对冲价值予以新评估,最大化共同利益。为此,中阿双方需要在如下方向形成合力。

一是中阿共建"一带一路"面对巨大需求空间,应以政治互信与沟通的进一步增进为务实合作增信赋能。一方面,中阿"一带一路"合作已在"五通"领域有了坚实的进展,双方对共建"一带一路"也有较高共识,应在"一带一路"谅解备忘录后迅速推动其他相关合作文件的签署。另一方面,中阿除了双边机制的沟通外,多边层面的定期沟通以G20机制最为突出,而类似于金砖国家、亚太经合组织之类的多边渠道相对缺乏。双方应创新机制,推动双方加强多层次政治交流与政策沟通。

二是中阿共建"一带一路"存在现实性短板,应推动贸易与投资便利化举措的进一步扩大。首先,中阿之间应尽快形成双边贸易救济合作机制,通过对话与磋商降低贸易摩擦带来的贸易损失。其次,中阿双方须在动植物检疫检验、通关等环节加强合作,并在私营部门对话、市场调研、生产性投资配套服务等领域加强合作，推动双方贸易与投资合作扩大。最后，鉴于南方共同市场对外签署自由贸易协定的一致性要求，中阿除了逐步共同推进形成中国—南方共同市场自由贸易协定外，应积极推动双边贸易与投资安排，推动贸易与投资自由化。

三是中阿共建"一带一路"存在创新领域，应形成与时俱进的新合作。中阿之间的现有合作创造了多项潜在提升空间：其一是人民币国际化合作的进一步空间，在人民币已在阿根廷发挥了一定清算和储备功能的基础上，进一步推动其计价和结算功能不仅能够满足双边投资、贸易扩大的需求，还能有效降低汇率波动风险，切实便利双方企业的当地经营；其二是新业务空间，新冠肺炎疫情流行期间，中阿之间食品、医药产品及游戏等文化类产品贸易有所增加，电子商务也有较大跃升，这表明中阿之间在相关领域出现了新的合作诉求，应通过"健康丝绸之路""数字丝绸之路"等填补这些空白；其三是国际合作新空间，在气候变化、南极科考和深空探测等领域，中阿具有共同领域，有条件拓展合作。

四是中阿共建"一带一路"存在认知缺口，应以沟通和认同消融合作障碍。彼此认知不足是约束中阿"一带一路"合作深入发展的深层原因，为此，在交流层面，中阿之间应该建立长期直接的政府、智库和媒体合作机制，实行开放的、多层次的交流和对接，尽可能建立起信息互通平台，避免受到外部干扰。

工业化进程：迈向高质量发展*

一 快速崛起的工业大国

坚持从中国国情出发的体制改革，坚持自主的市场开放，充分释放了中国的比较要素优势和大规模市场优势，使得中国制造业在改革开放以来的四十多年时间里实现了规模快速扩大，产业结构持续优化，技术能力显著提升。中国用几十年的时间走过了发达国家几百年的工业化道路，取得了举世瞩目的成就。

第一，在规模快速扩大的同时实现了产业结构持续优化。1978年中国工业增加值只有1621亿元，到2020年工业增加值达到313071亿元。工业增加值从2万亿美元到3万亿美元仅用了3年，美国用了9年；从3万亿美元增加到4万亿美元中国只用了2年，美国用了8年。在规模增长的同时，产业结构也不断优化。2019年，中国高技术制造业增加值占规模以上工业增加值的比重为14.4%，数字经济占GDP比重达到36.2%。

第二，构建了全球最为完备的工业体系。改革开放初期，中国制造业能力较为薄弱，制造业增加值占全球制造业增加值的比重可以忽略不计。2019年，中国制造业增加值达到3.82万

---

* 贺俊，中国社会科学院工业经济研究所研究员；江鸿，中国社会科学院工业经济研究所；李伟，中国社会科学院工业经济研究所。

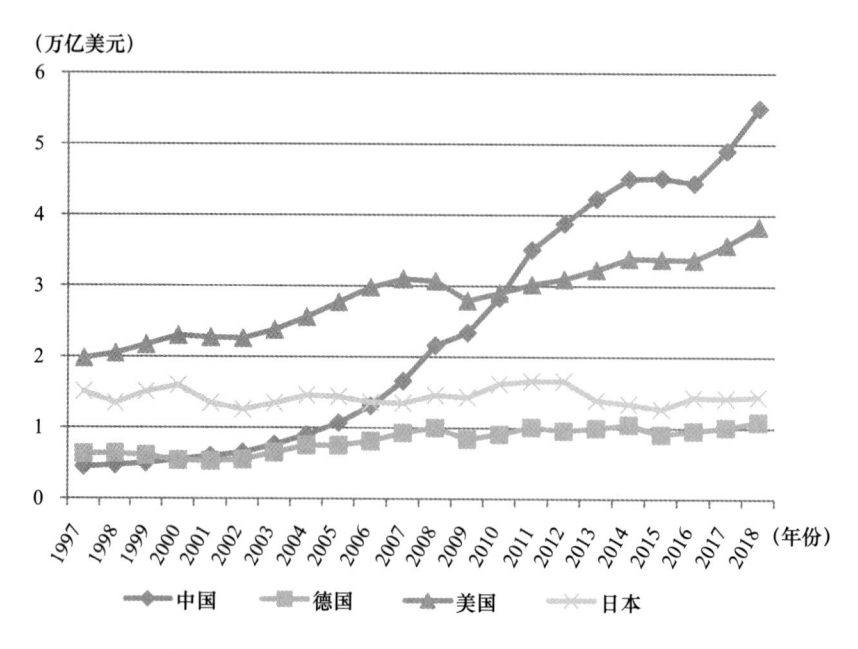

图 1 主要国家工业增加值变化

资料来源：中华人民共和国国家统计局：《中国统计年鉴》（历年电子版数据）。

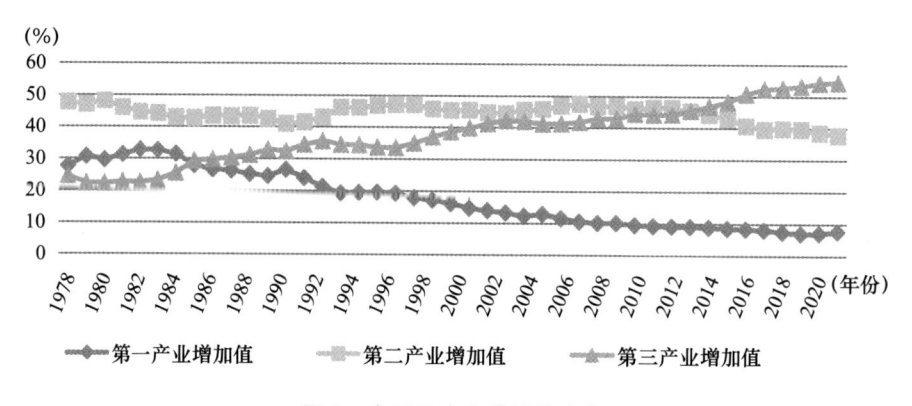

图 2 中国三次产业结构变化

资料来源：中华人民共和国国家统计局：《中国统计年鉴》（历年电子版数据）。

亿元，占全球制造业的比重达到 1/3 左右，成为名副其实的全球制造业中心。中国构建了全球最为完整的工业体系，拥有 41 个工业大类、207 个中类、666 个小类，是唯一拥有联合国产业分类中全部工业门类的国家；在 500 种主要工业品中中国有 220

多种产量位居全球第一,世界230多个国家和地区都可以看到"中国制造"的身影。

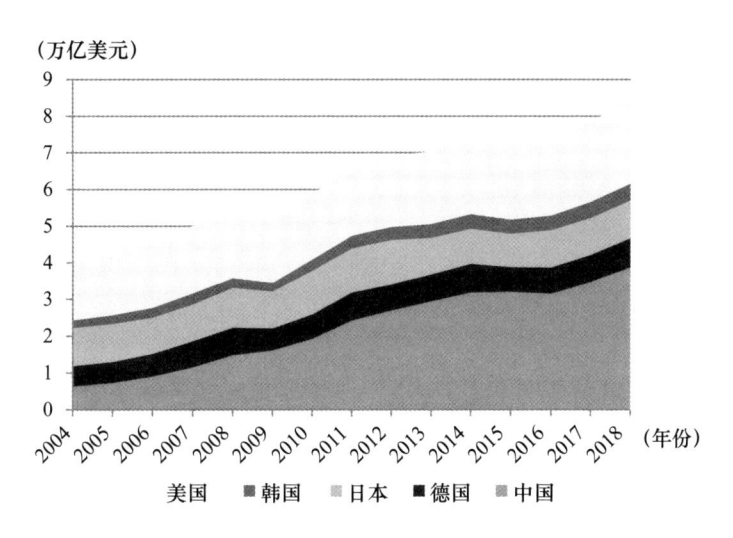

图3 主要国家制造业增加值变化

资料来源:中华人民共和国国家统计局:《中国统计年鉴》(历年电子版数据)。

第三,形成多种所有制企业充分竞争的产业组织结构。改革开放初期,国有企业主导了工业生产的各个环节。改革开放以后,随着市场开放和国企改革深入推进,多种所有制企业、大中小企业充分竞争,华为、中兴、联想、小米、海尔、美的、比亚迪、宁德时代、大疆等一大批本土企业成长为具有国际竞争力的制造业领军企业。2019年《财富》世界500强企业中中国企业数量达到129家,第一次超过美国成为上榜企业最多的国家。与此同时,高技术创业蓬勃发展,《2019胡润全球独角兽榜》的数据显示,中国独角兽企业数量达到206家,首次超过美国(203家),成为全球独角兽企业数量最多的国家。

第四,从技术模仿到原始创新。改革开放以来,中国工业技术实现了从技术引进到消化吸收再创新,再到自主创新的梯次跨越,正向设计能力和原始创新能力显著增强。1995年中国研发投入348.7亿元、研发强度只有0.57%,2019年研发投入激增到

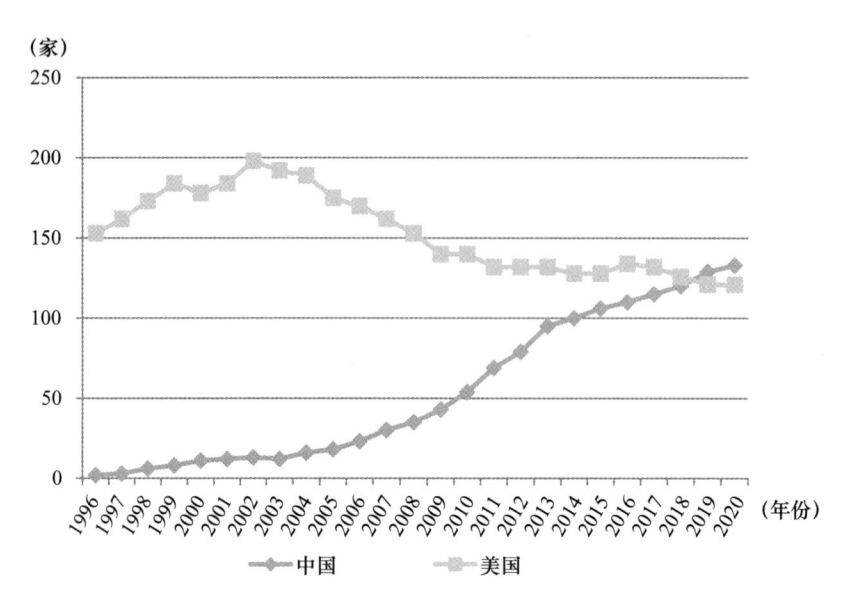

图4 中美《财富》世界500强上榜企业数量对比

资料来源:《财富》世界500强网站,http://www.fortunechina.com/fortune500/index.htm。

2.2万亿元,研发强度也达到2.23%,中国已经成为全球研发投入规模第二大的国家。1993年之前中国PCT专利数几乎为0,到2019年中国PCT专利数达到24010,占全球总量的13%。创新能力的提升显著促进了中国工业发展,根据《中国科技统计年鉴》的测算数据,1998—2003年中国科技进步贡献率为39.7%,2014—2019年科技进步对经济增长的贡献率达到59.5%。

第五,从引进来到走出去的对外开放格局。改革开放以来,中国超大规模的市场优势和成本优势吸引跨国公司持续来华投资,2003年中国超过美国成为全球吸引外资投资最多的国家。与此同时,中国进出口规模也快速提升,2020年,中国货物进出口总额达到32.16万亿元,连续12年位居全球货物贸易第一大出口国地位,是120多个国家的最大贸易伙伴以及约65个国家的第一大进口来源国。随着中国制造业技术能力的提升和中国"一带一路"倡议的引导,制造业企业对外直接投资开始快速增长，2003年中国制造业对外直接投资净额为6.2亿美元，2017年大幅上升到295亿美元。

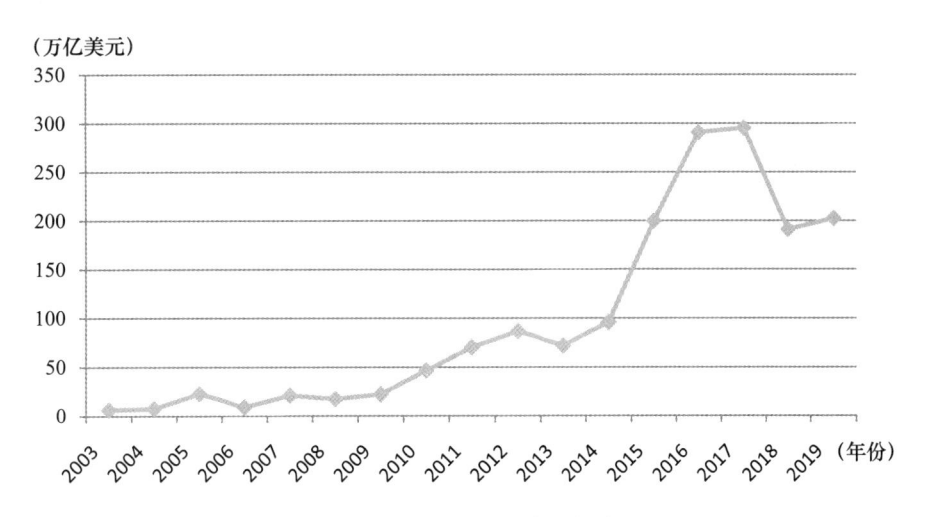

图5 中国对外直接投资净额变化

数据来源：Wind数据库。

二 中国制造业做对了什么？

著名经济学家张五常曾说："中国的高速增长持续了那么久，历史上从来没有出现过。中国一定是做了非常对的事才产生了我们见到的经济奇迹。那是什么呢？"[1] 制造业是支撑中国经济在过去四十多年实现高速增长的主要部门——直到2013年以前第二产业始终是中国最大的产业部门，中国制造业能够保持高速增长并最终取代美国成为全球最大制造业经济体，也一定是因为其特定的制度、经济条件和发展战略发挥了积极作用。

一是始终坚持工业自立的战略导向。中华人民共和国自成立以来始终坚持"工业立国"战略，在中国从站起来、富起

---

[1] 张五常：《中国的经济制度》，中信出版社2012年版。

来到强起来的伟大飞跃过程中,工业发展起到了举足轻重的作用。中国工业的快速增长出现在改革开放、特别是20世纪90年代以后,然而,改革开放等制度性因素之所以能够快速释放中国工业增长潜力的重要原因,是中国在改革开放前就已经在军工、机械、精密仪器、半导体、轨道交通、化工等领域形成了较为完整的生产制造能力,并发展起来较为完备的产业创新体系。由于在改革开放之初中国就存在一批具有技术能力的国有企业和科研院所,因此相比其他后发国家,中国在承接国际技术转移过程中的技术学习强度和技术学习效率更高。当制造业技术能力总体上实现了由模仿到正向设计(forward design)的跨越后,中国工业自立战略进一步实现由培育本土创新主体到形成原始创新能力的转变。2006年,中国制定了《国家中长期科学和技术发展规划纲要(2006—2020年)》,明确提出加强自主创新是中国科学技术发展的战略基点,确定了"自主创新、重点跨越、支撑发展、引领未来"的战略导向,提出通过原始创新、集成创新和在引进先进技术基础上的消化吸收再创新全面提升制造业竞争力。与中国实践形成对比,缺乏本土的技术学习主体,单纯依赖跨国公司技术引进,是部分后发国家在收割了市场开放红利后就长期陷入"中等收入陷阱"的根本原因。

二是通过制度改革不断释放地方政府和企业等各类经济主体的活力。国有企业改革、增强企业活力是中国经济体制改革的中心环节,也是中国改革过程中最具创造性的实践。中国国有经济结构调整大致经历了四个阶段：1978—1992年,通过"放权让利"激发国有企业的市场活力；1993—2002年,通过"抓大放小"和现代企业制度进一步提高国有企业的效率；2003—2012年在成立国资委的基础上实现"管资产"向"管资本"的转变；2013年以后国有企业分类改革和混合所有制经济快速发展。在整个国有企业改革过程中,国有经济的相对规模逐渐下降，而政府始终保持了对国有企业战略性控制和效率改进的最佳平衡。此外，中央政府不断塑造有利于激励地方政府发展地方经济的治理模式。相较发达国家和其他发展中国家，中国地方政府治理具有两方面的独特性，一是纵向从中央到各级地方的逐级行政分包体制，二是同级地方政府之间的横向晋升竞争。行政权力纵向层层分包使得地方政府能够获得发展经济所需的大量资源和自由裁量权；而地方官员的横向竞争则充分调动了地方官员发展经济的积极性，地方政府成为富有活力和创造性的行动主体，这是中国基础设施和工业能够快速发展的重要制度性基础。[①]

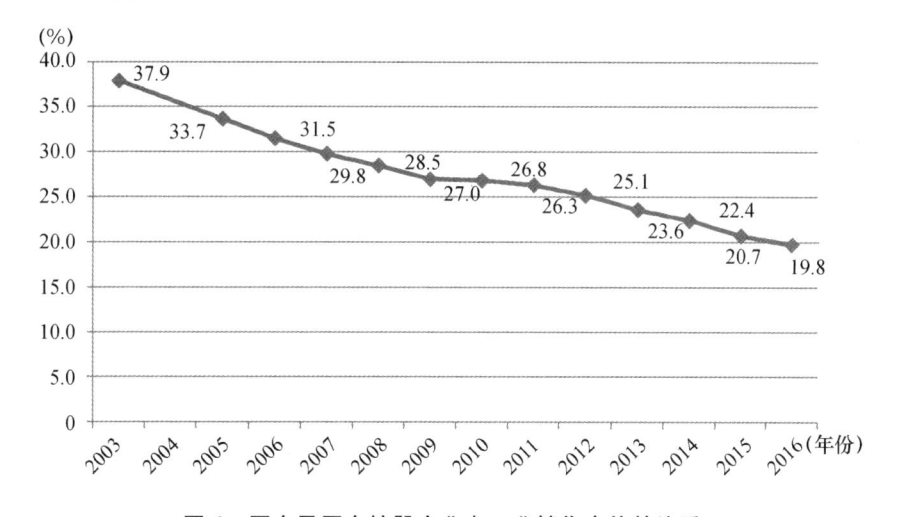

图6 国有及国有控股企业占工业销售产值的比重

数据来源：Wind 数据库。

三是采取渐次开放和自主开放的对外开放战略。与拉美的激进市场开放模式不同，中国采取了由点到线、由线到面的渐进开放战略，即通过选择符合条件的地区优先设立经济特区、开放沿海港口城市、经济技术开发区、内陆沿边开放等对外开放特区，

[①] 周黎安：《转型中的地方政府：官员激励与治理（第二版）》，上海人民出版社 2017 年版。

当"试点"经验成熟时再不断扩大到其他地区。以经济技术开发区为例，1984年到1986年，中国首次设立了14个国家级经济技术开发区，之后不断在全国各地新增设立国家级经济技术开发区，到2020年，中国共设立218个国家级经济技术开发区，实现地区生产总值10.5万亿人民币，占国内生产总值的比重高达10.6%，其中苏州工业园、广州经开区、天津经开区、青岛经开区等大型经济技术开发区的生产总值甚至超过了2000亿人民币。国家级经济技术开发区是中国对外开放地区的重要组成部分，大都是各省、市、自治区的省会、经济中心城市或沿海开放城市。在区位、产业基础条件较好的地区率先开放，有利于集中力量建设完善的基础设施，创建符合国际水准的投资环境，通过吸收利用外资，形成以高新技术产业为主的现代工业结构，有利于提高吸收外商投资的质量，促进产业集群化发展。除了区域层面，中国在产业层面也坚持渐进开放战略，即在符合国际多边贸易规则的前提下，根据产业结构升级的一般规律，逐步从低技术产业到资本密集型产业再到高技术产业渐次开放，保证了跨国公司管理和技术引入与外资对本土企业冲击之间的最佳平衡，实现了跨国投资与本土企业的协同动态效率。

  四是坚持基础设施适度超前建设和工业化协同推动战略。由于中国地方政府间存在激烈的招商引资竞争，地方政府具有强烈的基础设施投资动机，同时国有银行体系使得地方政府和国有企业能够获得低利率贷款，保证了中国基础设施得以高速发展。基础设施建设对地方经济增长的推动反过来又为基础设施投资提供了有力的财政支持，从而形成基础设施建设和地方经济发展相互增强的格局。1978年，中国的铁路营业里程和公路里程分别只有5万公里和89万公里，到2019年年底，铁路营业里程和公路里程分别达到14万公里和501万公里，是改革开放初期的2.8倍和5.6倍，分别位居全球第二和第三。中国高速公路里程在1988年以前、高铁营业里程在2007年以前几乎为零，然而到 2019 年，二者分别达到 15 万公里和 3.5 万公里，均位于全球第一，高速公路里程是位居第二位国家美国的近 2 倍，高速铁路里程是位居第二位国家日本的近 12 倍。基础设施适度超前建设使中国不仅能通过投资需求创造和降低物流成本带动制造业发展，还能充分利用高技术复杂度基础设施大规模建设的机会，通过"市场换技术"和"自主创新"战略将市场机会转化为技术机会，从而拉动高技术产业的快速发展。以高铁装备为例，中国在高速铁路建设规划的同时也战略性地部署了高铁装备技术的引进、消化和再创新。目前在衡量高铁速度水平的四个指标中，中国在实验室试验速度、线路试验速度和实际运营速度方面均保持全球领先，时速 350 公里的中国标准动车组具有完全自主知识产权，新车型开发周期居于全球领先水平，中国仅用不到 20 年的时间就实现了在高铁装备这一高技术复杂度产业的技术赶超。[①]

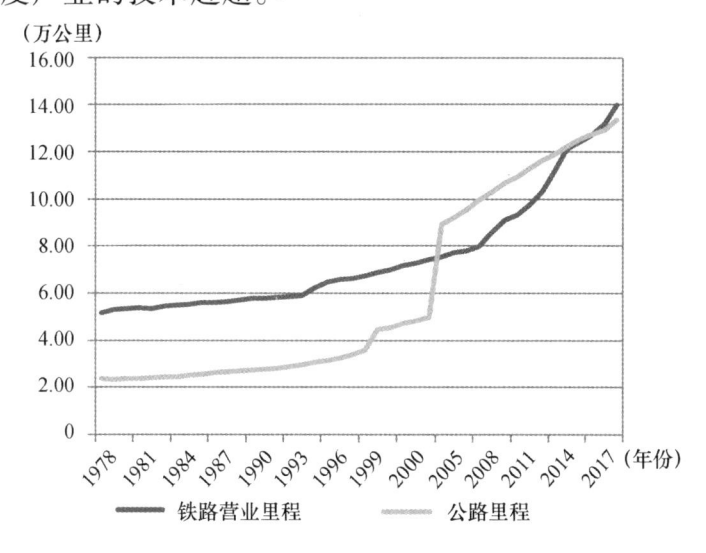

图 7 中国铁路（左轴）和公路（右轴）建设里程

数据来源：Wind 数据库。

---

① 吕铁、贺俊：《政府干预何以有效：对中国高铁技术赶超的调查研究》，《管理世界》2019 年第 9 期。

除以上因素外，各级政府对企业发展强烈的服务意识，特别是沿海地区地方政府常常能够灵活地与企业合作解决产业发展所面临的关键障碍①；对教育的高度重视和大规模投入，使工业发展和技术提升能够获得大量高技能人才；在欧美工作和学习过的海外华人"回溯"，使得企业可以通过人才流动掌握技术开发和产业化所必需的隐含知识，等等因素，对中国制造业赶超发展也至关重要。

三 更加广泛且深入的中阿工业与数字经济合作

在中国与阿根廷政府的合力推动以及全球供应链分工格局重构的背景之下，两国在工业产能合作、基础设施建设、创新创业发展等方面均有广阔的合作前景。

深化多领域工业产能合作，推动区域工业化进程。在可预见的未来，受到政治经济因素和新冠肺炎疫情的持续影响，全球供应链将朝着更加靠近终端市场的区域化方向发展。处于全球供应链中间环节的大量中国工业企业将加快布局海外产能，以适应区域化的市场需求。阿根廷是南方共同市场的主要国家，且近年来面临外商投资流出问题，接受中国工业直接投资的前景广阔。中国与阿根廷两国政府应致力于提升阿根廷公众对中国投资者的信任度，共同改善中国对阿根廷直接投资环境；同时积极支持阿根廷对华生产合作计划，共同寻求两国企业在第三方市场的项目合作机会，充分发挥两国在工业领域的多样化产能合作潜力。

提升具有资源效率和环境友好的基础设施承载能力。基础设施的结构直接影响一国经济结构和发展水平。新兴国家在基

---

① Rodrik, Dani, *One Economics, Many Recipes*, Princeton University Press, 2006.

础设施建设方面的重要优势之一，是可以参照先发国家技术路线选择的经验与教训，直接跃迁到适合本国条件的、先进适用的基础设施路线上。中国企业在阿根廷参与的基础设施建设项目并不是早期成熟技术在传统基础设施领域的简单再利用，而是因地制宜选用最新的适用性技术，发展更具资源效率、更加环境友好的可持续基础设施。截至2019年，阿根廷政府共批准了140多个可再生能源投资项目，其中有40%由中国投资建设。阿根廷第一个光伏电站即由中国企业承建，采用了中方的先进光伏发电技术以及国内积累的高海拔建设经验。未来中国与阿根廷应通过亚洲基础设施投资银行等渠道，加强对阿根廷基础设施建设的金融支持，促进中国基础设施建设能力与阿根廷基础设施改善需求高效对接，推动阿根廷基础设施实现结构性升级，提高内生增长动力。

建设面向未来的数字基础设施和数字经济合作伙伴关系。数字经济的发展既依赖于数字基础设施建设，也有赖于提高数字基础设施的包容性，促进广大人口和行业的普遍性互联互通，从而释放数字基础设施对经济发展的普遍促进作用。中国已经成为数字基础设施和数字经济领域的全球领先者，既有能力支持阿根廷建设民众可负担的高质量数字基础设施，弥合数字鸿沟；也有可供阿根廷借鉴的电子商务与数字经济发展最佳实践，以及对阿根廷开放的超大规模电子商务国内市场，能够有力带动阿根廷电子商务和相关行业发展。具体而言，在数字基础设施建设方面，阿根廷政府始终对两国企业合作建设通信5G网络秉承公开的积极态度，阿根廷三大通信运营商也已经与华为共同开展了5G网络测试，这为阿根廷利用中国通信技术建设高性价比、高覆盖率的包容性网络创造了有利条件。在跨国电子商务发展方面，基于中国与阿根廷2018年12月签署的《关于电子商务合作的谅解备忘录》，两国政府将积极加强政策沟通和协调，通过电子商务促进优质特色产品的双边贸易。中国庞大的电子商务市场规模和不断攀升的消费者在线购买率，将促进缺少营销渠道的阿根廷优质产品、中小企业与中国消费市场有效对接，充分发挥数字基础设施对阿根廷数字经济包容性发展与整体产出的带动作用。

打造更加紧密的创新创业合作纽带。在新一轮全球科技革命和产业革命的背景下，科技协同创新是促进中国与阿根廷产业合作可持续发展、提升两国科技能力与工业能力互补性的长期基础。近年来，在航空航天领域，两国基础科学研究合作关系与产业创新投资合作关系日益密切。中国企业通过技术支持、风险投资等多种方式，对阿根廷卫星遥感等高科技创业提供支持。阿根廷卫星逻辑公司（Satellogic）选择了中国长征系列运载火箭进行遥感卫星发射，并与中国科研人员密切配合，共同解决了卫星发射环节的许多关键技术问题。此外，中国腾讯公司还是该公司多轮投资的领投者。在数字经济与其他新兴产业领域，中国与阿根廷作为地区乃至全球性大国，应在新兴技术（如5G）的应用场景探索和应用标准制定方面开展更加广泛的合作，捍卫新兴经济体在全球前沿产业中的共同利益。

在经济全球化中育新机、开新局*

当今世界正面临百年未有之大变局,经济全球化也因此经历深刻转变。在新冠肺炎疫情冲击下,经济全球化面临前所未有的挑战。如何认识经济全球化的发展大势并在经济全球化中育新机、开新局,已成为当前摆在包括中国和阿根廷在内的世界各国面前的一项重大课题。

一 经济全球化发展潮流不可逆转

2018年4月,中国国家主席习近平在博鳌亚洲论坛2018年年会开幕式上发表题为《开放共创繁荣 创新引领未来》的主旨演讲指出,"综合研判世界发展大势,经济全球化是不可逆转的时代潮流"。[①] 一般来讲,经济全球化是指人类在经济上相互依存度不断提升的进程。从器物层面看,随着分工的深化和市场的扩大,商品和服务以及资本、劳动和技术等生产要素的跨国流动的规模和速度加大加快;从制度层面看,原本具有"地方性"的规则在全球范围内越来越得到普遍的尊重或日益具有普

---

* 徐秀军,中国社会科学院世界经济与政治研究所研究员。
① 习近平:《开放共创繁荣 创新引领未来——在博鳌亚洲论坛2018年年会开幕式上的主旨演讲》,《人民日报》2018年4月11日第3版。

遍适应性，同时世界的运转对非中性的国际规则高度敏感依赖；从观念层面看，借助于传媒革命，尤其是信息技术革命，不同人、不同族群、不同国家的价值观念和意识形态，在交流与碰撞中呈现出趋同与分化的趋势。[1]

在全球分工格局形成后，资本、劳动力、商品等在全球范围内向使用效率最高的国家或地区流动。从总体上看，经济全球化使资源配置从国家内部扩大到全球范围，能够提高资源配置的效率。更为重要的是，经济全球化以国际分工和市场经济为基础，把经济活力、生产效率和发展机会传导到世界各国，大大促进了生产力的发展和世界经济的增长，尤其是为一部分有潜力的发展中国家赶超发达国家经济提供了难得的历史机遇。在联合国日内瓦总部的演讲中，习近平主席指出，"经济全球化是历史大势，促成了贸易大繁荣、投资大便利、人员大流动、技术大发展。21世纪初以来，在联合国主导下，借助经济全球化，国际社会制定和实施了千年发展目标和2030年可持续发展议程，推动11亿人口脱贫，19亿人口获得安全饮用水，35亿人口用上互联网等，还将在2030年实现零贫困"。[2] 这充分说明，经济全球化符合世界各国的共同利益，其大方向是正确的。

从根本上讲，经济全球化是社会生产力发展的客观要求和科技进步的必然结果。按照生产力与生产关系、经济基础与上层建筑的辩证分析，经济全球化可以看作人类历史发展到一定阶段的必然结果。世界历史的形成和发展是以工业技术革命为代表的生产力自身运动的结果。随着生产力的发展，世界市场得以建立，全球经济日益紧密地联系在一起。经济全球化有赖于社会生产力的发展，而生产力的发展与科技进步密切相关。

---

[1] 张宇燕等：《全球化与中国发展》，社会科学文献出版社2007年版，第55页。

[2] 习近平：《共同构建人类命运共同体——在联合国日内瓦总部的演讲》，《人民日报》2017年1月20日第2版。

科学技术是生产力,是推动历史发展的革命力量。纵观世界经济发展史,人类先后经历了农业革命、工业革命和信息革命。历史经验表明,每一次产业技术革命,都给人类生产生活带来巨大而深刻的影响,都能够深刻改变世界发展格局。当今时代更是如此。尤其是,以互联网为代表的信息技术日新月异,使经济全球化在新的领域以新的形式加速推进,使世界各国人民更加紧密地联系在一起。

二 疫情严重冲击经济全球化进程

在疫情冲击下,世界经济出现了20世纪30年代大萧条以来的最糟糕局面。2021年1月,国际货币基金组织(IMF)数据显示,2020年世界经济萎缩3.5%,较2019年下降6.3个百分点。[①] 疫情不仅造成了世界经济的衰退,还使各国经济交往受到重大冲击,经济全球化因此面临重大挑战。新冠肺炎疫情对经济全球化进程的冲击,主要表现在对全球供应链、产业链、服务链和价值链的冲击。疫情发生后,商品、服务和人员等要素的跨国流动因各国的疫情防控措施而受阻,从而在客观上推动了世界经济"脱钩"。全球需求急剧萎缩不可避免地导致贸易的大幅下滑。

受部分国家贸易政策内顾倾向加重和突如其来的新冠肺炎疫情等因素影响,2020年世界贸易再次遭受重创。联合国贸易和发展会议(UNCTAD)数据显示,2020年世界贸易额下降了约9%,其中货物贸易下降了约6%,服务贸易下降了约16.5%。2020年上半年全球贸易受疫情的影响最为严重,贸易额下降约15%。[②] 并且,产业链较长的电子产品和汽车贸易可

[①] IMF, World Economic Outlook, January 2021.
[②] UNCTAD, Global Trade Update, February 2021.

能会下滑得更为剧烈。除了疫情在客观上导致的产业链断裂外，一些国家还出现了要求同其他国家实现产业链全面"脱钩"的呼声，甚至已转化为加速全球产业链"脱钩"的政策举措。

同时，疫情使增长持续乏力的国际直接投资陷入更为严重的困境。2008 年国际金融危机后，全球外商直接投资（FDI）大幅下滑，增长缺乏动力。UNCTAD 数据显示，2008 年金融危机爆发前的 10 年间，全球 FDI 流入额年均增速达 20.2%，而金融危机以来的 10 年间，全球 FDI 流入额年均增速为 -0.3%。全球 FDI 在经历 2015 年因全球跨境并购大幅增长而强劲复苏后[①]，2016 年起全球直接投资额连续 3 年下降，2020 年降幅创 2002 年以来新高。根据 2021 年 1 月 UNCTAD 发布的《投资趋势监测》报告估算，2020 年全球 FDI 流入额为 8590 亿美元，较上年的 1.5 万亿美元下降 42%，较金融危机爆发后的 2009 年下降超过 30%。[②]

从短期来看，全球经济出现一定程度的"脱钩"将难以避免。在经历疫情后，各国都提高了对经济过于依赖外部的警惕，这可能引起"脱钩"政策的盛行。甚至有人认为，疫情为全球经济"脱钩"提供了测试。一些经济上对外较为依赖的国家开始反思各自的产业政策，以减少对外部世界的过度依赖。这些情况都可能导致今后一段时间内全球经贸依存度下降以及全球产业链的断裂。但从长远来看，疫情中加速成长的新业态、新模式、新产业将会塑造经济全球化的新增长点。

三 在逆全球化挑战中培育新机遇

近年来，在线科技、人工智能、5G、大数据等数字化技术

[①] 2015 年全球 FDI 流入额较上年增长 38%。由于欧美等发达经济体跨国企业为避税等目的进行大规模企业重组，全球跨境并购成为全球 FDI 增长的主要驱动力，为全球 FDI 贡献了约 33 个百分点的增长率。

[②] UNCTAD, *Investment Trends Monitor*, No. 38, January 24, 2021.

的加快运用，推动了相关产业的迅速发展。疫情防控的常态化将倒逼各国新业态、新模式、新产业的加速成长，依托这些新技术，全球供应链、产业链、服务链和价值链将会在重构中建立更加紧密的联系，从而在更高层次上以新的形式推动经济全球化向前发展。数字经济将在疫情的推动下为经济全球化创造新的发展机遇。

作为一种新的经济形态，数字经济既包括将数据或数字化的知识与信息作为关键生产要素的经济，也包括以云计算、大数据、物联网、人工智能、区块链等数字技术为手段的经济。近年来，全球数字经济发展十分迅速。2019 年，全球 47 个国家数字经济增加值规模达 31.8 万亿美元，占 GDP 比重达到 41.5%。其中，2019 年产业数字化占数字经济比重达 84.3%，产业数字化成为驱动全球数字经济发展的主导力量。[①] 2020 年新冠肺炎疫情发生后，全球数字经济的发展步伐大大提速。经济合作与发展组织（OECD）报告显示，新冠肺炎疫情大流行病使数字转型的所有方面都取得很大进展，各国疫情防控措施进一步刺激了宽带通信服务的需求。在 OECD 成员国，估计有 13 亿人居家工作和学习；在整个互联网价值链上，各参与方的互联网流量比疫情暴发前增加了多达 60%。[②] 数字技术的广泛使用大大促进了产业的数字化转型，并且疫情对数字化转型的长期影响才刚刚开始显现。国际数据公司（IDC）报告预测，2022 年全球 65% 的 GDP 将由数字化推动；2020—2023 年，直接来源于数字化转型的投资将达到 15.5% 的年复合增长率（Compound Annual Growth Rate，CAGR），数字化转型的直接投资总规模将

[①] 中国信息通信研究院：《全球数字经济新图景（2020 年）》2020 年 10 月。

[②] OECD, OECD Digital Economy Outlook 2020, OECD Publishing, November 27, 2020.

超过6.8万亿美元。① IDC还预测，2020年全球大数据相关硬件、软件、服务市场的整体收益为1878.4亿美元，较上年增长3.1%。② 2019—2024年，大数据技术和服务相关收入将以15.6%的五年复合增长率增长。③

在中国等新兴经济体的带动下，全球数字经济快速增长。目前，中国数字经济总体水平已经稳居全球第二，数字产业化保持高速增长，产业数字化全面推进，数字经济发展环境日益优化。④ 尤其是在2020年新冠肺炎疫情暴发后，数字经济在推进复工复产和经济稳定等方面发挥了重要作用。中国国家统计局数据显示，2020年信息传输、软件和信息技术服务业增加值增长16.9%，增速高于第三产业14.8个百分点；全国网上零售额为117601亿元，比上年增长10.9%。⑤ 2020年，中国数字经济规模占GDP比重近四成，对GDP贡献率近七成。

在疫情背景下，很多国家都出台了推动数字经济转型的新举措，涵盖数字基础设施建设、数字产业化发展、产业数字化转型、数字化治理以及国际数字合作等多个方面。在数字基础设施建设方面，5G建设成为新亮点。在数字产业化发展方面，信息技术支撑服务疫情防控和经济复苏的作用凸显，大数据产业和物联网产业的支持力度加大，人工智能发展也驶入快车道。在产业数字化转型方面，数字经济与实体经济深度融合发展，

---

① Shawn Fitzgerald, et al., IDC Future Scape: Worldwide Digital Transformation 2021 Predictions, October 2020.

② IDC, Worldwide Big Data and Analytics Spending Guide, August 2020.

③ Chandana Gopal, et al., Worldwide Big Data and Analytics Software Forecast, 2020–2024, August 2020.

④ 尹丽波主编：《2019—2020数字经济发展报告》，电子工业出版社2020年版，第125页。

⑤ 中国国家工业信息安全发展研究中心：《2020—2021年度数字经济形势分析》，2021年1月。

数字农业、数字文化产业、"互联网+医疗健康""互联网+旅游"等蓬勃发展。在数字化治理方面，数字化公共安全联防联控、数字政务规范化管理、城市设施智能化升级、数字市场竞争等稳步推进。在国际数字合作方面，一些涵盖数字经济合作的区域和国际经贸合作取得新的进展。2020年4月，二十国集团数字经济部长特别会议，就运用数字技术加快新冠病毒相关研究、增强商业活动灵活性和创造就业机会等达成共识。

总之，疫情让各国更加充分认识到数字经济的价值，并推动了数字经济的加速发展。后疫情时代，数字经济将成为继农业经济、工业经济与信息经济之后影响世界经济与国际关系的关键力量，也将为经济全球化创造更大的发展空间。

四 共同推动经济全球化持续前行

伴随经济全球化出现的各种全球性问题，并非经济全球化的必然产物，它只是深刻反映了当前经济全球化缺乏有效的治理。因此，不能将困扰世界的问题简单归咎于经济全球化，搞"逆全球化"的各种保护主义和单边主义。在全球性问题凸显和挑战加大的今天，任何国家都不可能独善其身，仅凭单个国家的力量也不可能妥善处理和应对，而应不断加强国际经济协调与合作，共同探讨推动经济全球化进程的新方案。

首先，坚持多边主义和自由贸易，应对全球化驱动力不足。当前，经济全球化面临巨大障碍，正是由于多边贸易体制和区域贸易安排对经济全球化的驱动作用未能得到有效发挥。为此，世界各国要维护世界贸易组织规则，支持开放、透明、包容、非歧视性的多边贸易体制，构建开放型世界经济。让贸易成为推动经济全球化的基本动力，意味着世界各国不仅应成为现行多边贸易体制的支持者、维护者，还应在国际贸易规则制定、全球制度建设中推动实现各国权利平等、机会平等、规则平等。

正如世界经济论坛创始人兼执行主席克劳斯·施瓦布（Klaus Schwab）所言，自由贸易仍然是全球经济发展和社会进步的最强动力，当今世界各国领导人的责任是既要对抗贸易保护主义，又要让贸易成为包容性增长的原动力。面对经济全球化驱动力不足的困境，中国多次承诺"中国开放的大门只会越开越大"，努力推动形成全面开放新格局，其全球性的重要意义和作用将是巨大而深远的。

其次，积极参与全球经济治理，应对全球治理赤字。在一个相互依存度达到前所未有高度的时代，人类面临着日益紧迫的全球问题。加强全球经济治理，是解决经济全球化引发的市场失灵和全球治理赤字问题的药方之一。新的历史阶段，全球经济治理应该以平等为基础、以开放为导向、以合作为动力、以共享为目标。这是推动建设开放、包容、普惠、平衡、共赢的经济全球化的根本途径。为此，世界主要国家要推动二十国集团等发挥国际经济合作功能，积极参与世界贸易组织改革，推动新兴领域经济治理规则制定，推动完善更加公正合理的全球经济治理体系。

最后，推进共建"一带一路"，不断夯实经济全球化的坚实基础。中国提出"一带一路"倡议的目标在于促进互利共赢，其出发点和落脚点是所有参与国家的共同繁荣。在当前世界经济形势下，"一带一路"建设对于经济全球化的重大意义在于，它有利于推动经济全球化向包容普惠方向发展。面对疫情考验，"一带一路"展现出强大的韧性和活力，相关项目持续推进，合作成果亮点颇多，贸易和投资逆势增长，成为疫情阴霾中的一抹亮色。中国商务部数据显示，2020年中国与沿线国家货物贸易额为1.35万亿美元，较上年增长0.7%；同期，中国企业在"一带一路"沿线对58个国家非金融类直接投资177.9亿美元，同比增长18.3%，较上年同期提升2.6个百分点。自疫情发生以来，各种线上交易方兴未艾，线上线下融合程度不断加深，实体经济和虚拟经济相互促进，使"一带一路"更具活力，更具吸引力。截至 2021 年 1 月，中国已与包括阿根廷在内的 130 多个国家、31 个国际组织签署 200 余份共建"一带一路"合作文件。"一带一路"合作成就表明，促进互联互通、坚持开放包容，才是应对全球性危机和实现长远发展的必由之路，才能从根本上推动人类社会的共同发展和繁荣。

疫情后经济社会发展[*]

一 打赢抗击新冠肺炎疫情战役

新冠肺炎疫情是百年来全球发生的最严重的传染病大流行，是中华人民共和国成立以来遭遇的传播速度最快、感染范围最广、防控难度最大的重大突发公共卫生事件。党中央和国务院高度重视疫情扩散，果断作出封城决策，实行了严格的社交距离管控措施，全国从中央到地方迅速形成统一指挥、全面部署、立体防控的战略布局，有效遏制了疫情大面积蔓延势头，有力改变了病毒传播的危险进程，最大限度保护了人民生命安全和身体健康。我国用1个多月的时间初步遏制疫情蔓延势头，用2个月左右的时间将本土每日新增病例控制在个位数以内，用3个月左右的时间取得武汉保卫战、湖北保卫战的决定性成果，此后又有效处置多起局部地区聚集性或散发疫情，截至2021年3月底累计确诊10.27万人，累计治愈9.74万人。

中央迅速成立了应对疫情工作领导小组，派出中央指导组，建立国务院联防联控机制。提出"四早"（早发现、早报告、早隔离、早治疗）的防控要求，确定"四集中"（集中患者、集中专家、集中资源、集中救治）的救治要求，着力提高收治率和治愈率、降低感染率和病亡率。对待每一个患者都全力以赴，

---

[*] 孙兆阳，中国社会科学院大学国际教育学院副院长，副研究员。

不放弃每一位病患者，费用全部由国家承担，最大程度提高了治愈率、降低了病亡率。我国首先研发出核酸检测试剂盒，加快有效药物筛选和疫苗研发，2021年年初正式启动国产疫苗接种，全国已经超过1亿人接种疫苗，率先全面控制住疫情。

各级党委和政府、各部门各单位、全国民众积极响应中央疫情防控政策。社会主义高动员能力优势发挥重要作用，举全国之力实施规模空前的生命大救援，用十多天时间先后建成火神山医院和雷神山医院、大规模改建16座方舱医院、迅速开辟600多个集中隔离点，346支国家医疗队、4万多名医务人员、19个省区市对口帮扶，在最短时间内实现了医疗资源和物资供应从紧缺向动态平衡的跨越式提升。460多万个基层党组织全心投入，400多万名社区工作者在全国65万个城乡社区日夜值守。各类民营企业、民办医院、慈善机构、养老院、福利院等积极出力，广大党员、干部带头拼搏，人民解放军指战员、武警部队官兵、公安民警奋勇当先，广大科研人员奋力攻关，数百万名快递员冒疫奔忙，180万名环卫工人起早贪黑，千千万万名志愿者和普通人默默奉献，为抗击疫情做出不可磨灭的贡献。

二 推动经济快速恢复并有序发展

疫情在全球暴发后，国际贸易和供应链受到巨大冲击，在严格疫情防控条件下，2020年我国第一季度GDP增长率出现负增长，仅有-6.8%。在保障人民健康安全、控制疫情蔓延基础之上，中央立足国情实际，科学把握规模性政策的平衡点，加大宏观政策应对力度，在"六稳"（稳就业、稳金融、稳外贸、稳外资、稳投资、稳预期）工作基础上，明确提出"六保"（保居民就业、保基本民生、保市场主体、保粮食能源安全、保产业链供应链稳定、保基层运转）任务。各级政府精准有序复工复产，着力抓好农业生产，使经济运行持续稳定恢复，经济发展的内生动力、平衡性和可持续性进一步增强。我国经济第三季度在全球率先实现正增长，2020年GDP达到101.6万亿元，全年增长率达2.3%。

实施助企纾困政策，积极推动企业复工复产，使经济快速恢复。实施阶段性大规模减税降费，出台7批28项减税降费政策，从增值税、企业所得税、社会保险、公积金、物流成本、房屋租金、用电用气征信费用等方面予以阶段性减免，全年为市场主体减负超过2.6万亿元。创新宏观政策实施方式，中央财政对新增2万亿元资金建立直达机制，省级财政加大资金下沉力度，共同为市县基层落实惠企利民政策及时补充财力。通过降低存款准备金率、中期借贷便利、公开市场操作、再贷款再贴现、创新直达实体经济的货币政策工具等方式，推出的货币支持措施达9万多亿元。降低企业融资成本，创设普惠小微企业贷款延期支持工具和信用贷款支持计划，2020年银行业累积对7.3万亿元贷款实施延期还本付息，累计发放普惠小微信用贷款3.9万亿元。为企业持续注入动力，解决了企业融资和经营困难，增强了企业活力。

坚定实施扩大内需战略，充分发挥国内市场作用。中国有巨大的内部市场规模，截至2019年年底，城镇居民人均消费3.62万元，农村居民消费1.49万元。在疫情隔断国际产业链和市场情况下，国内市场的恢复和潜力对于经济复苏至关重要。我国坚持增强消费基础作用，积极支持以新业态新模式引领新型消费加快发展，加快培育建设国际消费中心城市，有序推进文化和旅游消费、信息消费试点，扩容养老托育等服务消费，稳定和扩大汽车等大宗消费，提振餐饮消费，进一步释放农村消费潜力。2020年全年社会消费品零售总额达39.2万亿元，全国网上零售额达11.8万亿元，增长10.9%，其中实物商品网上零售额增长14.8%，占社会消费品零售总额的24.9%。

发挥投资关键作用。出台《关于推动基础设施高质量发展的意见》《关于推动都市圈市域（郊）铁路加快发展的意见》，加大"两新一重"（新型基础设施建设，新型城镇化建设，交通、水利等重大工程建设）领域投资力度。调整优化中央预算内投资计划结构，重点支持公共卫生等疫情暴露的短板弱项，加强重大铁路、公路、水运、机场、水利工程、重大科技和能源基础设施、城镇老旧小区改造等领域建设。2020年全社会固定资产投资（不含农户）达52.7万亿元，增长率达2.9%，资本形成总额对GDP增长贡献率达2.2%，对经济恢复增长发挥了重要作用。

三 脱贫攻坚和全面建成小康社会取得新胜利

面临疫情冲击不利局面，脱贫攻坚战取得了全面胜利。针对疫情、汛情对脱贫攻坚带来的不利影响，优先支持贫困劳动力务工就业，多渠道扩大以工代赈实施规模，加大产业扶贫和就业扶贫力度，强化产销对接和科技帮扶，开展消费扶贫行动，及时落实兜底保障等帮扶措施。出台易地扶贫搬迁后续扶持若干政策措施，790万户、2568万贫困群众的危房得到改造，累计建成集中安置区3.5万个、安置住房266万套，960多万人"挪穷窝"，摆脱了闭塞和落后，搬入了新家园。着力巩固"两不愁、三保障"（不愁吃、不愁穿，保障义务教育、基本医疗和住房安全）成果，统筹运用基本医保、大病保险和医疗救助等制度保障，有效减轻贫困人口就医费用负担。现行标准下9899万农村贫困人口全部脱贫，全国832个贫困县全部摘帽，12.8万个贫困村全部出列，绝对贫困和区域性整体贫困得到解决，提前10年实现《联合国2030年可持续发展议程》减贫目标。

坚持就业优先政策，居民收入稳步提升。2019年，我国就业人口为7.75亿人，其中非农产业就业占比74.9%，城镇就业占比达 57.1%。疫情初期封城期间，这些群体的就业难以实现，造成收入和生计困难。就业是最大的民生，保市场主体也是为稳就业保民生。帮扶受疫情影响的重点行业、中小微企业和个体工商户等市场主体纾困，加大减负、稳岗、扩就业支持力度，扩大有效投资增加就业，支持大众创业万众创新带动就业，全年日均净增市场主体4.1万户，其中企业1.3万户。政府在严格疫情防控基础上，加速复工复产，通过支持多渠道灵活就业，扩大个体经营、国有企事业单位招聘、基层项目招聘、升学入伍、就业见习等方式吸纳就业规模，多渠道做好毕业大学生、农民工、退役军人等重点群体就业工作。2020年城镇新增就业1186万人，年末城镇调查失业率为5.2%，就业形式基本稳定。居民人均可支配收入32189元，比上一年增长4.7%，其中城镇和农村居民收入分别为43834元和17131元，增长率为3.5%和7.2%，在疫情中实现收入增长更加难能可贵。

进一步完善社会保障体系。参加城镇职工基本养老保险和城乡居民基本养老保险人数分别达4.56亿人和5.42亿人，两者基金累计结余超6.28万亿元。企业职工基本养老保险基金中央调剂比例从3.5%提高到4.0%，实现省级统收统支，退休人员基本养老金稳步提高。通过工伤保险为185万名工伤职工及供养亲属提供待遇保障。失业保险保障范围进一步扩大，阶段性实施失业补助资金政策、阶段性扩大失业农民工保障范围，全年共有1337万人领取到各种项目的失业保险。全年向608万户企业发放失业保险稳岗返还1042亿元，惠及职工1.56亿人。出台救助"扩围"政策，及时启动社会救助和保障标准与物价上涨挂钩联动机制，对因疫致困、未参保失业人员加大救助帮扶，实现"应救尽救"，因疫情新纳入低保、特困供养近600万人，实施临时救助超过800万人次。继续实施残疾人两项补贴制度，惠及1153万名困难残疾人和1433万名重度残疾人，为残疾人提供服务设施数4400多个。

四　全面开启社会主义现代化建设新征程

2021年是"十四五"规划开局之年，国际疫情形势不容乐观，国际贸易摩擦、单边主义此起彼伏，我国经济社会发展的方向是构建以国内大循环为主体、国际国内双循环的发展模式。第一，大力提升科技创新能力，强化国家战略科技力量。新型基础设施建设应成为重点发展方向，加快推进人工智能、量子技术、脑科学、生物育种等领域科技创新。实施不同规模企业融通创新示范工程，鼓励大企业向中小企业开放资源、开放应用、开放场景、开放创新，打造基于产业链、供应链的创新创业生态。使用税收优惠机制激励激发企业加大研发投入，完善金融支持创新体系，引导更多资金进入基础研究、自主研发、成果转化等领域。

第二，着力振兴和发展实体经济，提高产业核心竞争力。实体经济是生产率增长的主要动力，我国需要增强制造业核心竞争力，推动重大技术装备、高端新材料、机器人技术与智能制造等领域关键核心技术国产化和产业化。努力扩大制造业设备升级更新和技术改造，推动传统制造产业智能化、高端化、绿色化，促进全产业链优化升级。对先进制造业企业实行税收优惠，提高制造业贷款比重，扩大制造业设备更新和技术改造投资。加快壮大新能源等产业，促进新能源汽车健康有序发展，加快构建智能汽车基础设施、产业生态等支撑体系。培育壮大生物经济，推动生物技术融合发展，加快临床急需用药和高端医疗装备开发及产业化。

第三，推动"一带一路"高质量发展，建设更高水平开放型经济新体制。坚持共商共建共享原则，秉持绿色、开放、廉洁理念，深化务实合作。提升境外投资质量效益，促进对外投融资基金健康发展。深入推进与重点国家和地区规划对接，加强产能合作，推动铁路、港口、能源等互联互通重大项目取得积极进展。继续深化与国际组织共建"一带一路"合作，积极做好风险防范和处置应对。积极参与全球经济治理，坚定维护多边贸易体制，推动二十国集团发挥国际经济合作功能，积极参与世界贸易组织改革，推动国际金融体系改革。

第四，发挥大国担当，为国际疫情防控贡献力量。疫情初期，我国本着公开、透明、负责任的态度，认真履行国际义务，最早向世界通报疫情，第一时间发布新冠病毒基因序列等信息，公布诊疗方案和防控方案，坚定支持世界卫生组织发挥领导作用。发起新中国成立以来规模最大的全球人道主义行动，向世界卫生组织和联合国全球人道主义应对计划提供支持，为有需要的 34 个国家派出 36 支医疗专家组，向 150 个国家和 13 个国际组织提供抗疫援助。发挥抗疫物资最大供应国优势，全年向 200 多个国家提供了超过 2200 亿只口罩、23 亿件防护服、10 亿人份检测试剂盒。根据国家卫健委数据，截至 2021 年 3 月 27 日，我国已经累计接种新冠病毒疫苗超过 1.02 亿剂次，迈出建立群体免疫的坚实一步。

五 加强与阿根廷多层次合作

阿根廷是拉美第三大经济体，也是重要的发展中国家，具有丰富的自然资源、较高的人力资本、开放的对外政策和多元的工业体系。阿根廷是中国在拉美地区的重要贸易伙伴，双方在机电产品、高新技术产品、通信产品、大豆、原油、肉类等商品进出口方面具有互补关系。在目前国际贸易环境下，发展中国家要实现更大范围的合作，才能突破发达国家设置的贸易壁垒。2020 年中国与"一带一路"沿线国家货物贸易额为 1.35 万亿美元，较 2019 年增长 0.7%，占中国对外贸易总额比重达到 29.1%。中国愿意，也有能力与阿根廷扩大贸易范围，持续推进贸易创新发展，优化国内国际市场布局、商品结构、贸易方式，提升出口质量，加强在粮食、资源、能源、产业、基建等方面与阿根廷的合作，增加优质产品进口。

加强对阿根廷疫苗供应与接种。根据工业和信息化部数据显示，我国已批准四款新冠疫苗上市，日产量约500万剂左右，其他的技术路线的疫苗也取得显著进展，一旦产品获批上市供应，我国疫苗产能还将进一步提升。这有助于积极推进药物、疫苗研发合作和国际联防联控，支持世界卫生组织协调整合资源，公平有效分配疫苗，向应对疫情能力薄弱的国家和地区提供帮助，发挥全球抗疫物资最大供应国作用，推动构建人类卫生健康共同体。中国和阿根廷可以在疫苗制造、运输、接种等方面加强合作，在航运、进出关、税收等方面建立快速通道，以互惠互利、互相帮助的方式，尽快推广疫苗接种普及，推动大范围的群体免疫体系建设。

社会科学研究及其作用：
阿根廷的视角*

一 阿根廷社会科学的演变与发展

关于阿根廷国情的社会研究可以追溯到百余年前。19世纪末，资产阶级圈子及社会中先进的知识分子思考和讨论的主要是文明与落后之间的种种矛盾关系。社会知识的生产主要掌握在律师和医生手中，主要意识形态表现为社会达尔文主义和实证主义。

1880年至1930年间，约有500万外国移民来到阿根廷，特别是从欧洲和地中海前往阿根廷，这些外来移民造成了新的社会矛盾和压迫。国家迅速城市化，到第一次世界大战时，大部分人口已居住在城市。

---

* 本研究团队人员包括：福图纳托·马利马奇（Fortunato Mallimaci），阿根廷国家科技研究理事会高级研究员、布宜诺斯艾利斯大学教授；马里奥·佩切尼（Mario Pecheny），阿根廷国家科技研究理事会首席研究员、布宜诺斯艾利斯大学教授；卡罗琳娜·梅拉（Carolina Mera），阿根廷国家科技研究理事会首席研究员、布宜诺斯艾利斯大学教授；维克多·拉米罗·费尔南德斯（Victor Ramiro Fernandez），阿根廷国家科技研究理事会独立研究员、国立海岸大学教授；克里斯蒂安·洛伦索（Cristian Lorenzo），阿根廷国家科技研究理事会兼职研究员、国立火地岛大学教授。

1916年，通过当时实施的普选，阿根廷激进公民联盟首次被推选为执政党，增加了公民权及其他各项权利。与此同时，新兴劳工运动中的所有不同派别，包括无政府主义者、社会主义者和天主教徒，都在关注研究食品和住房成本与低工资之间的关系。这便是阿根廷长期关注国内市场粮食价格的开端，这一历史一直延续到今天。必须指出的是，这些商品，即肉类和谷物，是大型农牧业生产者的主要出口产品，也是国家外汇收入的主要来源。因此，粮食生产一直处于政治和社会关注与争端的中心。

1930年，一场军事政变终结了首次民选政府统治，开启了阿根廷社会的军事化。这次政变以及1930年和1943年的全球经济危机致使国家动荡，破坏了以出口为主导的自由主义增长模式，为另一种基于进口替代的工业化模式和不温不火的政府管制创造了空间。政府对物价和地方生产（肉、粮、油、煤等）的监管机构应运而生，并开始对这些问题进行研究。在那时，以民众贫困化、自由保守主义和英国帝国主义统治为基础的国家治理模式成为了各种民间社会和宗教组织的社会批判对象。

1946年至1955年期间，阿根廷迎来第二次民主统治。当时庇隆政府在动员起来的劳工和社会运动部门的大力支持下，通过民选上台。国家实现了工业化和多元化，工会组织几乎扩展到整个工农界。国家内部设立了社会研究机构，关注教育、人居、基础设施、人口普查、工人组织、卫生、军事制造、国有和私营工业企业等问题，这使得关于上述领域冲突和需求的已有社会知识得到进一步拓展。

这种新模式支持了社会权利的扩大，并推动了对阿根廷社会的新研究。1954年成为整个20世纪财富分配最公平的一年。此外，基于有关政治主权、经济独立和社会正义的提案以及不结盟的第三方立场，阿根廷与整个拉丁美洲的联系不断扩大，反帝国主义使得工人阶级动员起来反对新殖民主义。然而，在

1955 年，阿根廷的主要国家部门与商人、军队及天主教团体联合起来，推翻了第二次民选政府统治。

20 世纪 60 年代，一些军事独裁政权和文官政府在设法约束工人阶级和民众的同时，在公立大学为历史学、人类学、社会学、教育学、经济学、城市学、心理学、社会工作、人居学等社会科学学科的发展拓展和创造了新空间，这也为旧有的文哲学院、法学院和社会科学院注入了新活力。

在这些年里，阿根廷社会科学界与拉美其他地区的社会科学界保持着广泛对话。从发展主义理论，到发达国家与不发达国家之间不平等交流的理论，再到坚持与资本主义大国保持依附关系的理论，这些理论使阿根廷的社会科学焕发了活力。20 世纪 60 年代的社会和政治热潮以及随后 70 年代工人阶级、民众、学术界、学生和宗教界的激进主义，对资本主义统治提出了质疑，并在不同的社会主义和群众性民族主义经验基础上提出了改革方案。

1976 年，一场由商界、宗教界和军方发动的新政变结束了这段历史，并实施了一项消除所有形式的社会抗议和社会反抗的系统性计划。由此，在阿根廷出现了成千上万的被捕失踪人员、流亡者和政治犯，也出现了阿根廷社会有史以来最严重的城市贫困化、去工业化、债务增加和生产剧变。大学受到军事力量干预，社会科学学科也被压缩到最低限度。"颠覆性"一词被用来使这种镇压合法化。阿根廷批判性的社会科学研究被政治及军事镇压所摧毁。

自 1983 年以来，阿根廷经历了本国历史上最长的民主时期。从 20 世纪 80 年代开始，在各大学和国家科技研究理事会，社会科学关于批判性知识教学和生产方面的学术和科研空间得以逐渐恢复。由于恢复了民主，国内主要城市中心的公立大学和研究中心重新开设了各主要社会科学学科学位课程，这些课程在上一次军事独裁时期被迫停止或减少了活动。此外，还开设了许多新的社会科学学位课程。

到了21世纪，随着布宜诺斯艾利斯省乃至阿根廷全国不同地区新成立的高校不断开设新的学士、硕士和博士学位课程，社会科学的机构扩张得以加强。同时，阿根廷国家科技研究理事会也为社会科学和人文科学创造了新的发展空间。今天，社会科学已成为国家科技研究理事会的四大研究领域之一（其他三个领域分别为农业科学、工程学和材料学，生物科学和健康科学，精密科学和自然科学）。在过去20年间，全国各地的社会科学研究中心和大学的本科生、研究生课程都有了重要拓展，实现了多样化和制度化，研究人员和教师的代际基础也在扩大。

最后但同样重要的一点是，1980年开始的公民权利的逐步扩大尚未成功扭转源于前独裁统治时期的财富分配不均。目前，阿根廷近一半人口仍处于贫困状态，且几乎都是长期持续的城市贫困案例。阿根廷的社会科学对这些进程并不陌生，这些问题是对阿根廷的过去、现在和未来进行反思的核心。

二 阿根廷社会科学现状与面临的挑战

如今，阿根廷的社会科学因其高水平的专业人员培训、卓越的科研成果以及广泛融入拉丁美洲国际网络而引人注目。公立大学的社会科学课程为学生提供了扎实的概念、方法论和历史学培训，且以不同学科之间的对话为基础。全国各地的大学和研究中心都在从事研究工作。同时，社会科学界、民间社会组织和政府机构之间的对话也很通畅。事实上，许多受雇于国家、省、市等各级政府机构的专业人员都曾接受过社会科学领域的本科生和研究生教育。

（一）社会科学研究的理论、方法和领域

在阿根廷的社会科学界，各种正统或非正统的理论传统以不同分支学科的形式并存着。自20世纪50年代以来，结构功

能主义和发展主义、欧洲和拉丁美洲的历史唯物主义、解释性思潮和文化研究等分析方法一直占据着主导地位，这些分析方法都因阿根廷和拉丁美洲的政治、社会和文化现实而经历了重新诠释和定义。

在方法论方面，定量调查方法与生活故事、访谈、社会民族志、参与式观察和案例研究以及实证性检验等定性研究方法并存，且互为补充。研究方法具有很强的多元性，包含批判性、反思性的研究方法。

最受青睐的研究领域包括经济与社会发展、贫困、不平等、社会阶层、集体行动、政党与政治生活、教育、卫生、环境、宗教、媒体、国际关系、移民与文化认同、农村研究以及政治经济学。

（二）后疫情时代阿根廷社会科学面临的挑战

阿根廷等半边缘国家在考虑参与世界经济时面临着挑战，新冠肺炎疫情的持续蔓延更是加剧了这一挑战。

1. 发展挑战

新冠肺炎疫情带来了毁灭性影响，进一步加剧了国内危机，需采取短期应对措施；同时也带来了重要的机遇，推动将针对产业和技术政策作用的讨论提上议程。面对全球性的生产资本过度积累和流动性过剩，这些政策问题的紧迫性也显露出来，且这一情况并非阿根廷独有。这些问题伴随着信息和通信技术及生物技术革命步入新阶段而出现，并在一定程度上得到加强。

在这种情况下，阿根廷面临着一个历史性的困境，即如何以及在何处重新构建产业升级所需的专业化生产模式。虽然阿根廷经济起步处于被动，但却拥有"后发优势"，这来自于可以在模仿他国基础上开发本国独有的解决方案，即创造性地采用新技术，并在此基础上加速工业化进程。尽管如此，在新模式的初始阶段，经济落后还是带来了一些局限性。虽然后发经济体拥有小规模和低学习门槛的优势，但在缺乏科技基础设施的情况下，模仿的成本可能很高，而这对于成熟的工业国家则并不高。正如 Freeman（2002）所说，发展中国家是否建设这些基础设施，取决于该国的创新体系和在体系中占主导地位的新技术浪潮的性质。最终，这些国家面临的挑战还在于必须创建不同的体系条件。如果其他国家在产业中的领导地位已经稳固，新兴国家就应该采取不同的能力建设路径，以达到相同目标。

工业化的战略维度是指内核的设计和推广（Fajnzylber, 1984）。寻找可作为产业轴心的生产活动是工业化进程中需要考虑的重要因素之一。尽管国际形势充满破坏性和不确定性，但也似乎为阿根廷某些产业在生产层面创造了历史性机会。这些产业依赖与信息通信和生物技术"部分共有"的科技基础，彼此具有强大的互补潜力。

2005—2015 年间，阿根廷引进和巩固了一整套方法与机制，为制造业创造机会，提升技术能力（Abeles 等人，2017）。由于 2016—2019 年期间政府执政问题，相关体系和预算被认定的优先级较低，产业和技术政策的推进陷入僵局。尽管存在资金上的困难，但这套方法与机制是阿根廷产业和技术政策的一个重要起点，政策方向是发展以生物技术和信息通信技术为基础的相关产业。

2. 全球化挑战

20 世纪 70 年代的危机引发了金融和生产部门的深刻变革，带来了我们今天所知道的经济全球化。随着新自由主义的兴起，金融领域开启了自由化进程，这一进程在整个十年间不断深化，首先始于中心国家，随后逐渐蔓延至世界其他地区（Basualdo 等人，2016）。这一进程在国际层面得到体现，在国际货币基金组织和世界银行等国际金融机构的建议下，资本流动的障碍和规制得以逐步去除。这些国际组织认为，金融改革是消除当地市场既有缺陷的必要途径，也是各国获得支撑本国经济发展所需资源的唯一途径。

金融领域的变革也对生产领域产生了类似影响，这一点从大型工业企业两个紧密相连的深刻行为转变中可以看出。第一个转变是，生产过程的国际化进程日益加快。在这个过程中，大型工业企业逐渐不再以旨在供应当地市场的子公司的逻辑来运作，而是决定开始在生产成本较低的地方生产其产品零部件，并根据其不同战略在不同地方进行产品组装。第二个转变是，大型工业企业发展了一种新型投资模式，这种投资有赖于全球或区域层面的承包商和分包商网络的衔接。在这种情况下，大型企业的管理越来越集中，不仅对生产性投资的可行性进行评估，还对财务投资的可行性进行评估（Santarcángelo，2019）。这一进程在随后的几十年间得到巩固，产生了一种前所未有的生产、区域和全球一体化现象，而世界范围的金融部门在其中得以紧密相连。

3. 新冠肺炎疫情挑战

新冠肺炎疫情社会科学委员会（MINCYT-CONICET-AGENCIA）于 2020 年 3 月开展了一次全国调查。来自全国各地 800 余名社会研究人员在最脆弱地区和群体中向重要知情人收集信息，并根据委员会成员设计的问卷和要求撰写报告。该调查的组织得到了社会与人文科学院长理事会（CODESOC）、全国人文与教育学院协会（ANFHE）、阿根廷科学技术研究委员会（CONICET）和全国大学理事会（CIN）的支持。

第一份报告根据 1487 名阿根廷境内调查对象提供的信息撰写而成。研究人员就主题领域的情况向这些关键知情人收集信息。报告反映了民众在遵守预防措施方面面临的困难、产生的问题以及对新冠肺炎疫情可能持续蔓延的预期。同时，报告也指出并分析了应对疫情相关政策中的关键问题，以全面审视当前及未来亟需政府干预的关键事项。

从社会科学和公共卫生的角度来看，最重要的社会和政治问题是历史性和结构性的不平等、不公正问题不断深化。此外，另一个关键方面是卫生系统，主要问题包括社会和区域不平等、防疫资源的获取、护理和治疗机会、疫苗与药品的生产和提供，以及地方、省、国家、区域和全球各级的治理和沟通问题。

三 阿根廷社会科学的新议题

（一）工业化组织的整体经济研究

1. 世界生产和技术现状的分析与概括

这包括信息通信技术与生物技术之间的关系，范式概念的相关性及其与长期资本积累的关系。大量文献已经研究了技术革命与资本的长期积累周期之间的关系（Kondratief, 1925; Mandel, 1981）。尽管当前争论的焦点在于重振世界经济的可能性以及信息通信技术、生物技术和旧范式之间的连续性和不连续性，但南半球国家面临机遇与挑战的核心，仍然在于确定新旧关键投资领域及其本地化进程，以及基础设施（4G、5G 等）与相关支持机制的创建、移位与共存，尤其是主要参与者的所在地。

2. 科学、技术与国家

这具体指新国际背景下半边缘国家应对结构性变化、挑战及限制的产业与创新政策路径。调动相关资源和能力并非易事，这需要在共同战略核心中提出发展科技系统和提高生产能力的明确产业政策。公共干预不应被视为"良好计划者"所导致的外部因素，因为行动者至少也是变革结果的一部分，不能假设资产阶级的存在是为了国家的发展与变革。

（二）从生物医药进口国到（地区）出口国

应对新冠肺炎疫情需要国家对多种卫生需求作出紧急反应，这凸显了科学技术政策和产业政策的重要性。过去30年的发展表明，阿根廷已经达到了模仿生物技术药物赶超战略所必需的

（生物）技术能力的最低门槛（Lavarello，Gutman&Sztulwark，2018）。少数阿根廷公司与国家科研机构紧密合作，不同程度地融入国际研发和生产网络，已经达到复杂生物技术活性药物成分（API）开发、治疗性药物生产（包括单克隆抗体）以及DNA和RNA疫苗研发所要求的技术水平。

选择阿根廷是因为其生物技术能力可以在区域范围内生产一种活性物质，这一物质由新冠肺炎疫苗的龙头跨国公司之一开发。这很好地说明了阿根廷在该领域的内在潜力。然而，科技政策与产业政策的脱节限制了制造阶段的规模化（包括填充和精加工）。因此，有必要加快在这些领域的建设技术和生产能力，以便在国家层面进一步整合卫生产业综合设施，并探索新的专业化道路，以融入国际市场。这一研究成果为中国和其他国家（如拉丁美洲和加勒比国家、印度、俄罗斯）在治疗药物和疫苗的规模化，以及寻求生物技术与4.0技术融合等领域提供了广泛的南南合作机会。

（三）在区域和全球层面提供农业生物技术

阿根廷大量采用全球农业生物领域的重大创新技术。阿根廷采用的主要是进口技术，但在这些技术的非核心环节也具备一定开发能力。通过采用这些技术，阿根廷建立了较强的初级产品和农产品生产能力，并完成了一定程度的产业转型。尽管阿根廷仍是技术采用者，与发达国家的知识生产体系相比也有一定距离（Sztulwark & Girard，2020），但阿根廷拥有的科研基础能够生产惠及全球的生物技术产品。阿根廷的市场也在不断扩大（在南方共同市场地区），能够有效推动其创新转型。然而，如果产业政策不能较好地部署国家级企业，引导其达到与全球巨头企业竞争所必需的最低生产门槛，这种创新潜力就无法发挥。

这一领域的知识基础与卫生领域的生物技术应用互通，在扩大国内市场和与中国进行南南技术合作方面都有巨大潜力。阿根廷国内有一家大型的中国种子研发和粮食贸易公司，但同时也有必要发展新的国家级公私合营行为体，构建南南战略联盟模式是政策导向研究的一项重要课题。

（四）农业机械作为在农业中普及信息通信技术的载体

农业机械是最有可能在全球推广的"农业4.0"的产业之一。目前，"农业4.0"的普及在国际上还比较有限，在美国和欧洲的普及程度较高，在中国等其他国家有望迅速增长。普及"农业4.0"的主要挑战之一是发展通信网络和采用确保设备之间的互操作性、兼容性和通信性的标准。

因此，阿根廷正处在产业定位的关键时刻。从历史上看，农业机械产业的发展与金属加工技术发展的轨迹重合，有潜力在多个领域参与国际竞争（Lavarello & Goldstein，2011）。然而这种作为区域（或全球）生产者参与国际竞争的潜力尚未得到发挥，该产业也持续遭受贸易逆差。同时，中国正在推进电信公司和农工产业链的战略衔接。随着"农业4.0"初创公司的出现，对于企业"工业4.0"能力建设的政策支持也将同步进行。

在这一领域有若干主题可以开展共同研究，具体包括：5G和其他通信网络在农业中的共存；两国之间进行南南技术转让的可能性；在机器和工具间采用电子互操作性标准的共同策略（如ISOBUS）。

（五）气候变化的人文与社会维度、环境保护、可持续发展与自然资源

在全球环境变化背景下，气候变化、环境保护和可持续发展问题紧密关联，这对各个国家和地区的未来提出了挑战（Lorenzo，2020）。气候变化是当今时代最大的挑战之一，从气候科学与政治、经济之间的交织程度就可见一斑。在《联合国气候变化框架公约》和《巴黎协定》框架下,我们在气候变化缓解、气候变化适应、融资、技术和能力建设政策方面寻求共识与长期合作,促进谈判各方积极参与（Klöck,2020；Bueno Rubial,Siegele,2020年）。由于气候问题的紧迫性,以及确保《巴黎协定》的所有要素在全球盘点中得到公平呈现的必要性,这些行动的价值更加凸显（Winkler,2020）。同时,这一合作可以在二十国集团中得到加强,期望各国能在这一领域有更远大的目标,加强气候领导力（Hughes,de Jong,Thorne,2020）。阿根廷担任二十国集团轮值主席国期间,在增强适应性方面留下了宝贵遗产,可以通过采用将研究与政策制定联系起来的永久性工作计划进一步巩固。同时,在国家和次国家层面开展更多有关缓解气候问题和适应性政策的比较研究也很有意义。

人类在南极的活动已经广泛影响了多个地区的生物多样性（Leihy等人,2020）,并引发了人们对南极在全球生态系统中作用的关注。在这片地球最后的净土上,气候变化、环境保护和自然资源的合理利用等问题需要认真审视。要增强《南极条约》体系的韧性,关键在于加强南极合作,而中国和阿根廷都是该体系中的积极成员。过去几十年中,新的挑战和困境不断涌现。更具体地说,气候变化对南极的影响是迄今为止最重要的关切之一。南极冰盖的加速消失以及温度和降水量的变化证明了这一点（Chown&Brooks,2019）。此外,南极海洋生物资源养护、南极保护区以及疫情影响等挑战也亟待解决,应重视南极地区的科学、决策和商业活动带来的短期和长期影响。尽管研究南极地区的主要是自然科学各领域的科学家,但这也为开展社会科学研究提供了宝贵机会（Chaturvedi,2016）。

四 中阿社会科学合作的可行性

在过去50年间,各国所走的发展道路并不一样。一方面,东南亚国家和中国的案例是，国家作为发展驱动力在关键源头具有强大参与和决策能力，并以非常有效的科技创新为支撑，成功巩固了高度良性的发展模式。中国也正是凭借这种发展模式在世界范围内取得领先地位。

另一方面，大多数拉美国家在20世纪70年代中期放弃了进口替代的工业化模式，开始实行新自由主义政策。这些政策最初在军事独裁统治下实行，后来被民主政府所巩固。许多拉美国家深陷经济自由化、放松市场管制和私有化的道路，在21世纪初导致了深刻的经济和社会危机。制造业矩阵的逆转破坏了增长能力，加深了以自然资源为基础的生产专门化进程，导致其累积的核心力量薄弱、日益跨国化且从属于外部需求，在本国及生产国保留盈余的能力不足。

这两个地区不同的发展战略产生了若干后果，其中最重要的就是它们在全球价值链中的参与度不同。拉丁美洲和阿根廷在全球价值链中完全被边缘化，而中国则占据非常重要的地位。在全球价值链的一些环节上，中国的参与度非常高，乃至起到主导作用。阿中两国经济具有强大的互补性，这为阿根廷创造了一个巨大的机会窗口。阿根廷与中国的双边贸易额由2003年的32亿美元增长至2019年的155亿美元。尽管自2008年以来，阿根廷对华贸易逆差不断扩大，但2019年阿根廷对华出口大幅增长，达到64亿美元的历史高点，比2018年增长64%，这使其对华贸易逆差降至29亿美元，是自2010年以来的最低点（联合国贸易委员会，2021年）。

在商品构成方面，两国在生产上的互补性有利于深化双边贸易往来，带动产业间贸易（初级产品及衍生品的工业制成品）。在这种结构下，阿根廷对华出口主要集中在大豆、冷冻牛肉、海鲜、家禽、豆油和花生油，占2019年对华出口总额的64%。受2018年阿中签署的贸易协议影响，2020年牛肉超过大豆成为阿根廷主要对华出口产品。

中国在阿根廷提供了多方面金融工具。在贷款方面，2007年至2018年期间，阿根廷与中国达成的协议金额约为169亿美元（Gallagher 和 Myers，2019）。双方承诺实施的一些项目包括：（1）2017年达成协议的考查里（胡胡伊省）太阳能发电站开发项目，中方贷款金额为3.31亿美元（由中国进出口银行提供）；（2）2010年、2014年和2018年达成协议的阿根廷铁路系统现代化项目，协议总金额为132亿美元（Gallagher 和 Myers，2019年）；（3）圣克鲁斯省"秃鹰崖"和"La Barrancosa"水电站建设项目，中国国家开发银行、中国工商银行和中国银行贷款约47亿美元（Rius，2017；Marchio，2019）。中国加强对基础设施的投资，将能够加强南南经济合作，以配合正在进行中的相关发展规划。

这一切为阿根廷社会科学界与中国同行之间的联系提供了一个独特的机会，使我们能够反思在社会知识的全球和国家生产过程中所涉及的认识论和地缘政治假设。特别是，阿根廷社会科学界需要在没有欧洲和盎格鲁—撒克逊学派的认识论和理论中介的情况下，接触到中国社会科学界的多样化思想。深化阿根廷及拉美地区同中国在社会科学领域的联系，将有助于使其认识论立场从概念化的所谓全球进程的立场上分离开来。

我们相信，跨文化对话能够产生由多种知识来源滋养的多元认识论。这意味着要从主客体认识论转向主体认识论，在这种认识论中，研究者和被研究群体都会产生情境化的、相关的和历史化的知识。这种认识论的基础是，一个已知主体在生产关于社会世界的思想和概念时，承认他者是平等的，从而评估不同的人在认知互动中所拥有的相同的认知能力。

因此，我们把社会生活知识的生产过程设想为学术研究与社会行为者自身的反思性之间的一种共同生产。我们认为，在大学和学术中心创造科学知识的方式与在社会中创造常识和人类信仰的方式之间，尽管存在着矛盾，但也确实有着很大的互补性。

五 中阿社会科学合作的方向与选题

加强阿根廷与中国在社会科学领域的学术和科研联系,关键是要促进两国间学生、教师和研究人员的流动。科研和学术流动有助于促进跨文化知识发展,建立友谊和互信的纽带,这对于建立持久的社会和机构联系至关重要。因此,我们对阿中交流合作可采取的不同工作模式提出如下建议。

1. 访学研修

组织相关人员赴对方国家的大学和研究中心进行为期 6 个月至 1 年的访学研修,期间参加课程学习,开展实证和文献研究,参与科研项目,举办讲座和课程,指导当地本科生和研究生。可分别为赴阿根廷和中国访学人员设置西班牙语和汉语课程。

2. 暑期课程

在阿根廷为中国学生、教师和研究人员开设暑期课程,介绍阿根廷和拉美社会科学;在中国为来自阿根廷和拉美地区的学生、教师和研究人员开设与双方国家和地区相关主题的暑期课程。

3. 拉美—中国关系常设中心

设立由阿中两国研究人员和教师组成、与其他政府机构协调配合的"拉美—中国关系常设中心",在关于阿根廷及拉美地区与中国关系的问题上为学术议程和公共政策设计提供相关知识。

4. 围绕共同主题开展联合和比较研究项目

(1) 中国崛起和"一带一路"倡议下的阿根廷和拉丁美洲:建设性的一体化及面临的挑战和建议。分析两国在全球价值链中的一体化战略,以及国家在实现一体化方面所发挥的作用。探讨、确定并制定促进阿根廷不同地区特定生产部门发展的政策建议，以实现良性整合，通过工业化进程、技术经济模式和内生核心，促使其迈向高质量发展。

（2）中阿发展互鉴。探讨在阿根廷可再生能源、电信、研发等相关部门以及对出口增长和创造就业具有重要影响的生产部门进行投资的条件、能力和潜力。为全面了解中国的投资情况，建议按部门、省份和企业，对中国在阿根廷的投资项目进行调查、系统化和地图化。研究中国在可再生能源、电信和研发领域的促进和整合战略，以确定可行的发展战略以及两国之间可采取的互动方式。识别和分析中国的生产部门的推广以及土地发展政策，将其作为一种分享经验和加强相互了解的机制。

（3）中阿气候与环境合作。一是气候变化多边合作，即《联合国气候变化框架公约》和《巴黎协定》中的国家贡献、长期目标和目标周期；二十国集团在气候行动中的领导地位；谈判过程中的行动和执行手段，包括集团和联盟。二是气候变化政策，即能源转型的路径与场景，尤其是可再生能源；与适应性有关的政策（基于社区和生态系统的适应性）；国家、次国家以及区域层面的国家适应性计划（NAP）；国家适应性计划中的性别因素；监测、评估和学习系统（MEL）；金融体系中的气候因素。三是国际旅游关系，即国际旅游政策（双边、区域以及国际组织）；与旅游相关的交流，包括社会（游客）、文化象征（软实力和国家品牌战略）、环境（气候变化）、健康（新冠肺炎疫情）。四是南极治理，包括南极海洋生物资源保护、新冠肺炎疫情对南极环境保护的影响、南极旅游业以及气候变化对南极的影响。

（4）中阿社会问题研究合作。中国和阿根廷社会科学研究机构必须承担起研究和反思两国经验的责任，从而为理解和处理当代社会问题（如新的人口流动形式、环境挑战、新型社会与情感关系、新文化消费以及旅游业的发展）提出明智建议，将其作为跨文化交流的新领域。有必要针对这些问题开展比较研究：移民进程与移民身份；新的家庭组成、性别与家庭角色；女性在政治、商业、国家及家庭中的角色；包容女性和转性群体的战略与政策；信仰、宗教及其社会角色，社会援助与志愿工作；跨宗教对话；国家的价值与立场；跨文化对话与实践——外语学习、中国武术在阿根廷、舞蹈（探戈在中国）、传统食物与当地融合；作为经济发展重要领域的文化产业与旅游业，及其与新消费行为与消费流通平台的关系。此外，针对深受新冠肺炎疫情影响的多个社会群体类别（阶级、性别、年龄、种族、公民身份、宗教），研究应侧重于以下方面：疫情对社会平等的影响；人口挑战；疫情对卫生系统组织方面的挑战；疫情对护理理念与护理实践的影响，包括护理经济、家庭与社会政策、市场力量与社区团结、就业与工作；疫情对情感关系的影响；经济困难与不平等及性别关系（包括性别暴力）；疫情对数字经济的影响（电子商务、电子支付手段、电子货币）以及虚拟办公/虚拟医疗；疫情对城市空间使用的影响，包括人员活动和人口流动的变化；疫情对城市和人口迁徙的影响。

中国崛起和"一带一路"倡议下的阿根廷和拉美：建设性融合的相关挑战及建议[*]

一 霸权主义危机、中国崛起和"一带一路"倡议下的全球多极联通

新冠肺炎疫情加速了当代全球历史空间转型的一系列趋势，使当前国际关系迎来了一个新的变化与重构的时刻。在这些转型中，值得关注的包括：中国和亚太地区的相对崛起以及美国和西方的相对衰落；政治战略矛盾的上升，加剧了在多个领域和地区既已存在的冲突，威胁全球稳定；美国霸权危机及其引发的"全球混乱"；结构性经济危机，对全球资本主义的核心部分及其势力范围产生了一定影响，并加剧了融资困难；生产关系向新的技术范式转变；以及全球发展中国家为了向前发展而必须制定的战略路径所面临的重重困境。

充满活力的全球资本积累中心已经从西方转移到亚太地区，

---

[*] 本研究团队人员包括：维克多·拉米罗·费尔南德斯（Victor Ramiro Fernandez），阿根廷国家科技研究理事会独立研究员、国立海岸大学教授；朱莉安娜·冈萨雷斯·霍雷吉（Juliana Gonzalez Jauregui），拉美社科院研究员；加布里埃尔·梅里诺（Gabriel Merino），阿根廷国家科技研究理事会研究员、国立拉普拉塔大学教授。

产生了以中国为主要推动力的地缘经济转型。与发达国家相比，1978年至2010年期间，中国年均经济增长率为10%，2011年至2019年期间，中国年均经济增长率在6%—7%之间。2020年，由于新冠肺炎疫情导致的全球危机，中国经济只增长了2.3%，但与此同时，中国也是全球唯一实现经济正增长的大型经济体。

中国在全球贸易、投资和融资领域已占据核心地位。2013年，中国成为全球最大的出口国。2014年，中国超越美国，成为以购买力平价计算的GDP总量最高的国家经济体（以购买力平价计算，自1872年以来，美国一直是全球第一大经济体）。2020年，中国超越美国，成为欧盟最大贸易伙伴。同时，自2011年以来，中国已成为全球主要商品进口国，以及全球第一大能源、矿物和食品消费国。

在资本流动方面，中国是全球最大外资流入国和全球第二大对外投资国，累计外国投资存量超过9000亿美元，对于发展中国家发挥着越来越重要的作用。中国应对2008—2009年国际金融危机所作的努力及其相关产业政策，带来了信贷繁荣，也使中国商品在国际市场上占据更加重要的地位。2009年，中国从净债务国变为净债权国，发展融资在其国家现代化目标中占据关键地位。

此外，2019年，中国制造业GDP达4万亿美元（占GDP总量的28.4%），相当于美国、德国和日本的总和。如今，中国已不仅仅是北半球范围内最大的世界工厂，且能在设计、高级金融、顶尖技术和战略管理功能等领域参与竞争。中国已经成为专利申请的主要国家之一，引领着所谓"第四次工业革命"的一些前沿技术，并与其他亚太国家一道，在能源转型中处于领先地位。

中国和亚太地区在全球范围内的崛起，亦或其他力量的重现和强化，反映了世界力量版图的关键变化和向多极化现实的演变。南半球的半边缘地区和边缘地区浮现了新的困境和机遇，因此，出现了获取财富和参与全球决策相关民主化路径的新倡议。同时，也出现了有关国家和地区发展的新提议，对发达国家和发展中国家之间原有的中心—外围关系、国家间体系的传统等级制度以及基于不平等国际分工的经济变动提出了异议。

由于"华盛顿共识"框架下的单极新自由主义全球化的确立、影响生产和劳动部门的资本主义融资，以及主导发展模式带来的文明困境等因素的影响，其他全球化的愿景和形式正在不断涌现。改革现有多边机制的呼声越来越高，同时，许多新的区域和全球多边机制得以建立，这些新机制反映了发展中国家的新现实，例如金砖国家及其创立的新开发银行、上海合作组织、南美洲国家联盟等。其中，中国的"一带一路"倡议因其规模和特点脱颖而出。中国于2013年启动了"一带一路"倡议，得到俄罗斯、中亚国家和其他欧亚国家的支持，此后，世界不同地区的国家也陆续加入该倡议。目前，该倡议涵盖范围内涉及全球70多个国家和40多亿人口、全球已知能源储备的75%，以及以购买力平价计算的世界GDP的55%以上。

为了理解全球性力量更迭演变的背景，应当思考中国政策制定所基于的长期愿景，以及中国于1949年取得结束大国新殖民主义统治的新民主主义革命胜利后所开启的新征程。当前实现"中国梦"的目标，即实现中华民族伟大复兴。中国重回国际体系中央，即回到在18世纪之前中国在全球经济和文明中所处的位置。中国将在2049年前成为全球化、技术变革和知识社会的引领者。在中国共产党第十八次全国代表大会上确定的目标体现了2008—2009年发达国家爆发国际金融危机后，2009—2011年中国国内和外交政策的转型。自新中国成立以来，中国一直奉行与其他大国过去走过的道路所不同的发展道路，这种发展道路建立在"中国特色社会主义"这一独特生产方式之上。

"一带一路"倡议是这些总体目标的一部分，并为"走出去"战略提供了新的推动力。这些政策不仅是中国社会主义现代化战略以及随之而来的海外合作战略的中心内容，也是分析中国与拉美国家关系的轴心因素。与中国和亚太地区所走的发展道路相比，"华盛顿共识"统治下的拉美自20世纪70年代末以来遭受了重大发展挫折，尽管在21世纪初情况有所改变，但这一重大的边缘化过程很难得以逆转。

二 中拉合作及"一带一路"倡议在拉美地区的延伸

在拉美，包括南美洲的乌拉圭、厄瓜多尔、委内瑞拉、智利、玻利维亚、秘鲁和阿根廷，共21个国家已加入"一带一路"倡议。中拉相互关联度和合作水平的提高，与中国在该地区日益增长的影响力相吻合。中拉贸易额从2002年的170亿美元上升至2019年的3150亿美元。据估算，到2025年，中拉双边贸易额可能达到5000亿美元。在这一框架下，值得注意的是，中国已经成为南美洲的最大贸易伙伴。

此外，拉美成为中国外商直接投资（FDI）的主要目的地。2005年至2019年，中国在拉美的FDI达1300亿美元，也就是每年新增近100亿美元。2015年，在北京举行的中国—拉美和加勒比国家共同体论坛首届部长级会议上，习近平主席提出，2015年到2025年，要实现中国在拉美直接投资存量达到2500亿美元的目标。因此，中国投资作为拉美区域FDI的一部分，其相对加权份额从2003年的1.67%上升至2017年的6.30%。

近年来，并购成为中国在全球范围内进行外商直接投资的最主要渠道，在拉美也不例外。2020年之前，并购占中国对拉美投资的62%，其中涉及最多的国家是阿根廷和巴西，智利和秘鲁也变得越来越重要。2020年，中国公司在全球范围内的并购额连续第四年下降，这一趋势也随着新冠肺炎疫情的发生而不断加深。而在拉美，来自中国的并购非但没有减少，反而较此前有所上升，超过其在欧洲和北美的并购额总和。

中国在拉美的外国直接投资分布在不同领域，但在战略性领域的投资较为突出，包括基础设施、能源、原材料开采等。在这些投资项目中，有一些大型基础设施项目是推进拉美国家发展的核心，且与其他地区在"一带一路"框架内所开展的项目类似，包括桥梁、公路、隧道、输电网络、可再生能源园区、管道、大坝、核电站、横贯拉美大陆的铁路等，甚至还包括一条连接太平洋和大西洋的跨洋海路。

中国向拉美国家提供贷款，这种融资超过了世界银行和美洲开发银行在过去十年间所提供的贷款总和，这使得中国在拉美地区日益增长的影响力变得越发显著。自2005年以来，中国的两家政策性银行，即中国国家开发银行（CDB）和中国进出口银行（CHEXIM），已经向拉美地区国家提供了超过1400亿美元的贷款。与其他全球融资提供者不同，中国的贷款不需要宏观经济政策方面的制约性条款。此外，自2009年以来，中国中央银行实施了积极的互换政策，目的是促进人民币国际化，并增强中国金融实力。

关于中国和拉美的关系，中国在与拉美和加勒比国家共同体（拉共体）合作方面提供的支持也值得一提。2016年，习近平主席在访问智利、厄瓜多尔和秘鲁时首次表达了中国有意将拉美国家纳入"一带一路"倡议，到2017年，习近平主席宣布拉美是"一带一路"倡议、特别是"21世纪海上丝绸之路"的"自然延伸"。2010年创建的拉加共同体是在转向南南关系背景下推进拉美自主区域主义的一部分，近年来其影响力不断减弱，凸显了拉美区域一体化面临的挫折。某些情况下，有兴趣通过拉加共同体与拉美地区建立联系并加强该机制的似乎是中国，而非在该地区的国家。同样，需要指出的是，中国已经制定了与拉美接触的战略，并在过去二十多年间以各种不同方式加强与拉美的关系。事实上，中国不仅与该地区国家和拉加共同体分别建立了双边和区域战略伙伴关系，以及全面战略伙伴关系，而且还增加了赴拉美地区的高层访问次数。此外，中国还与智利、秘鲁和哥斯达黎加签署了自由贸易协定，并与该地区的一些国家签署了双边投资协定。同时，中国加大了对拉美区域和多边机制的参与度，发布了两份《中国对拉美和加勒比政策文件》，制定具体计划，促进中拉共同议程的建立和深化。而相较之下，拉美地区仍然缺乏一个联合战略以处理和规划与中国的中长期关系。

拉美地区一体化问题是改善拉美国家国际地位、增强拉美国家对其他大国发声、减少现有的不对称性和实现更大程度的相对自主所面临的核心障碍。同时，拉美各国在区域主义方面的碎片化，对于推进符合区域需求的发展项目，形成必要的生产规模以提升产业复杂化程度以及拓展国家战略能力等都造成了阻碍。

在中国和阿根廷的经济关系方面，双边贸易额从 2000 年的 20 亿美元增加到 2019 年的 163 亿美元，其中阿根廷出口达 70 亿美元，进口达 90 多亿美元。中国是阿根廷继巴西之后的第二大贸易伙伴。实际上，在 2020 年新冠肺炎疫情最严峻的时期，中国成为阿根廷第一大贸易伙伴，而南方共同市场伙伴之间的贸易额则有所下降，这反映了近年来南美国家的去工业化和初级产品出口专门化进程。值得注意的是，自 2008 年以来，阿根廷对中国一直保持着贸易逆差，这一贸易逆差在 2019 年大幅下降，但在 2020 年又再次上升，与阿根廷对其他国家和区域集团的贸易逆差相比，阿根廷对华贸易逆差额是最高的。

就中国在阿根廷的外国直接投资而言，中国在大豆领域进行的投资涵盖了生产链的各环节。中国在阿根廷的投资还涵盖金融业、肉类行业、汽车行业、零售业、渔业和电信业。此外，中国公司还投资于被认为具有战略意义的经济部门，如石油和天然气、采矿（铜和锂，以及其他相关矿物）、物流和运输基础设施、风能、水电和太阳能，同时签署了一项在阿根廷建设第四座核电站的协议。在2020年至2021年间，阿根廷与中国在能源和交通基础设施方面签署了几项投资协议，这些协议与"一带一路"倡议下的其他项目相类似。

在融资方面，阿根廷从中国国家开发银行、中国进出口银行和中国工商银行获得了贷款。这些融资协议主要涉及运输和物流基础设施项目以及能源领域。此外，阿根廷是亚洲基础设施投资银行的区域外成员，并从2009年起与中国签署了多项货币兑换协议。

还应指出的是，阿根廷和中国在2004年成为"战略伙伴"，并在2014年将双边关系提升为"全面战略伙伴关系"。两国学者应当对中阿双边关系的深化及其在阿根廷发展和国际嵌入方面的影响多加关注。从多极世界中的南南合作和双赢逻辑的角度来看，阿根廷加入"一带一路"倡议应考虑某些优先目标，减少存在的不对称性，扭转生产矩阵的"初级化"过程，建立互利经济交流。

三 全球新秩序和中国的"一带一路"倡议：融合共赢及面临的挑战

阿根廷和拉美融入"一带一路"倡议，以及总体而言中国进一步深化与拉美和阿根廷关系，也面临着相应的挑战。拉美地区民族国家的形成以及最初英国霸权和后来美国霸权在该地区的布局，构成该地区一体化特殊的历史背景。以此为背景，该地区一体化模式处于转变之中。这就需要在学术层面和公共政策领域，从阿根廷和拉美的角度来确定行动方向。

第一，基于自主的整合。这是拉美思想中具有悠久传统的一个侧面，是在与亚洲，特别是与中国关联中包含的一项重要因素。在它所涉及的多层面问题中，最相关的是在区域宏观层面，产生形成内生和动态的积累内核。

第二，从加强自身宏观区域融合出发的整合。自主性的构建需要宏观区域一体化进程作为支撑，它涵括整个拉美地区，且不仅限于投资和贸易协定，它还激发构建起一种积累模式，其主要载体是其宏观层面区域生产链的整合。当中有两个相互关联的子向量：工业化和技术发展，两个进程共同推进，从而强化和优化参与全球价值链的水平。

第三，基于通过工业化的融合。上述子向量中的第一个是工业化进程，这也是有关拉美发展结构主义思想的一项重要组成部分，布局非次要和"初级化"积累模式，在全球南方国际一体化中甚为盛行。在此布局中，以工业化为不可或缺的支柱，一批发展动力中心生成出来并得到加强。工业化是一个居于中心位置的方面。自20世纪70年代中期以来，特别是由于华盛顿共识，其在拉美和阿根廷呈现为短板。由此需要重新制定一种与新的生产和实现条件相适应的产业战略，这包括多重离岸经济活动，也包括在多重本地化生产链中依托分散与去中心化打造复合型发展动力；以及通过新技术的吸收与自主研发，提升在全球价值链中的位置。

第四，基于技术开发和对工业化过程的战略控制实现整合。在这些新的再生产条件下，在积累核心及工业化动力基础上，构建一个更加自主的、在全球和区域层面一体化的工业化，要求在战略部门部署协调一致的学习和创新进程（包括初级部门的工业化）。

第五，基于联邦/地方/次区域一体化的宏观一体化。宏观区域一体化进程作为在"一带一路"倡议下与中国进行反馈性一体化的条件，还需要在整个国家领土上，在分散的生产网络框架内，部署工业化和学习并举的进程。克服区域不平衡，将次国家空间纳入宏观区域联系是一个基本要求，以使"一带一路"框架内的相互关系不会加强空间不平衡，并有利于国家协调一致的多梯次发展进程，在这一进程中次国家空间、特别是那些边缘空间转变成为主角。

第六，与国家能力和国家发展方向的结合。在以扭转结构性弱点为目标的国家建设进程中，上述所有方面都变得可行。这一进程既影响一国的基础设施能力，促成实现更深入和更协调的社会空间渗透，也影响到一国具备管理技能的状况，从而为投资和学习过程提供了条件与引导。宏观区域一体化进程，如"一带一路"倡议，要求在国家能力建设方面取得进展；即克服这些弱点，设法形成充分的梯次链接（国家、地方和区域层次的），并从功能的角度，发挥其货币和金融系统作用，引导其在强化国家战略性生产和技术进程中发挥作用。

假设上述六点中的每一个对中国/阿根廷/拉美一体化战略的成功都有单独的和明确的相关性，那么将它们纳入一个互补性的研究议程，就有战略意义。这个议程可以为相关政策和行动提供支撑，使那些日趋总体上由亚洲、特别是中国引领的进程也能在拉美和阿根廷得以发展，这包括宏观区域一体化、工业化、知识和学习的发展、梯次链接以及国家能力建设。

Social Sciences: Play a Significant Role in China's Economic and Social Development*

Scientific research is an important way for mankind to know and change the world. Social sciences research reveals the laws of economic and social development, and serves economic and social development and promotes people's well-being with research results. Chinese social sciences are accompanied by the great practice of China's development, closely aligned with China's reality, and provide intellectual support for China's development in research and exploration that keeps pace with the times.

1　The Bases and Characteristics of the Theory of Knowledge of Chinese Social Sciences Research

The historical materialism and dialectical materialism created by Marx provide a scientific worldview and methodology for Chinese social sciences research, and constitute the underlying logic of the theory of knowledge of Chinese social sciences research.

---

* Wang Lei, Director-General, Bureau of International Cooperation, Chinese Academy of Social Sciences.

Matter and consciousness are the two basic phenomena of the world. Dialectical materialism points out that matter is the essence and foundation of the world, while consciousness is an active response to matter, and the world is unified on the basis of matter; matter determines consciousness, and consciousness has a reaction to material things. ① The concept of matter in the theory of knowledge refers to the objective reality that does not depend on human consciousness and is reflected by human consciousness. ②

The scientific nature of social sciences is fundamentally embodied in persisting in knowing the world as it is in the objective world, basing everything on facts, realizing the correct reflection of human consciousness about the objective reality, opposing book worship, and rejecting subjective imagination.

Practice is a core category in dialectical materialism and historical materialism. Its philosophical meaning refers to conscious activities that change society and nature. Mankind understands the material world through practice. Chinese social sciences research is closely connected with China's development practice, and in its close integration with China's development practice, it realizes its own scientific nature and thus effectively exerts the function it carries of promoting economic and social development. Chinese social sciences research has a distinctive practice-centered characteristic.

1.1 **From practice**

Chinese social sciences research is rooted in Chinese practice

---

① Yang He ed., *Outline of Marxist Philosophy*, Peking University Press, 2005, p. 40.

② Yang He ed., *Outline of Marxist Philosophy*, Peking University Press, 2005, p. 44.

and integrates theory with practice, which consists of its distinctive features. In terms of research topics, Chinese social sciences focus on major theoretical and practical issues facing China's economic and social development, and answer questions of the times and development. In terms of research methods, we follow the principle of seeking truth from facts, and emphasize investigation and research. We closely connect with rather than being divorced from national conditions and world conditions. We oppose working behind closed doors and do not engage in metaphysics. In terms of theory, we do not regard Western textbooks as the golden rule. We oppose mechanical transplantation and never blindly copy others. We are actively building a range of disciplines, academic system and discourse system of social sciences with Chinese features and style.

1.2 Serve for practice

It is the fine tradition of Chinese academics to learn for the purpose of application. Serving the country's development practice is the fundamental and essential purpose of Chinese social sciences research. All sectors of society and government departments constitute the demand side of social sciences research. Social sciences research institutions provide consulting services for the society, offer suggestions to policy making in various fields, and evaluate the effectiveness of policy implementation. Social sciences research conducts scientific analysis of empirical materials based on academic theories and scientific methods, thus providing the functional value of serving for practice.

1.3 Innovation in practice

Practice is the sole criterion for testing truth, and it is the creed followed by Chinese social sciences research. The objective world and people's practical activities are always changing in motion. Social sciences research should not stick to convention. We must constantly explore new situations, solve new problems, break through original limitations, and revise, expand, and enrich theories and research methods. Practice, knowledge, again practice, and again knowledge. This form repeats itself in endless cycles. This is the dialectics of the development of man's knowledge and the only way for innovation and development of social sciences. Theory can only come from people's practical activities, and theory in turn guides people's practice, and constantly improves and develops on the basis of practical tests.

The practice-centered Chinese social sciences research has embarked on a development path with its own characteristics, and is blooming in the gardens of the world social sciences with its practice-centered characteristic of theory of knowledge and theoretical characteristic.

2 Important Contributions of Social Sciences to China's Economic and Social Development Since Reform and Opening-up

Adhering to the practice-centered characteristic, Chinese social sciences are deeply rooted in the development practice of modernization in China. Soon after the founding of the People's Republic of China in 1949, the first generation of Chinese leaders set forth the ambitious goal of building a modern socialist country. The Third Plenary Session of the 11th Central Committee of the Communist Party of China held in 1978 made a strategic decision to shift the focus of the work of the party and the country to socialist modernization drive, and decided to focus on economic construction and set a policy of reform and opening-up. For more than 40 years, Chinese social sciences have been diligently pursuing a development path that is suitable for China's national conditions, unremittingly exploring the laws of China's modernization drive, and have made due contributions to the enrichment and development of the theory of socialism with Chinese characteristics. The contributions are prominently reflected in how to handle the following major relationships, and effectively promoting China's economic and social development.

2.1 The government and the market

Since the reform and opening-up, China has achieved a profound transformation from the traditional planned economic system to the unprecedented socialist market economic system. The fundamental direction adhered to is to see that the market plays the decisive role in resource allocation and that the government plays its role better under the premise of the path of socialism with Chinese characteristics. Chinese social sciences research actively draws on the experience of mature market economies in the world, and emphasizes the proper handling of the relationship between the government and the market in the construction of a socialist market economy with Chinese characteristics. On the one hand, it respects the general laws of the market economy and minimizes the government's direct allocation of market resources and its direct intervention in microeconomic activities, so as to stimulate the vitality of various market entities and promote productivity; on the other hand, it attaches importance to the "visible" role of the government to effectively make up for market failures.

2.2 The state-owned economy and the private economy

Since the implementation of reform and opening-up for more than 40 years, China has achieved a profound transformation from a single public ownership to maintaining the dominant role of public ownership while developing other forms of ownership. Thus, China's basic economic system has been established, namely a system that maintains the dominant role of public ownership while developing other forms of ownership. China's non-public sector has developed under the guidance of national policies, with the private economy accounting for more than 60% of China's economy. In China's economic structure, the state-owned economy and the private economy are not against each other, but instead cooperate with each other by leveraging their respective comparative advantages to jointly drive China's economic growth.

2.3 Urban and rural areas

After the founding of the People's Republic of China in 1949, we rested on the support of agriculture and rural areas as we pushed forward industrialization and urbanization from a foundation of utter destitution. In particular, over the past more than 40 years of reform and opening-up, we have achieved rapid progress in industrialization and urbanization with the backing of factors including rural labor, land, and capital, thus bringing vast changes to urban areas. In 1978, percentage of China's permanent urban residents of the population was 17.9%. By 2019, it had risen to 60.6%, with hundreds of millions of farmers entering cities and towns during that period. In 2021, China has won the fight against poverty as scheduled, with more than 700 million rural poor people completely lifted out of absolute poverty. By 2021, China has achieved a great leap from a traditional agricultural society to a modern industrial society with its three industrial structures changing from 33.4 : 44.8 : 21.8 in 1981 to 7.1 : 39.0 : 53.9 in 2019. [1] Chi-

---

[1] Xie Fuzhan, "The Theory and Practice of Building a Well-off Society in an All-round Way", *Social Sciences in China*, No. 12, 2020.

na is now the only country that has developed all the industrial categories of the UN's industrial classification with the world's most comprehensive industrial system. As the world's largest manufacturer, China has accomplished rapid industrialization in a short span of several decades, which took developed countries hundreds of years to accomplish.

2.4 Fairness and efficiency

As the ruling party, the Communist Party of China attaches great importance to continuously strengthening and improving national governance and has created two miracles of rapid economic development and long-term social stability at the same time. The fundamental reasons for creating "two miracles" at the same time can be attributed to making big cakes while dividing the cakes well, and properly handling the relationship between fairness and efficiency. Starting from achieving common prosperity, which is the essential requirement of the socialist system with Chinese characteristics, Chinese social sciences always pay attention to how to solve the income gap, urban-rural gap, regional gap, etc., conduct in-depth research on major issues, such as the reform of the income distribution system, equal access to basic public services, construction of a social security system, strengthening the rule of law, and improving the democratic system, and propose relevant development and reform plans. As a large country with more than 1.4 billion people, China has built the world's largest social security system including pensions, medical care, subsistence allowances, and housing, and people's sense of benefit, happiness, and security has continuously increased. Facing a sudden coronavirus epidemic, China put people and their lives first and adopted the most resolute and thorough prevention and control measures to effectively curb the spread of COVID-19. We treated patients scientifically, thus protecting people's lives and health to the maximum. Resumption of work and production was realized in an orderly way, and economic development remained stable with improvement. Based on the socialist system with Chinese characteristics, China has achieved healthy and sustainable economic and social development by continuously promoting social fairness and justice.

2.5 Domestic and international situations

A basic enlightenment from China's reform and opening-up for more than 40 years is that openness brings progress, whereas isolation leads to backwardness. ① China has established opening-up to the outside world as a basic national policy, which has further expanded space for China's development and brought opportunities for the world's development. Chinese social sciences have been studying in depth how should China make good use of both domestic and international markets and resources in the process of its proactive participation in economic globalization. After more than 40 years of reform and opening-up, China has achieved a historical transition from seclusion and semi-seclusion to all-round openness. China has been deeply integrated into the global economy. It has become the world's largest trader in goods and the second largest recipient of FDI, and has long been the world's largest holder of foreign exchange reserves, contributing over 30% to world economic growth for years in a row.

These important relationships above are also major issues common to many developing countries in their pursuit of economic and social development. Based on the practice of China's reform and open-

---

① Xi Jinping, *On Continuing to Comprehensively Deepen Reform*, Central Party Literature Press, 2019, p. 519.

ing-up, Chinese social sciences offer advice and suggestions on handling these significant relationships properly and have contributed wisdom to realize Chinese-style modernization through in-depth research and exploration.

3 Facing the Next 30 Years: Social Sciences Will Take on New Missions in the New Era of China's Development

President Xi Jinping pointed out that the next 30 years will be a new development stage for China to achieve the goal of building a modern socialist China.

President Xi Jinping stressed that "philosophy is the precursor of action, and a certain development practice is always led by a certain development philosophy; whether or not the development philosophy is correct fundamentally determines the effectiveness and even the success or failure of development". [1] Facing the new development stage, China has proposed to put into practice the vision of innovative, coordinated, green, open and inclusive development, which is known as the new development philosophy. In the next 30 years, Chinese social sciences will carry out research in the light of the systematic theoretical system of the new development philosophy, identifying new issues and providing new solutions on the basis of the outstanding challenges facing China's development in the new stage.

---

[1] Xi Jinping, *On Understanding the New Development Stage, Applying the New Development Philosophy, and Creating a New Development Dynamic*, Central Party Literature Press, 2021, p. 475.

3.1 The challenge of scientific and technological progress

In the new development stage, the goal of China's scientific and technological development is to notably improve China's innovation ability, significantly enhance its scientific and technological capabilities, achieve major breakthroughs in a number of core technologies in key areas and make China a country of innovators by 2035; ① and to build China into a world power in science and technology by 2050. ② To this end, on the key proposition of effectively enhancing China's capacity for scientific and technological innovation, Chinese social sciences urgently need to study how to make government and market forces work together and make good use of a variety of resources to overcome major scientific and technological challenges through improved institutional arrangements.

3.2 The challenge of demographic change

The basic trend of China's demographic change is that the natural population growth rate continues to decline, the average life expectancy increases, and the aging population grows rapidly. ③ In 2019, 12.57% of China's population are over 65 years old. ④ The period of

---

① Wang Zhigang, "Undertake the Mission of Self-reliance and Self-improvement in Science and Technology, and Accelerate the Pace of Building a Powerful Country in Science and Technology", *Science and Technology Daily*, November 30, 2020.

② Wang Zhigang, "China Will Become A World Science and Technology Power by 2050", www. Chinanews. com, March 11, 2019.

③ Han Baojiang ed., *New Concept of the Outline of the Fourteenth Five Year Plan*, People's Publishing House, 2021, p. 194.

④ According to international standards, if the population aged over 65 accounts for more than 7% of the population, it means the society has entered an aging society.

declining total social dependency ratio has come to an end, with demographic dividend cuts and a heavier burden of elderly care. Facing the multiple problems brought by the aging population, there is an urgent need for Chinese social sciences to find solutions on the basis of China's realities, mainly including how to form new demographic dividend by developing education and improving labor force quality; how to accelerate scientific and technological progress and structural adjustment to raise total factor productivity and potential growth rate; how to reform the household registration system to optimize the efficiency of labor force allocation between urban and rural areas; and how to improve the level of social security to provide a social safety net for economic transformation while balancing needs and possibilities to avoid falling into the trap of high welfare burden.

3.3 The challenge of ecological environment

In September 2020, President Xi Jinping announced at the UN General Assembly that China strives to peak its CO_2 emissions before 2030 and achieve carbon neutrality before 2060. Based on the experience of developed countries, it takes 40 – 70 years to go from CO_2 emissions peak to carbon neutrality. China aims to complete this process in 30 years, which will accomplish the world's largest reduction in carbon emissions. To this end, Chinese social sciences need to study in depth how to develop action plans to achieve carbon emissions peak and carbon neutrality, and how to effectively develop and implement local and industrial plans to address climate change and protect the ecological environment; with the fact that in 2019, clean energy accounted for 23.4% of China's total energy consumption while the proportion of coal consumption was 57.7%, [①]how to transform the current coal-based energy consumption structure in China into a clean and renewable energy-based structure; how to realize the restructuring and transformation of infrastructure and equipment in the energy industry; and how to provide sufficient financial support for the transformation of the energy structure and even the economic base.

3.4 The challenge of de-globalization

The sudden outbreak of COVID-19 has ravaged the world and disrupted the operation of the global industrial chain and supply chain, with trade and investment activities continuing to be sluggish. Economic globalization, which has already been experiencing headwinds since the financial crisis in 2008, is now facing even greater setbacks. China has always supported economic globalization, opposing unilateralism and protectionism as well as the use of the epidemic as an excuse for "de-globalization", isolation and decoupling. In the face of the various new conditions resulted from the growing de-globalization trend and the changing international environment, China has set out to speed up fostering a new development pattern in which domestic and international development can reinforce each other, with the domestic development as the mainstay. The new development pattern does not mean a development loop behind closed doors, but more open domestic and international circulations, emphasizing opening-up more sectors of the economy in a more thorough fashion and focusing on developing new systems for a higher-standard open economy. To this end, we need to explore how to transform the old development pattern

---

① The State Council Information Office of the People's Republic of China, *White Paper on Energy in China's New Era*, December 21, 2020.

based on external demand into a new development pattern based on domestic demand and endogenous growth, with expanding domestic demand as the strategic basis, so as to keep the fundamentals of the economy stable; how to pursue the strategy of expanding domestic demand and intensify supply-side structural reform, optimizing and upgrading the industrial structure while improving the quality of supply, so as to usher in a higher stage of well-adjusted balance where demand drives supply and supply, in turn, creates demand; how to actively make use of multilateral as well as regional and sub-regional cooperation mechanisms to build a global connectivity partnership; how to effectively promote international macroeconomic policy coordination as well as the reform and building of the global economic governance system to better achieve win-win cooperation between China and the rest of the world; and how to practice the principle of extensive consultation, joint contribution and shared benefits, and advance high-quality Belt and Road cooperation, making it an important link between domestic and foreign markets.

The development of productivity is the fundamental determining force of changes in economic and social patterns. The above-mentioned challenges involve the international flow and allocation of science and technology, demography, resources, commodities, capital and other factors, which are the key factors affecting the state and level of productivity as well as its changes. China, in its new development stage, faces the above-mentioned challenges, but at the same time, by proactively dealing with them, it can turn challenges into opportunities, which contain great development potential and prospects. Facing the new stage of China's development in the next 30 years, Chinese social sciences will continue to uphold the basic principles of linking theory with practice and seeking truth from facts, taking advantage of various disciplines such as economics, sociology, political science, and history to identify, analyze and solve problems in response to challenges and, in this process, continue to enrich theories and methods to better serve China's economic and social development.

4 Conclusion

Since the Industrial Revolution, human society has been moving forward in the historical change of modernization. After the Second World War, classical modernization theory, dependency theory, world systems theory, post-modern theory and the second modernization theory have emerged one after another, and the international academic community has gradually expanded and deepened its understanding of the modernization process. China, like many other developing countries and emerging economies, has been exploring the path of modernization with great difficulty. Based on its own national conditions, China firmly follows the path of socialism with Chinese characteristics as its fundamental choice to achieve modernization. Since the reform and opening-up in 1978, Chinese social scientists have been working on the basic theme of what kind of socialism with Chinese characteristics to build and how to build socialism with Chinese characteristics, going deep into practice to objectively understand China's development practice, explore the laws of China's modernization drive and answer the theoretical and practical questions facing China's economic and social development, and have made due contributions to the pursuit of a development path that is suited to China's national conditions.

There is no one-size-fits-all pattern or standard for modernization. Each country can only take the modernization path that fits its own characteristics according to its own national conditions. With the great diversity of modernization paths, we should actively promote extensive and in-depth dialogues among social sciences of different countries to exchange and learn from each other's development experiences, while exploring the common interests in the development of different countries to promote common development and prosperity.

Demographic Transition, Urbanization and the Trend Towards Smaller Household Size in China[*]

1 Demographic Changes in China

China has the world's largest population. The changes of its population's age distribution do not only exert impacts on the country's labor market and consumption demand, but also play an leading role in the world's industrial structure and distribution, as well as the migration trends. China has already shifted from an adult society to an aging society. The country has also gradually adjusted its one-child policy and is expected to lift all birth restrictions soon.

The average life expectancy of Chinese citizens was around 35 in 1949. The figure has been gradually increased as China has enjoyed social stability and growing economic strength. With lower infant and child mortality rates, China's total population started shooting up. In 1953, the total population was 580 million, climbed to 690 million in 1964. In 1982, at the beginning of the reform and opening-up, it

---

[*] Zhang Yi, Director of National Institute of Social Development, Chinese Academy of Social Sciences.

rose to 1.003 billion, then reached 1.13 billion in 1990, 1.267 billion in 2000, 1.34 billion in 2010, about 1.39 billion at the end of 2017,① and over 1.4 billion in 2019.

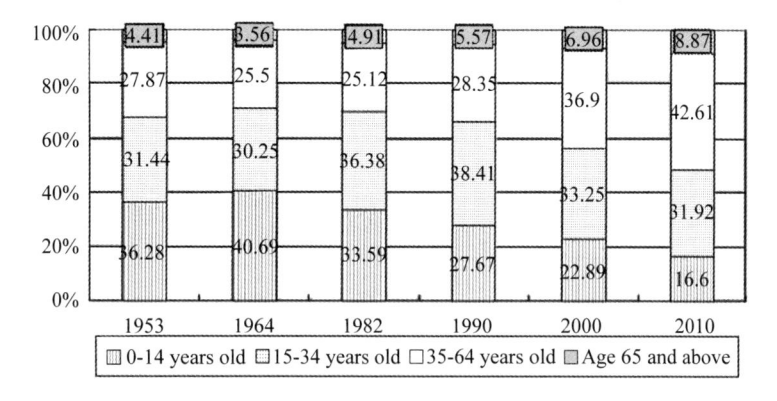

Figure 1 Population structure of China's six censuses by age group

As for the age distribution, in the first national population census in 1953, the children aged under 14 accounted for 36.28% of the total population. The young people aged from 15 to 34 accounted for 31.44% and the figure was 27.82% when it came to adults aged from 35 to 64. The share of the elderly aged 65 and older in the population were 4.41%. By the second census in 1964, the share of children aged under 14 was 40.69%. The share of young people aged from 15 to 34 was 30.25%. The population aged from 35 to 64 accounted for 25.50% in the whole and the proportion of the elderly

---

① These are statistics of the National Bureau of Statistics. The total population was 1.016 billion in 1982, 1.143 billion in 1990, and 1.267 billion in 2000, according to Table 2 – 1 of the *2017 China Statistical Yearbook*. That is, since the fifth census in 2000, the data are consistent with those originally published. The data for the end of 2017 are from the *Statistical Bulletin of the People's Republic of China on National Economic and Social Development in 2017*.

population aged 65 and older was 3.56%. However, during the fifth national population census in 2000, the share of children aged under 14 in the population declined to 22.89% and people aged from 15 to 34 dropped to 33.25%. Meanwhile, the proportion of adults aged from 35 to 64 increased to 36.90% and the elderly aged 65 and older rose to 6.96%. In general, the academic community believes that China has witnessed the coming of an aging society since 2000.

Table 1   Population structure of China, 2019

Indicators	Population by the end of 2019 (million)	Percentage (%)
Total population	1400.05	100.00
Cities and towns	848.43	60.60
Rural Areas	551.62	39.40
Male	715.27	51.10
Female	684.78	48.90
Age:		
0—15	249.77	17.80
16—59	896.40	64.00
Above 60	253.88	18.10
Above 65	176.03	12.60

At the end of 2019, when it came to the share in the total population, the figure was 17.8% and 64.0% respectively, among those the aged under 16 and from 16 to 60. The proportion of the elderly people aged 60 and older grew to 18.1%, and the share of the elderly aged 65 and above rose to 12.6%. It is predicted that in 2022, China's population share of the elderly aged 65 and older will probably reach around 14%.

Internationally, the aging society is defined as an economy in which the share of population aged 65 and older reaches or exceeds 14% of the whole population. This means that from 2000 to 2022, China could possibly take only 20 to 22 years to complete the process.

Among the most populous countries across the world, China has the fastest growing aging populations by far. China has enjoyed a compressed modern development and, in several decades, it realized demographic transition which took developed countries centuries to realize. While this helps China enjoy demographic dividend in the development of manufacturing industries, it also exerts extremely great pressure on the country's future development.

The reasons why China could maintain rapid economic growth rates for over 40 years since the reform and opening-up are as follows. First, the rapid decline in the number of children reduced the child dependency ratio and expanded the absolute and relative supply of the labor force. Second, it also relieved family stresses. With greater accumulation of wealth, parents could concentrate the limited resources on fewer children, which has swiftly enhanced the value of human capital. Third, the reform and opening-up has attracted foreign investment, which efficiently combined capital and labor force. Along with cheap supplies of resources such as land, China has achieved economic growth. The fourth is that the reform of household registration system has facilitated the flow of internal migrants, which released the dividend it brought. The allocation of resources in China's labor market has boosted economic efficiency. In the circumstance where other human and natural environment has remained unchanged, these changes could provide credible explanations for China's long-term rapid growth. Till now, the share of the juvenile population (from 0 to 15 years old) in the total population is still low, while the proportion of the labor force between 16 and 59 years old is relatively large. The share of the people aged 60 and older has increased, but the total dependency ratio remains low. This is the fundamental support force that enables China to build a moderately prosperous society in all aspects.

Based on recent observations, it is also clear that China's total population will peak at over 1.42 billion probably between 2025 and 2028 (if we evaluate the recent births as 14 million babies per year, the estimates nowadays would be different), and then start to drop and enter a period of population shrinkage. Therefore, after building a moderately prosperous society, the aging populations increase sharply. And by around 2035, the proportion of population aged 65 and older in the total will exceed 20%. Thereafter, it keeps growing quickly and goes beyond 30% by 2050.

Why China's population has been aging so fast? The answers may be as follows.

First, the rapid aging of population in China is due to double factors—one-child policy and economic and social development. Both result in the transition of China from an adult society to an aging society. In more than 40 years since the reform and opening-up, family planning policy has gone through three stages, from moderate to strict control to moderate liberalization. After the 1980s, in urban areas, every couple were permitted to have only one child. While in rural areas, depending on the population density and the total number of ethnic minorities, they selectively applied the "one-child policy", the "two-child policy", or a policy of no birth control. However, the overall trend is to become increasingly strict. It was only after 2013 that the policy began to be relaxed, especially, from the "two-child fertility policy for couples where either the husband or the wife is from a single-child family" to the "universal two-child" policy in 2016. But the dividends of the reform policy were limited, with 17.86 million births in 2016, 17.23 million births in 2017, and only 14.65 million births in 2019, which run counter to the expectation of the policy (according to the policy expectation, there should be 3 million to 4 million more births per year than before the reform). The decline in the proportion of the marriageable youth population would be responsible for the result directly.

Second, the high population mobility has affected young people's fertility desire and thus made China's fertility pattern realize the significant transition from that of the agricultural society to industrial society. This was followed by another transition to the pattern of post-industrial society. In agricultural society, because of the high mortality rate, the only way to sustain the productivity of the family is to have more children. While in industrial society, the mortality rate decreases rapidly, the birth rate goes up, and the natural growth rate rises significantly. And in post-industrial society, low birth rates, low mortality rates, and low natural growth rate will become the normalcy. This is the reason why we should recognize the ongoing and long-term effects of social transformation on demographic transition, rather than attributing the current decline in birth rates solely to an increase in the cost of living.

The third reason is the major transition of family model which was resulted by human capital, women's liberation and urbanization. Since the reform and opening-up, China's education equality has contributed to a rapid rise in female human capital. The increase in the women's years of schooling and the population mobility brought by urbanization have greatly delayed the age of first marriage for women. At the beginning of the reform and opening-up, the age of first marriage was once delayed in urban areas because of the influence of "postponing marriage and childbearing", but in rural areas it was limited. In the 1980s, the age of first marriage dropped for a while. However, after the 1990s, the age of first marriage for Chinese women increased in total significantly, and was delayed to about 23 to 24 years old around 2005. Currently, in large cities and mega-cities, the age is delayed to 27 to 28 years old, and in some cities, even to 29 to 30 years old. The increase in women's years of schooling has raised their social status in the family. The broad coverage of the social security system has also increased women's ability to live independently. Nowadays, the proportion of "voluntary non-marriage" and "passive non-marriage" is climbing among the population under 30 years old, which leads to the coexistence of an "empty nest for the young" and an "empty nest for the old". One of the most significant changes is that not only is the unmarried population increasing, but the divorce rate among the married population is also rising rapidly. In 1985, at the beginning of the reform and opening-up, the number of married pairs was 8.313 million and the number of divorced pairs was 0.4579 million; in 2010, the figures were 12.41 million and 2.678 million; in 2015, the number of married pairs continued to fall to 12.2471 million and the number of divorced pairs rose to 3.841 million; in 2019, the amount of married pairs dropped to 9.272 million and the amount of divorced pairs reached 4.70 million. According to these, it is clear that the number of divorced pairs tends to go up and the number of married pairs tends to decline.

Under such circumstances, China's population strategy has to focus on the shift from a country with a large population to a country rich in human resources. It also needs to attach great importance to the demographic dividend transformation from one with a relatively high labor force population to a new one that depends on human capital and scientific and technological innovation. China has to change from a manufacturing power to a powerhouse of innovation. Only in this way can we complete the blueprint drawn by the 19th CPC National Congress for the basically realization of modernization in 2035 and the realization of the Chinese dream of modernization in 2050.

2 Population Migration, Urbanization and Small-sizing Tendency of Family

In 1949, the urban population of China accounted for 10.64% of the total population. In 1978, the starting year of the reform and opening-up, the figure was 17.92%, while the rural population accounted for 82.08%.

After the reform and opening-up, urbanization has been driven by several factors: first, the pull of cities or towns—rural population moves from countryside to city or town; second, the local urbanization of rural areas, that is, under the influence of urban expansion or the non-agricultural, rural areas were transformed into cities or towns; third, the separation between household registration and actual residences existed in cities and towns and the migration of population between cities—under the pull of large cities, China has accelerated its urbanization.

Affected by this, as shown in Table 2, China's urbanization rate is increasing year by year, reaching 23.71% in 1985, 26.41% in 1990, 29.04% in 1995, 36.22% in 2000, 42.99% in 2005, 49.95% in 2010, 56.10% in 2015, and 60.6% in 2019. This is a judgment based on the distribution of the resident population, which is defined as a person having lived in a place for at least 6 months. If we take 3 months as the standard, the urbanization rate would be higher. However, if we take into account the hourly population in the daytime, the urbanization rate in China is likely to be over 75%, which would be the urban-rural distribution in developed countries after the realization of industrialization.

The changes of China's urban and rural structure do not only affect the distribution of the population between cities and countryside, but also change people's lifestyle. It means China has managed to liberate the majority of its population from farm and enabled them to migrate to cities or towns in just a few decades. The variation in residential morphology also changes people's lifestyle to a large extent, transforming it from a sedentary society to a migratory society, from a society of acquaintances to a society of strangers, from a self-sufficiency society to a society depending on market transactions, and from an extended family structure to a small one or an individualized mode of existence.

Table 2　Evolution of China's urban-rural structure on population

Year	Total population by the end of year (million)	Percentage of cities (%)	Percentage of rural areas (%)	Year	Total population by the end of year	Percentage of cities (%)	Percentage of rural areas (%)
1950	551.96	11.18	88.82	1978	962.59	17.92	82.08
1955	614.65	13.48	86.52	1985	1058.51	23.71	76.29
1960	662.07	19.75	80.25	1990	1143.33	26.41	73.59
1965	725.38	17.98	82.02	1995	1211.21	29.04	70.96
1970	829.92	17.38	82.62	2000	1267.43	36.22	63.78
1971	852.29	17.26	82.74	2005	1307.56	42.99	57.01
1972	871.77	17.13	82.87	2010	1340.91	49.95	50.05
1973	892.11	17.20	82.80	2015	1374.62	56.1	43.9
1974	908.59	17.16	82.84	2017	1390.08	58.52	41.48
1975	924.20	17.34	82.66	2019	140005	60.60	39.4

Note: 1. 1981 and earlier data are household registration statistics; 1982, 1990, 2000, 2010 data are projected from the census data of that year; the remaining years data are projected from the annual population sample survey (the same as the relevant table below). 2. The total population and the population by gender include active military personnel, and the population by urban and rural areas include active military personnel in the urban population.

For those who live in rural areas, they no longer rely merely on agriculture-based income, but probably on non-farm earnings. In other words, China's countryside has changed a lot. Now, the class structure formed in rural areas is manifested as: the class of agricultural enterprise owners, the class of village cadres, the class of rural residents, the class of migrant workers and the class of professional farmers. Therefore, the proportion of Chinese traditional peasants has been rapidly declining, and the share of professional peasants is still rising slowly. The progress of agricultural science and technology and the increase of mechanization level, as well as the accelerated transfer of farmland, have largely improved the productivity of agricultural production. In the future, the farming ability of professional farmers will be promoted rapidly. After automation technology is used by the agricultural sector, about 3% to 5% of professional farmers will be able to meet the farming needs of the transferred land. China no longer has to devote its main labor force to agricultural production; it can fully feed China's people with its own land in the modernization process. China has only 1.8 billion mu of arable land, and if you take away the barren slopes and arid lands, less than 1 billion mu of fertile land is left. If land continues to be transferred as it has been in the past few years, it will not take long for the countryside to be transformed into a residential-leaded, rather than continuing to behave as a predominantly peasant countryside. Thus, the last generation of traditional farmers is standing at the crossroads of modernization, choosing the future career.

After over 40 years of blind urban expansion across China, the construction land area of Chinese cities enjoyed a significant increase. However, household registration system is still playing a dominant role in allocating basic public service resources. Because of this, separated living conditions between registered population and non-registered population have gradually emerged in cities. Almost all major cities and mega-cities, or merely mega-cities, have formed a city pattern where registered residents live in the urban center and non-registered residents live in the outskirts. Non-registered population mainly consists the ones who move between cities and those who migrate from rural areas to cities. The bigger the city, the larger proportion of its non-registered population. For example, Beijing and Shanghai both have almost 8 million and 9 million non-registered population. In Shenzhen, the number of the non-registered population greatly exceeds the number of the household population. In addition, in mega-cities like Beijing and Shanghai, the total number of the registered population is slightly higher than the non-registered population. The non-registered population lives in clusters, creating a situation where the local household population is less than the non-registered population and the social form of large separation and small residence. Thus, the original urban-rural dual structure is transformed into a new dual structure of the registered population and the non-registered population within the city.

While pursuing modernization, China has increased the urbanization ratio to tackle the issue and thus made registered residents and non-registered residents live in harmony. It has also fully realized the aim of equalization of the basic public services.

Due to the population mobility and migration across regions, a new kind of family which is made up mainly by migrant workers has formed. Meanwhile, those who are not able to migrate into cities such as children and the elderly have formed a kind of family called left-behind family. After forming nuclear families in rural areas, many couples migrate into cities to earn a living while leaving their children behind. This rural-urban division of family members has increased the proportion of conjugal family in cities and directly led to the small-sizing tendency of family in China. In 2019, about 2.92 people were living in an average Chinese household. The number was even smaller in cities like Beijing (2.56), Shanghai (2.38) and Tianjin (2.65). And the family size is quite small all across the northeast. For example, the number of people living in an average household dropped to 2.54 in Liaoning Province, 2.60 in Jilin Province and 2.47 in Heilongjiang Province. The long-term trend of declining family members resulted from lower birth rates and population migration. And the major factors driving the recent declines are the falling marriage rates and delayed marriage.

China's Basic Experience on Environmental Protection and China-Argentina Cooperation Opportunities*

1 Introduction

China and Argentina are two countries with unique national conditions. In order to achieve the goal of modernization, China and Argentina have explored different development paths according to their own national conditions. In terms of economic development, both countries have made great achievements, and are currently at a critical stage of realizing modernization. The two countries are both members of the Group of 20 (G20) and have important influence in the world. At the same time, the two countries are also facing ecological and environmental problems. After the reform and opening-up in 1978, China has gone from a poor country with a per capita GDP of only USD 156 to the world's second largest economy with a per capita GDP of more than USD 10,000. By 2020, it lifted the entire population out of poverty and achieved the goal of building a moderately prosperous society in all respects. However, due to the inherent conflict between environment and development under the traditional industrialization

---

* Zhang Yongsheng, Director of Research Institute for Eco-civilization, Chinese Academy of Social Sciences. This report referred Zhang Yongsheng (2020) and materials in his relevant research projects.

model, China is also facing a severe environmental crisis. Argentina's geographical and natural conditions are superior. In the early 20th century, per capita income in Argentina was once among the top ten in the world. Until the middle of the 20th century, it was still the fifteenth largest economy in the world. Later, due to various reasons such as political instability and exchange rate fluctuation, the economy experienced decline and volatility. In 2019, Argentina's per capita GDP was about USD 10, 000, and in 2020 it dropped to the level lower than USD 10, 000 due to the COVID-19.

In the process of rapid industrialization, a large number of environmental problems have appeared in China. Before the 18th National Congress of the Communist Party of China, China's understanding of the relationship between environment and development experienced a tortuous process of exploration. The different policies adopted by China to solve environmental problems in different periods with different experiences and lessons are a process of deepening the understanding of the relationship between environment and development. After the 18th National Congress of the Communist Party of China, China put forward a new development concept and formed a complete ecological civilization concept. It is not only due to the special problems faced by China's development model, but also the general problem of the unsustainable traditional development model established after the Industrial Revolution. The report of the 19th National Congress of the Communist Party of China further pointed out that the modernization that China wants to develop is a modernization with "humans developing in harmony with nature".

The thought and practical experience produced in this exploration process in China can become the public knowledge of all mankind, which has reference significance for the cooperation between China and Argentina. This article, as a background knowledge for China-Argentina cooperation in environmental protection, aims to introduce China's basic practices and experience in environmental protection, and reveal its general implications to China-Argentina cooperation. As for the specific areas and methods of cooperation, further identification and in-depth research are yet to be conducted.

2   The Exploration and Practice of Environmental Protection in China[①]

2.1   The evolution of the understanding of the relationship between environmental protection and development

For a long time after the founding of the People's Republic of China in 1949, due to the low level of industrialization, industrial pollution has not yet appeared universally. Coupled with the influence of classic textbooks, people believe that only capitalism societies have environmental problems, and socialism society does not have environmental pollution problems. It has not attracted enough attention. Participating in the United Nations Conference on the Human Environment in 1972 and convening the first national conference on environmental protection in 1973 have enlightenment and milestone significance. China's environmental protection work is largely synchronized with the rest of the world, and both started in 1972 at the United Nations Conference on the Human Environment. Later, although it was seen that socialism society also had environmental problems, China generally believed that the superiority of socialism could

---

① Zhang Yongsheng, "The Reform of Ecological Civilization System", in Xie Fuzhan ed., *The Great Practice of China's Reform and Opening Up*, China Social Sciences Press, 2020.

solve the environmental problems arising in development.

After the reform and opening-up in 1978, China's work has shifted its focus to economic construction. For a long time, due to the small size of the economy, the above understanding has not been seriously tested. With the increasing effectiveness of reform and opening-up, especially after Deng Xiaoping's Talks in the South in 1992 and joining the WTO in 2000, China's economy has developed rapidly and has become the "world factory" (see Figure 1). The previously set target for reducing the total amount of pollutants has not only been impossible to achieve, but the environmental problems will be difficult to curb even with great efforts. In view of these realities and the development experience of Western industrialized countries, China has begun to see firsthand the dilemma between environment and development.

Gross Domestic Product, 1960 to 2017
Gross domestic product adjustod for price changes over time(inflation)and expressed in Us-Dollars.

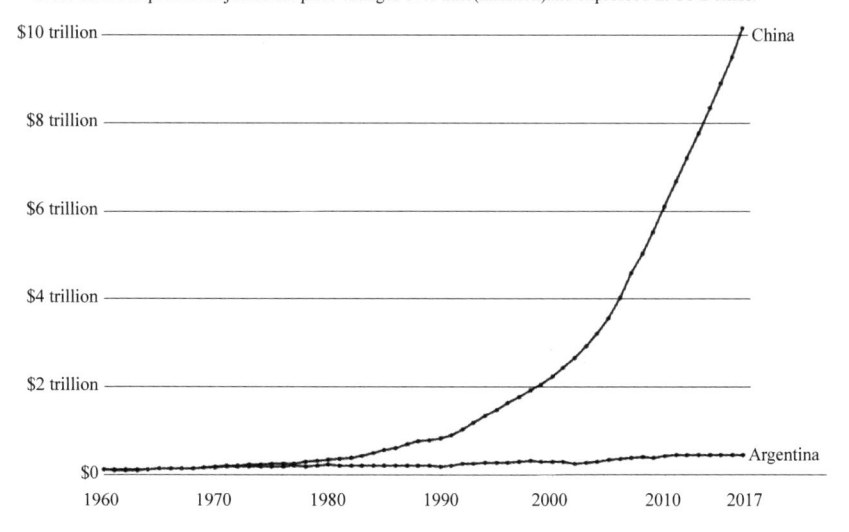

Figure 1　GDP Growth in China and Argentina

Source: The figure is made by author according to the data from https://ourworldindata.org.

In China, the environmental problems caused by the overall acceleration of the economy in the 1990s have become increasingly intensified. It is difficult to have both of economic growth and good environment (the so-called inverted U-shaped environmental Kuznets curve). China began to believe that it is difficult to avoid environmental problems before the economic development matures. This subtle change in epistemology is reflected in both of its domestic and international policies.

In 2007, the 17th National Congress of the Communist Party of China formally proposed the concept of ecological civilization for the first time as one of the new requirements for building a well-off society in an all-round way: "Promote a conservation culture by basically forming an energy-and resource-efficient and environment-friendly structure of industries, pattern of growth and mode of consumption. We will have a large-scale circular economy and considerably increase the proportion of renewable energy sources in total energy consumption. . . . Awareness of conservation will be firmly established in the whole of society." This means that although economic development has brought serious ecological and environmental problems, as long as we adhere to the so-called "scientific development", environmental problems and economic development can be achieved side by side. This is a major advancement in China's epistemology on environment and development.

2.2 Breakthroughs in development concepts and environmental protection after the 18th National Congress of the CPC

After the 18th National Congress of the Communist Party of China in 2012, the concept of ecological civilization has new connotations and a fundamental breakthrough has been made in environmental protection. The understanding of the relationship between environment and development has been improved from the previous compatibility to the mutual promotion of the two. A major improvement in epistemology has brought about major changes in actions. China's environmental protection efforts have been unprecedentedly increased, and remarkable results have been achieved in both the environment and development. After the 18th National Congress of the Communist Party of China, China started the comprehensively deepening reforms. As an important part of the "five in one" overall development strategy, ecological civilization has been raised to an unprecedented height. In October 2015, at the Fifth Plenary Session of the 18th Central Committee of the Communist Party of China, Xi Jinping further put forward the new development concept of innovation, coordination, green, open and sharing. Green development has become the core content of the new development concept.

At the Eighth National Ecological Environment Protection Conference on May 18, 2018, Xi Jinping gave a report on "Pushing China's Developmant of an Ecological Civilization to a New Stage", marking the formal establishment of Xi Jinping's thought on ecdogical progress. The important content of the thought of ecological civilization is the concept of "lucid waters and lnsh mountains are invaluable assets" and the modernization with "harmonious coexistence between man and nature".

The concept of "lucid waters and lnsh mountains are invaluable assets" means that the underlying value concept of development has undergone a major change, and the GDP with material wealth as its core content is no longer overemphasized. The relationship between environmental protection and economic development has changed from conflicting in the past to mutual promotion. With the change of development concepts or values, a good natural ecological environment itself has become an indispensable content of development. This will transform environmental protection from a burden in the past into a new development opportunity.

The harmonious coexistence of "man and nature" reflects the new concept of modernization. In the report to the 19th National Congress of the Communist Party of China, General Secretary Xi Jinping defined the modernization that China wants to build from the perspective of ecological civilization, which is different from Western modernization standards: "The modernization that we pursue is one characterized by harmonious coexistence between man and nature. In addition to creating more material and cultural wealth to meet people's ever-increasing needs for a better life, we need also to provide more quality ecological goods to meet people's ever-growing demands for a beautiful environment." This means that the modernization of China in the future will be different from the development content formed in the traditional industrial era in the industrialized countries today.

3 China's Basic Practices and Experience on Environmental Protection

3.1 Establish a strong system guarantee for environmental protection

Since the Third Plenary Session of the 18th Central Committee, China has established an overall institutional framework for the ecological civilization construction system from different levels including the Constitution, the Constitution of the party, the national development strategy, the modernization of the national governance system and governance capacity, the legal system, and the design of specific mechanisms.

First, China is the first country in the world to provide legal system guarantees for the construction of ecological civilization and environmental protection with the Constitution, the Constitution of the ruling party, and the national development strategy (the Five-sphere Iutegrated Plan). It is also one of the countries with the greatest determination to protect the environment. The core of ecological civilization is the mutual promotion of environment and development. The supreme legal status of ecological civilization in China means that China has a firm belief and confidence in promoting economic development through environmental protection.

Second, the ecological civilization system has become an important part of the modernization of the national governance system and governance capacityies. The Fourth Plenary Session of the 19th Central Committee of the Communist Party of China put forward "a 'dual circulation' development pattern in which domestic economic cycle plays a leading role while international economic cycle remains its extension and supplement" as a content that must be adhered to in the national governance system and governance capacityies, including the implementation of the most stringent ecological and environmental protection system, comprehensively establish a system for efficient use of resources, a sound ecological protection and restoration system, and a strict responsibility system for ecological environmental protection.

Third, a complete institutional system has been established at the implementation level. The reform of the ecological civilization system mainly involves the reform and design of the system in the three major areas of natural resource asset management, natural resource supervision, and ecological environment protection. In general, it includes the system of natural resources and natural property rights, the system of land development and protection, the system of spatial planning, the system of total resource management and conservation, the system of paid use and compensation of resources, the system of environmental governance, the market system of environmental governance and ecological protection, and performance appraisal and the accountability system.

3.2 A series of reform breakthroughs have been achieved

First, breakthroughs have been made in environmental legislation concept. In April 2014, the "Environmental Protection Law" was revised in accordance with the new concept, and for the first time the comprehensive legal status of the Environmental Protection Law and the principle of "protection first" were clarified. This law is known as the most stringent environmental protection law in history, and for the first time the ecological protection red line is written into the law. In areas such as key ecological protection areas, ecological environment sensitive areas and vulnerable areas, ecological protection red lines are delineated and strictly protected.

Second, breakthroughs have been made in the ecological protection and restoration system, the efficient use of resources system, and the reform of the ecological environment management system. Mainly include: natural resource asset property rights system, natural resource asset confirmation registration, natural ecological space use control reform, multi-regulations in one, red line delineation, national park system construction, departmental institutional reform, and national natural resource asset management system pilot projects. The continued advancement of the paid use of resources and the ecological compensation system has further promoted the gradual improvement of the price formation mechanism of natural resources and their products, and has effectively promoted the rational development, efficient use, strict protection and systematic restoration of natural resource assets.

Third, breakthroughs have been made in the reform of the ecological environment governance system. The establishment of the Ministry of Ecology and Environment in 2018 has changed the situation in the field of pollution prevention and control for many years, and fundamentally realized the unified supervision and law enforcement of ecological protection. In terms of management mechanism, the implementation of the vertical management of environmental protection agencies and the central ecological and environmental protection inspection system not only optimizes the organizational structure, but also effectively improves administrative efficiency and promotes the construction of a responsible government.

Fourth, breakthroughs have been made in the reform of the target responsibility system and accountability mechanism. On the one hand, build a target assessment system oriented to specific indicators such as total pollutant emission reduction and environmental quality improvement, including the resource and environment binding indicators in the "Five-Year Plan" and special assessments by relevant departments. On the other hand, the accountability mechanism based on the target responsibility system, including the central ecological and environmental protection inspection system, the accountability system for the ecological environment damage of the officials of the party and government, and the auditing system for the natural resource assets as officials leave their posts, has promoted the solution of the long-term accumulated environmental pollution problems.

Fifth, establishing different types of compulsory, incentive, and guiding systems. Compulsory systems include: ecological protection red line system, natural resource asset property rights system, etc. Incentive systems include: promoting the reform of resource tax and environmental tax, and advancing the pilot trading system of ecological compensation, water rights, energy use rights, pollution emission rights, forest rights, and carbon emission rights.

3.3 **Resolutely "declare war on pollution"**

With the major change in epistemology, concerns that pollution control will affect economic development have been largely eliminated. After the 18th National Congress of the Communist Party of China, the central and local governments have taken unprecedented environmental governance and ecological restoration actions, including pollution prevention and control, water environment governance, soil governance, agricultural non-point source pollution control, the Yangtze River protection strategy, the Yellow River Basin protection, ecological red line, national parks system, clean energy, energy saving and emission reduction, etc.

In particular, the 19th National Congress of the Communist Party of China put forward "prevent and control pollution", together with the "forestall and defuse major risks", and "targeted poverty alleviation", as the three major battles for building a well-off society in all respects. On June 24, 2018, the Central Committee of the Communist Party of China and the State Council issued the "Opinions on Comprehensively Strengthening Ecological Environmental Protection and Resolutely Fighting Pollution Prevention and Control". The three major defense battles of the Blue Sky, Clear Water and Pure Land and the seven iconic battles include winning the blue sky defense battle, fighting pollution control of diesel trucks, water source protection, black and odorous water control, protection and restoration of the Yangtze River, comprehensive control of the Bohai Sea, and tough battles for agricultural and rural governance. The "Opinions" set 2020 as the time node, taking into account 2035 and the middle of this century, and formulated specific targets for pollution prevention and control and ecological environmental protection.

3.4 Leading the actions fighting climate change for green transformation with the carbon neutrality target by 2060

The Chinese government has been actively responding to climate change. Before the Copenhagen Climate Change Conference in 2009, China announced a goal of reducing its carbon emission intensity by 40% - 45% from 2005. In the "11th Five-Year Planning" and "12th Five-Year Planning" periods, energy consumption intensity and carbon emission intensity were set to decrease by 20% and 17% respectively. In the Nationally Determined Contribution submitted by China to the United Nations in 2015, the carbon intensity in 2030 will be further reduced by 60% - 65% on the basis of 2005.

In his speech at the Paris Climate Conference in 2015, President Xi Jinping put forward two "win-win" views. One is that green recovery can achieve a win-win situation between economic development and addressing climate change; the second is that addressing climate change can achieve a win-win situation among countries, and countries can share opportunities instead of zero-sum games.

On September 22, 2020, President Xi Jinping announced at the United Nations General Assembly that "We aim to have CO_2 emissions peak before 2030 and achieve carbon neutrality before 2060". The proposal of the 2060 carbon neutrality target is basically a result of change in China's development philosophy. At the same time, China has a clear understanding of the daunting challenges facing the goal of achieving carbon neutrality. Carbon neutrality is an inevitable choice to solve the unsustainable crisis of the traditional development model. It is not a question of whether or not it is necessary, but a question of how to achieve it. Regarding the challenge of carbon neutrality, when he announced China's 2060 carbon neutrality goal at United Nations, President Xi Jinping pointed out that "mankind needs a self-revolution to accelerate the formation of green development methods and lifestyles, and build an ecological civilization and a beautiful planet earth".

China's stringent environmental protection actions have not affected economic development as some people feared. According to the National Bureau of Statistics, from 2013 to 2019, China's GDP growth rate was 7.8%, 7.3%, 6.9%, 6.7%, 6.8%, and 6.6% respectively. In 2020, when the COVID-19 broke out globally, China became the only country in the world to achieve positive growth, with a GDP growth of 2.3%, reaching RMB 101 trillion, and a per capita GDP exceeding USD 11, 000.

In the "14th Five-Year Plan" period, China will increase efforts to protect ecological environment. In 2020, the Fifth Plenary Session of the 19th Central Committee of the Communist Party of China deployed the long-term goals of ecological civilization construction in the 14th Five-Year Plan period and 2035 and proposed "building an ecological civilization system, promoting a comprehensive green transformation of economic and social development, and building a modernization in which man and nature coexist harmoniously". Compared with the 2030 National Determined Contribution target issued in 2015, China's carbon emission intensity reduction target has been raised from "60% −65%" to "over 65%", and the target for the proportion of non-fossil energy sources has increased from "about 20%" to "about 25%". The target for increasing forest stock volume will be increased from

"4. 5 billion cubic meters" to "6 billion cubic meters". In particular, the carbon peak time has changed from "around 2030" to "before 2030". During the "14th Five-Year Plan" period, the energy intensity per unit of GDP will drop by 13. 5%, and the intensity of carbon dioxide emissions per unit of GDP will drop by 18%.

4 Basic Experience of China's Environmental Protection

First, the new development concept is the most critical to reform. Green development is a fundamental change in the development paradigm. This change is a leap forward, facing a dilemma similar to "chicken and egg". That is, if there is not enough evidence of green success, the risk-averse governments will not take strong actions; if they do not take strong actions, green evidence will not appear. At this time, the leader's foresight, vision and courage to reform play a decisive role. Under the concept of "lucid waters and lush mountains are invaluable assets", the vision of mutual promotion of ecological environmental protection and economic development provides a guarantee for breaking this dilemma.

Second, the development concept of "Never forget why you started" and centering on the people. The fundamental purpose or original intention of development is to enhance the well-being of the people, rather than the supremacy of commercial interests. An important consequence of the traditional development model is that, to a certain extent, the purpose and means of development are upside down. GDP is only a means of development, and the improvement of people's well-being is the fundamental goal of development, and a good ecological environment is the inclusive of people's livelihood and is an indispensable part of " growing expectation for a better life".

Third, ecological civilization is a new civilization after industrial civilization. It is not just a repair and patching of the old one, but a comprehensive system transition that requires comprehensive top-level design and overall advancement. Green transformation is a typical public choice and coordination issue, which requires strong promotion by the government. The promotion of the government is equivalent to providing a public product necessary for transformation. In promoting green transformation, the Chinese government's strong mobilization ability has become its unique advantage.

Fourth, give full play to the advantages of big size of the country and give full play to the innovative spirit of various regions through regional competition. "First pilot, then promote." Carry out various ecological civilization system experiments in regions with different conditions, and then upgrade effective regional experiments to national reform measures. It includes following types of pilots: comprehensive ecological civilization pilots; specific ecological civilization construction pilots for various ministries. An important feature of these pilots is that the country usually conducts the same type of pilot work in multiple regions.

Fifth, an effective market mechanism. In the construction of ecological civilization, "the market plays a decisive role". The transformation of "lucid waters and lush mountains" into "invaluable assets" basically relies on an effective market mechanism. Many emerging products and services based on a good ecological environment and culture are difficult to realize their value with the business model and corporate organization model that established in the traditional industrial era, and they need to rely on innovative business models. In this regard, a flexible and dynamic market mechanism becomes the key.

5 Historical Opportunities for China-Argentina Cooperation in Environmental Protection

At present, the formation of a global consensus on carbon neutrality marks the end of the traditional industrialization model established after the industrial revolution and the opening of a new era of green development. This new era of development characterized by green development and the Internet has provided a new foundation and broad prospects for China and Argentina to carry out environmental protection and green development cooperation. First, the new development concept brings new opportunities. The new green development model means new green development concepts, new green supply and demand, and new green resources. For example, a new green service economy can be developed based on a good ecological environment and culture. China and Argentina are rich in ecological and cultural resources, and there is broad room for cooperation in this regard. Second, the Internet has broken the traditional time and space barriers in the past and provided conditions for overcoming the long geographic distance between China and Argentina. A high-level international division of labor between the two countries can be achieved under the new green development model.

China's economy is much larger than Argentina, but their per capita GDP are at the similar level. The two countries have a lot of room for cooperation in environmental protection. Taking climate change as an example, it can be seen from Figure 2 that the greenhouse gas emissions and composition of the two countries are very different, reflecting the differences in the economic structure of the two countries. For example, the largest sources of GHGs emissions in Argentina are agriculture and land use, while in China it is electricity, heating, manufacturing and construction. These differences indicate that the two countries have broad room for cooperation in economy, trade and emission reduction.

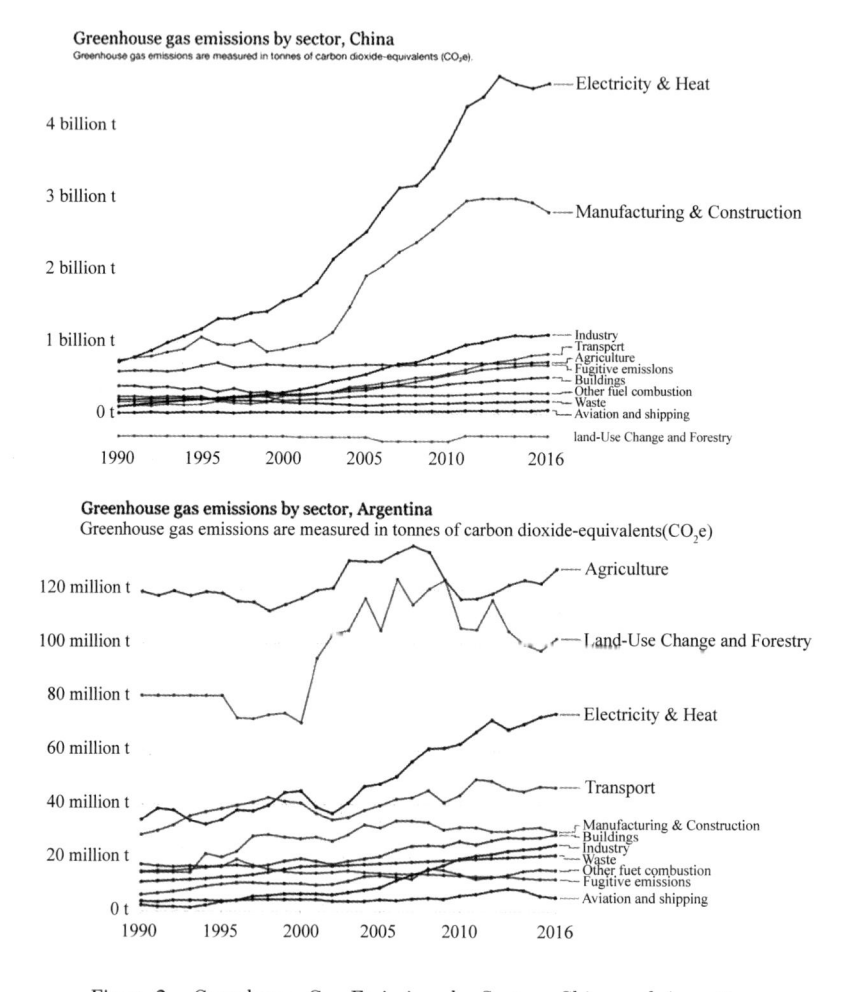

Figure 2　Greenhouse Gas Emissions by Sector: China and Argentina

Specifically, the two parties can explore the possibility of cooperation in the following aspects:

First, address global climate change. Cooperate in technology, knowledge, and funding, and promote the establishment of an international climate governance mechanism with equity and effectiveness.

Second, cooperation in environmental protection. China and Argentina can share knowledge and best practices in environmental protection and promote cooperative research in environmental protection.

Third, green infrastructure cooperation. China has strong infrastructure construction capabilities. China's high-speed rail, expressway, and 5G are leading in the world. China can provide the necessary technology and funds for the construction of various infrastructures in Argentina.

Fourth, carry out cooperation in green development.

China's goal of carbon neutrality by 2060 will bring tens of billions of investment opportunities. These opportunities will be shared with Argentina.

China has world-leading R&D and manufacturing capabilities in solar energy, wind energy, electric vehicles, and 5G, which can help Argentina develop a green economy.

Green agriculture cooperation. China has a huge demand for green agricultural products, and Argentina has very good conditions for green agriculture, and the two sides can carry out a lot of cooperation.

Cooperation in culture, tourism and sports. Culture, tourism and sports are important contents of the green economy. In these respects, Argentina has good advantages and can develop various sports industries including soccer with China.

Fifth, maritime economic cooperation. China and Argentina are both big maritime countries. China's marine economy accounts for nearly 10% of its GDP. Argentina is located in the southern hemisphere, and the use of Antarctica is of great strategic significance to it. In particular, under the conditions of marine pollution and global climate change, how to realize the sustainable open use of the marine economy is an important opportunity and challenge facing both China and Argentina.

China-Argentina Cooperation under Belt and Road Initiative[*]

Since its launch in 2013, BRI has gradually made its way to Latin America. In January 2018, the Second Ministerial Meeting of the China-CELAC Forum adopted a "Special Declaration on the Belt and Road Initiative" and other important outcome documents, agreeing that "BRI will provide important opportunities for the countries concerned to strengthen development cooperation", indicating that priority areas of cooperation between China and CELAC include the docking of BRI. This indicates that the BRI has begun to enter Latin America and the Caribbean (LAC) in a comprehensive manner. In line with this, and in accordance with Argentina's unique national conditions, the China-Argentina BRI cooperation is also moving forward, catering to the common development needs of both sides and pushing their cooperation into a new phase of high-quality development.

---

[*] Yue Yunxia, Ph. D. in economics, professor, Director of Economic Department of the Institute of Latin American Studies (ILAS), Chinese Academy of Social Sciences.

1 China-Argentina Cooperation under the BRI Framework

As the international recognition of BRI continues to grow, international BRI cooperation is developing rapidly. As of July 2022, China has signed more than 200 cooperation documents with over than 170 countries and international organizations, covering countries in Asia, Africa, Europe, LAC and the South Pacific.[1] Meanwhile, China has signed 21 BRI cooperation documents among the 24 LAC countries that have diplomatic relations. This is making LAC an indispensable and important participant and realistic co-constructionist in the global BRI cooperation.

As a global initiative, China's BRI cooperation focuses on the universal needs of world development, as well as on the different needs of individual countries and regions. China-LAC BRI cooperation has been recognized at the regional level within the CELAC. It shows, at the bilateral level, in three forms: first, the signing of BRI cooperation documents; second, official participation in the BRI International Cooperation Summit, joining the Asian Infrastructure Bank (AIIB)[2] or other related cooperation mechanisms, or specifying cooperation intentions in official

---

[1] Central Government Network of the People's Republic of China, "China has signed 205 BRI cooperation documents", http://www.gov.cn/xinwen/2021-01/30/content_ 5583711.htm.

[2] Serrano et al. consider this format as a concrete expression of LAC countries' participation in BRI cooperation. See Serrano, J. E., D. Telias and F. Urdinez, "Deconstructing the Belt and Road Initiative in Latin America", Emerald Insight, 2020, https://www.emerald.com/insight/2046-3162.htm.

documents; third, the docking of projects or plans with the spirit of BRI①.

China and Argentina have signed the cooperation document. In 2018, during President Xi Jinping's state visit to Argentina, China and Argentina issued a Joint Statement, which clearly stated that "BRI will give impetus to China-Argentina cooperation, and the bilateral comprehensive strategic partnership can be extended to BRI". In a communication with Argentine President Alberto Fernandez in January 2021, President Xi Jinping said, "China is ready to work with Argentina to promote high-quality BRI cooperation and to promote the building of a community with a shared future for mankind". In February 2022, when Argentine President Fernandez attended the opening ceremony of Beijing Winter Olympic Games and visited Beijing, China and Argentina signed the MOU on BRI cooperation. The BRI consensus has led to the deepening of practical cooperation between the two sides, resulting in a number of early achievements in the "Five Links".

Firstly, in the field of Policy Coordination, the Argentine head of state attended the two sessions of BRI International Cooperation Summits; Argentina is a signatory to the BRI Financing Guiding Principles; and the Chinese and Argentine governments have decided to strengthen communication and cooperation under the framework of BRI and to dovetail the development plans of both countries.

Secondly, in the field of Financial Integration, Argentina is a founding member of the Asian Infrastructure Investment Bank (AIIB), and the Argentine Bank for Investment and Foreign Trade

---

① From a practical perspective, it is generally considered that projects that meet the requirements of the five-links are BRI projects.

(BIAF), as a founding bank, has joined the China-Latin America Development Finance Cooperation Mechanism (CLAF).

Thirdly, in the fields of Unimpeded Trade and Facilities Connectivity, Argentina is a relative front-runner in LAC in terms of trade, investment, finance and economic cooperation with China. In the trade sector, China has become Argentina's second largest trading partner, accounting for 9.8% of its total exports (USD 54.884 billion) and 20.4% of its total imports (USD 42.356 billion) in 2020. The meat from Argentina accounts for 12.1% and soybeans for 7.5% of China's imports, while the share of seafood and shellfish, animal fats and oils, beverages, leather and other products exceeds 2%. Argentina plays an important role in China's food and raw material supply as well as in the leather manufacturing industry, which is of outstanding importance for the stability of the supply and production chains of related industries. In the field of investment, China is one of the main sources of foreign investment in Argentina. By the end of 2019, the stock of Chinese investment in Argentina reached USD 1.8 billion, involving various sectors such as agriculture, energy and manufacturing. In the field of financial cooperation, five currency swap agreements have been signed between China and Argentina, with the latest one reaching RMB 130 billion in August 2020. Argentina's RMB reserves accounted for about 43% of its foreign exchange reserves during the same period. With these, Argentina has become an important cooperation partner for RMB internationalization. In the field of economic cooperation, Chinese enterprises have participated in several infrastructure and energy projects in Argentina, such as China Machinery Engineering Corporation (CMEC) signed a general contract with the Argentine for the renovation of the Belgrano Cargas rail line, providing building materials, locomotives and carriages for the whole line in addition to the renovation; Power China and Shanghai Electric Power Construction jointly constructed the largest photovoltaic project in Argentina-Cauchari 300 MW photovoltaic power project, which is now in commercial operation; China Goldwind invested and Power China constructed the largest wind power project group in Argentina—the first and the third phases of the Helios wind power project group Loma Blanca phase I, which has been integrated into the Argentine national grid system and officially put into commercial operation; Gezhouba Group is in charge of the construction of two hydroelectric power plants in Santa Cruz Province in southern Argentina.

Fourthly, in the field of People-to-people Bonds, China and Argentina have jointly recorded documentaries such as *Charming China*, *Charming China & Argentina*, *Crossing Over*, and etc. Argentina also broadcasted the series of *Brilliant 70 Years—China TV Month* on the occasion of the 70th anniversary of the founding of the PRC, which deepened the mutual Understanding of the two countries and promoted people-to-people communication.

2 Matched China-Argentina Demand and Supply under BRI Framework

The Fifth Plenary Session of the 19th CPC Central Committee proposed to build "a new development pattern with the domestic circulation as the main body and the domestic and international circulation promoting each other", while BRI is the general platform for China's opening-up and external cooperation in the new era, and internally connects with the new round of reform. Under the framework of BRI, Sino-Argentina cooperation can meet the needs of mutual development of both sides.

First of all, Sino-Argentina cooperation can help Argentina get out of its economic difficulties. For nearly a decade, Argentina's economy has lagged behind the average of emerging markets and developing economies, and for most of the time has been below the average growth of developed economies. The year 2020 saw the worst recession in Argentina's history, with a GDP growth rate of − 11.78% (Figure 1). During the same period, data from Argentina's National Institute of Statistics and Census showed that its unemployment rate exceeded 11%, poverty and extreme poverty rates reached 42% and 10.5%[①], both peaks in the last 16 years. Meanwhile, the debt pressures were relatively prominent. With limited endogenous growth momentum, external cooperation is the main support for Argentina to get out of the crisis, and the BRI project built by China and Argentina can help support Argentina's economic growth and employment expansion, becoming an important option to get out of its difficulties.

Secondly, Argentina has the realistic capacity to undertake China's outbound investment cooperation. Since 2014, China has become a net FDI outflow country; since 2016, it has become the second largest outward investor in the world. Outward investment is a natural result of the accumulation of capital, technology and experience under China's reform and opening-up strategy of "bringing in" and "going global", and also undertakes the important mission of promoting international production capacity cooperation. Argentina is the third largest economy in Latin America, a major member of MERCOSUR. It has a complete range of industries and the ability to provide supporting industries for Chinese investment. Therefore, it

---

① CCTV News, the official new media account of CCTV News Center.

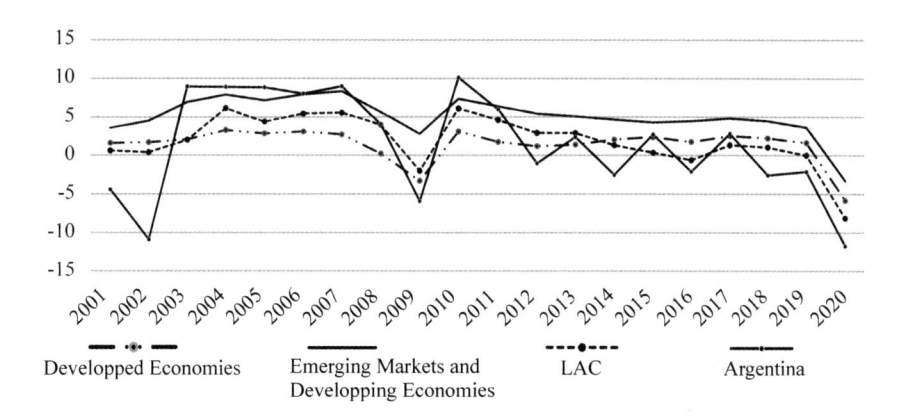

Figure 1 Argentina's Economic Growth in a World Perspective
Source: IMF, World Economic Outlook.

has the power and ability to undertake Chinese investment and production capacity transfer. Thus, the Sino-Argentine investment cooperation under the framework of BRI has the basic conditions for stable expansion.

Thirdly, Argentina has a strong demand to undertake the export of China's infrastructure construction capacity. An important part of BRI is the infrastructure interconnection. China has relatively mature technology, experience and manpower advantages in related fields. Argentina, on the other hand, is relatively backward in terms of infrastructure, and the cost of transportation, storage and other productive services accounts for a high proportion of the production cost of enterprises, which compresses the profit margin of the manufacturing industry and inhibits industrial development. In order to improve infrastructure, Argentina is promoting the largest infrastructure renovation program in its history. Under the framework of BRI, focusing on investment in infrastructure construction, China's advantageous production capacity and technology can be introduced into Argentina to achieve a win-win situation for both sides.

Fourthly, Argentina has the feasibility of carrying the RMB's going abroad. RMB internationalization is an important vehicle for China's new round of opening-up. It has the conditions to be implemented in Argentina. At current, China has successfully promoted the local currency swap program in Argentina and has a regional clearing bank. The country thus has the transaction scale and operational experience to carry RMB internationalization and can become a possible pilot region. Under the framework of BRI, China-Argentina production capacity cooperation and infrastructure interconnection construction are beneficial to the formation of a good situation of product flow and capital flow cycle interaction.

3　Challenges toward China-Argentina BRI Cooperation

While the practical BRI cooperation between China and Argentina continues to expand, the internal and external market environment is constantly changing, and the bilateral cooperation is facing structural frictions in the trade field, as well as the external barriers.

First, the volatility of Argentina's macroeconomy and policies has created certain disturbances to bilateral pragmatic cooperation. Due to the weak global economic recovery and stagnant internal growth, Argentina has been facing high inflation, foreign exchange shortage, exchange rate fluctuation and fiscal imbalance in recent years. It therefore has been forced to introduce a series of foreign exchange control measures to prevent financial market shocks, and to impose higher tariffs on major export products such as soybeans and soybean oil to increase revenue. These measures have objectively created an adverse impact on Chinese enterprises' investment and trade in

Argentina.

Second, Argentina's frequent trade remedy measures against China have had a certain impact on bilateral trade. Due to the high concentration of domestic production in Argentina and the existence of certain competition between the products of the two sides, Argentina is one of the countries that have initiated the largest number of trade protest measures against China. As of mid-2020, Argentina is the fourth largest country in the world after India, the U. S. and the EU in terms of anti-dumping investigations against China (124 initiations); ranks 3rd after U. S. and Canada in terms of countervailing measures initiated against China (20 initiations); and also relatively leading in LAC in terms of the use of safeguard measures (6 initiations) ①. In contrast, China has not initiated any trade remedies against Argentina under the WTO framework. Trade frictions have to some extent affected the trade between China and Argentina and have had a negative effect on the smooth flow of trade between the two countries.

Third, Argentina's traditional infrastructure construction sector and new emerging areas such as 5G are highly competitive, and the game of interests is complex. The long-term economic downturn coupled with debt pressure has made the Argentine government face financial constraints, making it difficult to use public financial resources to expand the scale of investment. It can only rely on external financing to achieve investment in infrastructure. As a latecomer, Chinese enterprises face multiple disturbing factors. They thus have to adapt to the international engineering bidding model and

---

① WTO trade topics, https://www.wto.org/english/tratop_e/tratop_e.htm.

engineering standards under the European and American paradigms, as well as to meet the multi-level demands of local owners, competitors in the same industry, environmental organizations and communities. All these put forward high requirements for project operation and management. The rapid development of Sino-Argentina cooperation has inevitably triggered the concern and vigilance of traditional interest groups, which has also put pressure on the project progress.

4 Direction of Future China-Argentina BRI Cooperation

BRI provides a new platform and new impetus for Sino-Argentina cooperation. It can promote a good situation of dynamic upgrading and continuous breakthrough. China and Argentina have the same development aspirations, but also face certain realistic challenges. Both sides should make a new assessment of the value of risk hedging that can be generated by BRI cooperation to maximize common interests. To this end, China and Argentina need to form a joint effort in the following directions.

First, China-Argentina BRI cooperation faces huge demand space, which should be further enhanced by mutual political trust and communication, so as to enhance confidence and empowerment. On the one hand, China-Argentina BRI cooperation has made solid progress in the field of "Five Links". Both sides have a high consensus on cooperation. The signing of detailed bilateral cooperation documents and the promotion of further cooperation planning are already in place, and should be promoted as soon as possible. On the other hand, apart from bilateral communication, regular communication at multilateral level is most prominent in the G20 mechanism, while multilateral channels like BRICS and APEC are relatively lacking. The two sides should make mechanism innovations to strengthen multi-level political exchanges and policy communication.

Second, China-Argentina BRI cooperation faces with realistic chronic problems, which should promote the further expansion of trade and investment facilitation initiatives. First, China and Argentina should form a bilateral trade remedy cooperation mechanism as soon as possible, through dialogue and consultation to reduce the trade losses caused by trade friction. Second, China and Argentina must strengthen cooperation in animal and plant quarantine inspection, customs clearance and other aspects, and strengthen cooperation in the areas of private sector dialogue, market research, productive investment support services, etc., to promote the expansion of trade and investment cooperation between the two sides. Once again, in view of the consistency requirements for the signing of free trade agreements by MERCOSUR to the outside world, China and Argentina should actively promote bilateral trade and investment arrangements, in addition to jointly and gradually pushing the formation of a China-MERCOSUR FTA.

Third, there are innovative areas for China-Argentina BRI cooperation, which should form a new cooperation with the times. The existing cooperation has created a number of potential spaces for improvement: the first is the further space for cooperation on RMB internationalization. On the basis of the RMB's function in Argentina's clearing and reserve, its function of denomination and settlement can not only meet the needs of bilateral investment and trade, but also effectively reduce the risk of exchange rate fluctuations, which will effectively facilitate the local operation of enterprises on both sides. The second is the space for new business. During the COVID-19,

China and Argentina have increased connections on food, medical products and games and other cultural products, while the e-commerce also has a large jump. These indicate that China and Argentina are facing new cooperation requirements, which should be met through the Health Silk Road and the Digital Silk Road. The third is the new space for international cooperation. In the areas of climate change, Antarctic research and deep space exploration, China and Argentina have common interests and the conditions to expand cooperation.

Fourth, there is a cognitive gap in China-Argentina BRI cooperation, which should be dissolved by communication and recognition. The lack of mutual awareness is the deep-seated reason that constrains the deep development of China-Argentina BRI cooperation. For this reason, at the level of communication, China and Argentina should establish a long-term direct government, think-tank and media cooperation mechanism, implement open and multi-level communication and docking, and establish an information exchange platform as far as possible to avoid external interference.

Industrialization Process: Toward High-Quality Development[*]

1 A Fast-Rising Industrial Power

Pursuing structural reforms based on China's national conditions and pursuing an independent open market have fully released China's comparative factor advantages and large-scale market advantages. Thus, China's manufacturing industry has achieved rapid expansion, continued to optimize its structure and significantly improved its technical capabilities in the 40-odd years since the reform and opening-up. In a short span of several decades, China has accomplished industrialization which took developed countries hundreds of years to accomplish, and has made world-renowned achievements.

First, China has achieved continuous optimization of the industrial structure while rapidly expanding its scale. In 1978, China's industrial value added was only 162.1 billion yuan, and in 2020, the industrial value added reached 31,307.1 billion yuan. It took only 3 years for China's industrial value added to go from USD 2 trillion to USD 3 trillion, and 9 years for the United States; it took

---

[*] He Jun, Jiang Hong, Li Wei, Institute of Industrial Economics, Chinese Academy of Social Sciences.

(trillion US dollars)

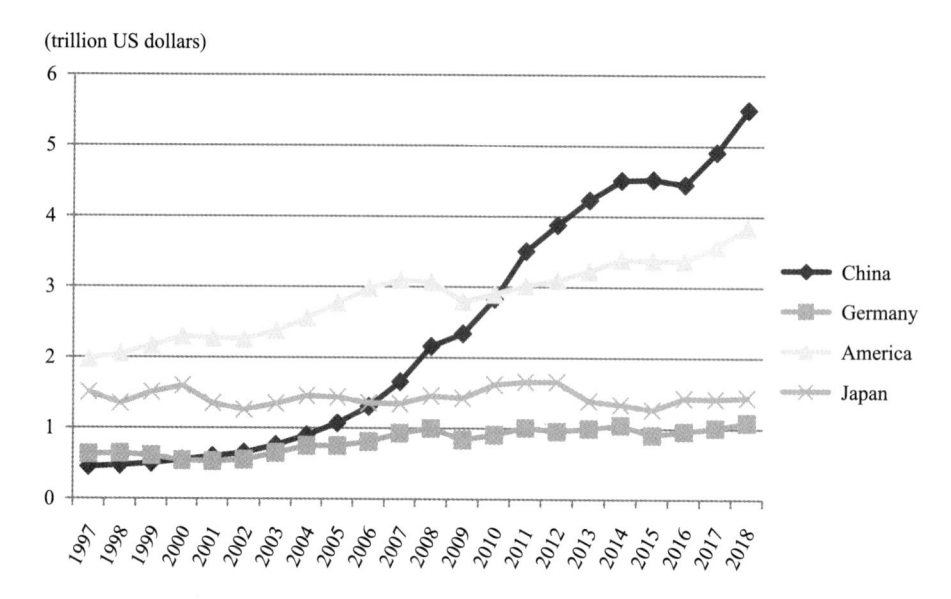

Figure 1   Changes in industrial value added of major countries

Source: *China Statistical Yearbook* (calendar year).

only 2 years for China to increase from USD 3 trillion to USD 4 trillion, and 8 years for the United States. While the scale has grown, the industrial structure has also been continuously optimized. In 2019, the value added of China's high-tech manufacturing industry accounted for 14.4% of the total value added of the industrial enterprises above designated size, and the digital economy accounted for 36.2% of GDP.

Second, China has built the most comprehensive industrial system in the world. At the beginning of reform and opening-up, China's manufacturing capacity was relatively weak, and the proportion of its manufacturing value added in the global manufacturing value added was negligible. In 2019, the value added of China's manufacturing industry reached 3.82 trillion, accounting for about one-third of the global manufacturing industry, making

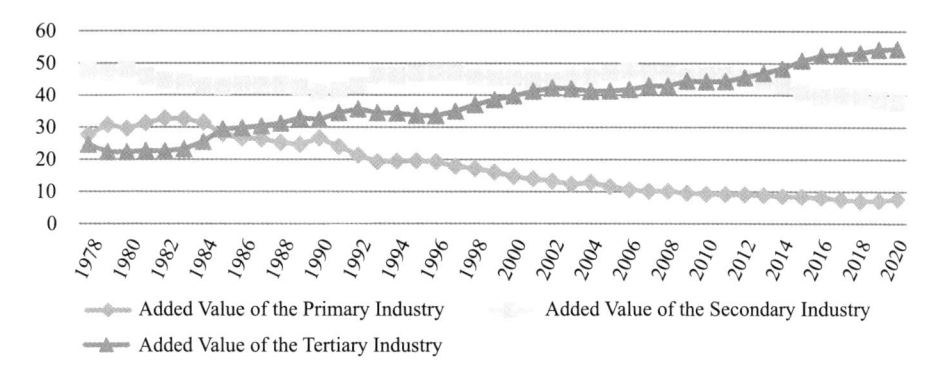

Figure 2　Changes in China's three industrial structures

Source: *China Statistical Yearbook* (calendar year).

China a veritable global manufacturing center. With 41 major industrial categories, 207 medium industrial categories, and 666 industrial sub-categories, China has built the world's most comprehensive industrial system and is the only country that has developed all the industrial categories of the UN's industrial classification. Among the 500 major industrial products, China has 220 major industrial products whose outputs rank first in the world. "Made in China" brands can be seen in more than 230 countries and regions in the world.

Third, China has formed an industrial organization structure in which enterprises of diverse ownerships fully compete. In the early stage of reform and opening-up, state-owned enterprises dominated all aspects of industrial production. After the reform and opening-up, with the opening of the market and the deepening of the reform of state-owned enterprises, enterprises of diverse ownerships, small, medium and large enterprises have fully competed. A large number of local enterprises such as Huawei, ZTE, Lenovo, Xiaomi, Haier, Midea, BYD, CATL, DJI, etc. have grown up into internationally

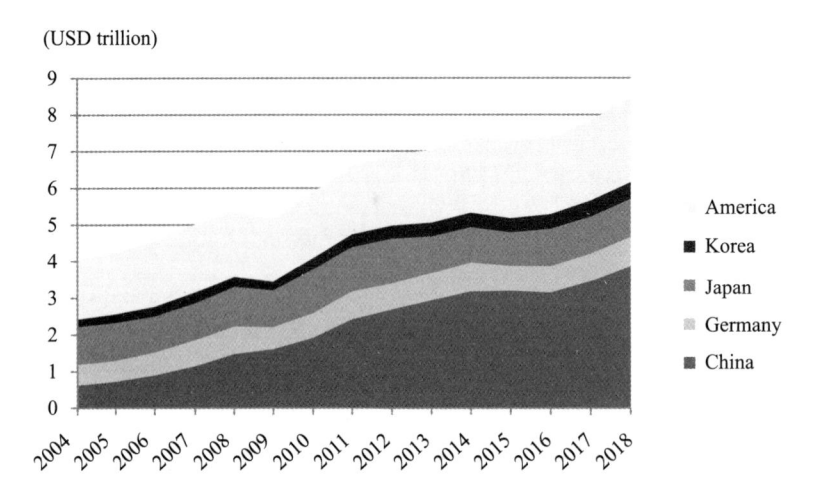

Figure 3 Changes in the value added of manufacturing in major countries

Source: *China Statistical Yearbook* (calendar year).

competitive manufacturing leaders. In 2019, China had 129 companies on the list of Fortune Global 500, surpassing the United States for the first time to become the country with the most companies on the list. At the same time, high-tech entrepreneurship is booming. Data from the Hurun Global Unicorn List 2019 shows that the number of Chinese unicorn companies has reached 206, surpassing the United States (203) for the first time, making China a country with the world's largest number of unicorn companies.

Fourth, from technological imitation to original innovation. Since the reform and opening-up, China's industrial technology has achieved stepwise development from technology introduction to digestion, absorption and re-innovation, and then to independent innovation. The forward design capabilities and original innovation capabilities have been significantly enhanced. In 1995, China's R&D investment was 34.87 billion yuan, and the R&D intensity was only 0.57%. In 2019, the R&D investment surged to 2.2 trillion yuan, and the R&D

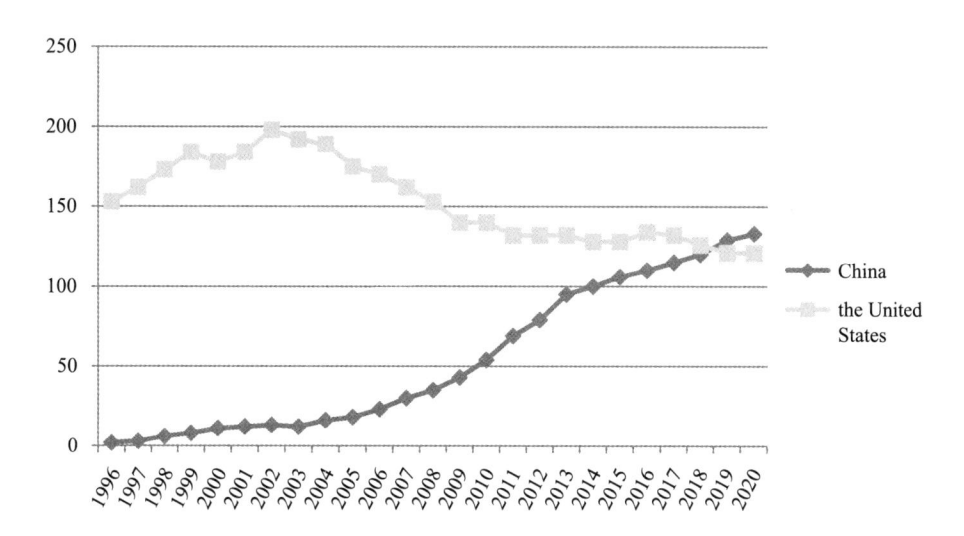

Figure 4 Comparison of the number of companies on the
Fortune Global 500 list between China and the United States

Source: Fortune Global 500 website, http://www.fortunechina.com/fortune500/index.htm.

intensity also reached 2.23%. China has become the second largest country in the world in terms of R&D investment. Before 1993, the number of PCT patents in China was almost zero. By 2019, the number of PCT patents in China reached 24,010, accounting for 13% of the global total. The improvement of innovation capabilities has significantly advanced China's industrial development. According to the data of *China Statistical Yearbook on Science and Technology*, the contribution rate of China's scientific and technological progress to economic growth was 39.7% from 1998 to 2003, and the contribution rate rose to 59.5% from 2014 to 2019.

Fifth, the pattern of opening-up to the outside world from "bringing in" strategy to "going global" strategy. Since the reform and opening-up, China's super-large market advantages and cost advantages have attracted continuous investment from multinational companies. In 2003, China surpassed the United States to become the country attracting the most foreign investment in the world. At the same time, China's import and export scale has also increased rapidly. In 2020, China's total volume of trade in goods reached 32.16 trillion yuan, making China the world's largest exporter of goods for 12 consecutive years, and the largest trading partner of more than 120 countries as well as the largest source of imports of about 65 countries. With the improvement of China's manufacturing technology capabilities and the guidance of China's Belt and Road Initiative, manufacturing enterprises' foreign direct investment began to grow rapidly, rising sharply from USD 620 million net in 2003 to USD 29.5 billion in 2017.

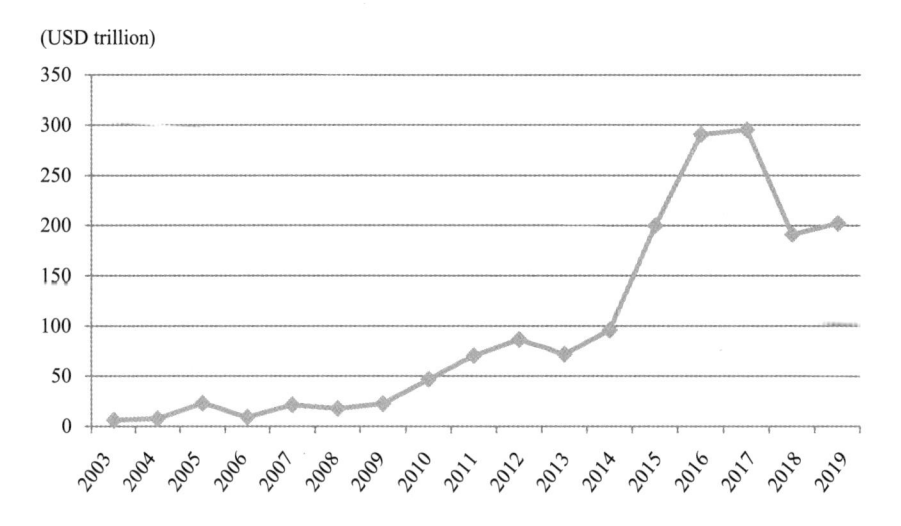

Figure 5　Changes in China's net foreign direct investment

Data source: Wind database.

2　What Did China's Manufacturing Industry Do Right?

The famous economist Zhang Wuchang (2012) once said:

"China's rapid growth has lasted for so long, which is unprecedented in history. China must have done something very right to create the economic miracle we have seen. So what is it?" Manufacturing is the main sector that has supported China's rapid economic growth over the past 40 years. Until 2013, the secondary industry has always been China's largest industrial sector. The reason why China's manufacturing industry can maintain rapid growth and eventually replace the United States to become the world's largest manufacturing economy must be attributed to the positive roles played by China's special system, economic conditions and development strategy.

First, we always adhere to the strategic orientation of industrial self-reliance. Since the founding of the People's Republic of China, China has always adhered to the strategy of "building the country based on industry". Industrial development has played a pivotal role in China's great leap from standing up, growing rich, to becoming strong. The rapid growth of China's industry appeared in the period of reform and opening-up, especially after the 1990s. However, the important reason why the reform and opening-up and other institutional factors were able to quickly release the growth potential of China's industry was that China had already formed a relatively complete manufacturing capacity and developed a relatively comprehensive industrial innovation system even before the reform and opening-up in fields like military, machinery, precision instruments, semiconductors, rail transit, and chemical industry. Since there were a number of state-owned enterprises and scientific research institutes equipped with technical capabilities in China at the beginning of reform and opening-up, China has higher technological learning intensity and efficiency when undertaking international technology transfer compared with other countries with late development. After the overall technological capability of the manufacturing industry has achieved a leap from imitation to forward design, China's industrial self-reliance strategy has further transformed from cultivating local innovation subjects to forming original innovation capabilities. In 2006, China formulated The National Medium and Long-Term Program for Science and Technology Development (2006 – 2020) (An Outline), which clearly placed the strengthening of indigenous innovation capability at the core of S&T undertakings and set the guiding principles for our S&T undertakings, namely: "indigenous innovation, leapfrogging in priority fields, enabling development, and leading the future". The outline also stated that we need to enhance original innovation, integrated innovation, and re-innovation based on assimilation and absorption of imported technology, in order to improve our national innovation capability. In contrast to China's practice, the lack of local technology learning subjects and the pure reliance on multinationals' imported technologies are the fundamental reasons why some countries with late development have fallen into the "middle-income trap" for a long time after reaping the dividends of open markets.

Second, we continuously release the vitality of various economic entities such as local governments and enterprises through reforms of system. The reform of state-owned enterprises and boosting business dynamism are central to the reform of China's economic system, and are also the most creative practice in China's reform. The restructuring of China's state-owned economy has roughly gone through four stages: from 1978 to 1992, stimulating market vitality of state-owned enterprises through "decentralization of power and transfer of profits"; from 1993 to 2002, further improving the efficiency of state-owned enterprises through "invigorating large enterprises while relaxing control over small ones" and the modern enterprise system; from 2003 to 2012, the transformation from "managing enterprises" to "managing capital" was realized on the basis of the establishment of the State-owned Assets Supervision and Administration Commission. After 2013, the classification reform of SOEs and the mixed ownership economy developed rapidly. Throughout the reform of SOEs, the relative size of the state-owned economy has gradually declined, and the government has always maintained the best balance between strategic control of SOEs and efficiency improvement. In addition, the central government continues to shape governance models that help stimulate local governments to develop local economies. Compared with developed countries and other developing countries, local governance in China is unique in two aspects: one is the vertical subcontracting administration system from the central government to all levels of local governments, and the other is the horizontal promotion competition among local governments at the same level. The vertical subcontracting administration system allows the local government to obtain a large amount of resources and discretion for economic development; while the horizontal competition among local officials has fully mobilized their enthusiasm for developing the economy, and the local governments have become dynamic and creative actors, which is an important institutional basis for the rapid development of China's infrastructure and industry. [1]

Third, we adopt an opening-up strategy featuring gradual opening-up and indigenous opening-up. Different from the radical market opening model, China has adopted a gradual opening-up

---

[1] Zhou Lian, *Local Government in Transition: Official Incentives and Governance*, Shanghai People's Publishing House, 2017.

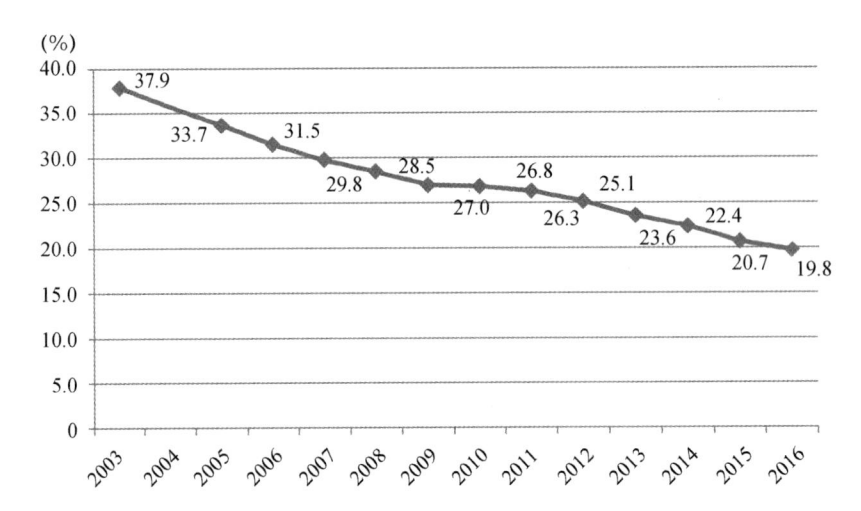

Figure 6 The proportion of state-owned and state-holding enterprises in industrial sales value

Data source: Wind database.

strategy from the sample to the whole, that is, to give priority to eligible regions which are selected for establishing special economic zones, open coastal port cities, economic and technological development zones, inland open zones and border open zones, etc. When the "pilot" experience is mature, such practice will be expanded to other regions. Take the economic and technological development zone as an example. From 1984 to 1986, China first established 14 national-level economic and technological development zones, and then continued to establish new ones throughout the country. By 2020, China has established a total of 218 national economic and technological development zones, with a gross regional product of RMB 10.5 trillion, accounting for 10.6% of GDP. In particular, the total output value of large-scale economic and technological development zones like Suzhou Industrial Park, Guangzhou Economic Development Zone, Tianjin Economic Development Zone, Qingdao Economic Development Zone, etc. has even exceeded RMB 200 billion. National-level economic and technological development zones are an important part of China's opening-up areas, and most of them are the capitals of various provinces and autonomous regions, municipalities directly under the central government, economic centers, or coastal open cities. Implementing the opening-up strategy first in areas with better location and industrial infrastructure conditions is conducive to concentrating on building complete infrastructures, and creating an investment environment that meets international standards. By absorbing and utilizing foreign capital, we can form a modern industrial structure with high-tech industries as the mainstay, which is conducive to improving the quality of foreign investment and promoting the development of industrial clusters. In addition to the regional level, China also adheres to the gradual opening-up strategy at the industrial level, that is, under the premise of complying with international multilateral trade rules, according to the general law of industrial structure upgrading, gradually opening-up from low-tech industries to capital-intensive industries and then to high-tech industries. Such opening-up ensures the best balance between the management and technology introduction of multinational companies and the impact of foreign investment on local companies, and realizes the synergetic dynamic efficiency between multinational investment and local companies.

　　Fourth, we adhere to the strategy of moderately advanced construction of infrastructure and the coordinated promotion of industrialization. Due to the fierce competition among local governments in China for attracting businesses and investment, local governments have strong motives for infrastructure investment. In addition, the state-owned banking system enables local governments and state-owned enterprises to obtain low-interest loans, ensuring the rapid development of China's infrastructure. Local economic growth boosted by infrastructure construction has also provided strong financial support for infrastructure investment, thus forming a pattern of mutual reinforcement of infrastructure construction and local economic development. In 1978, China's railway operating mileage and highway mileage were only 50,000 and 890,000 kilometers, respectively. By the end of 2019, railway operating mileage and highway mileage had reached 140,000 and 5.01 million kilometers, 2.8 times and 5.6 times that of the beginning of reform and opening-up, and ranking second and third in the world respectively. The mileage of expressway in China was almost zero before 1988, so was the mileage of high-speed railway before 2007. However, by 2019, the two reached 150,000 and 35,000 kilometers respectively, both ranking first in the world. China's expressway mileage is nearly twice that of the United States which ranks second in the world, and China's high-speed railway mileage is nearly 12 times that of Japan which ranks second in the world. The moderately advanced construction of infrastructure promotes the development of manufacturing industry by creating investment demand and reducing logistics costs. China also makes full use of the opportunities to build high-tech and complex infrastructure on a large scale, and transforms market opportunities into technological opportunities through "trading market for technology" and "indigenous innovation" strategies, thereby driving the rapid development of high-tech industries. Taking high-speed rail equipment as an example, China has also strategically deployed the introduction, digestion, and re-innovation of high-speed rail equipment technology while planning the construction of high-speed railway. In terms of the four indicators measuring high-speed railway speed, China has maintained a global lead in laboratory test speed, line test speed and the actual operating speed. China-EMU with a speed of 350 kilometers per hour has completely independent intellectual property rights. The development cycle of new models is at the global leading level. It only took less than 20 years for China to achieve technological catch-up in high-speed rail equipment, a high-tech and complex industry. ①

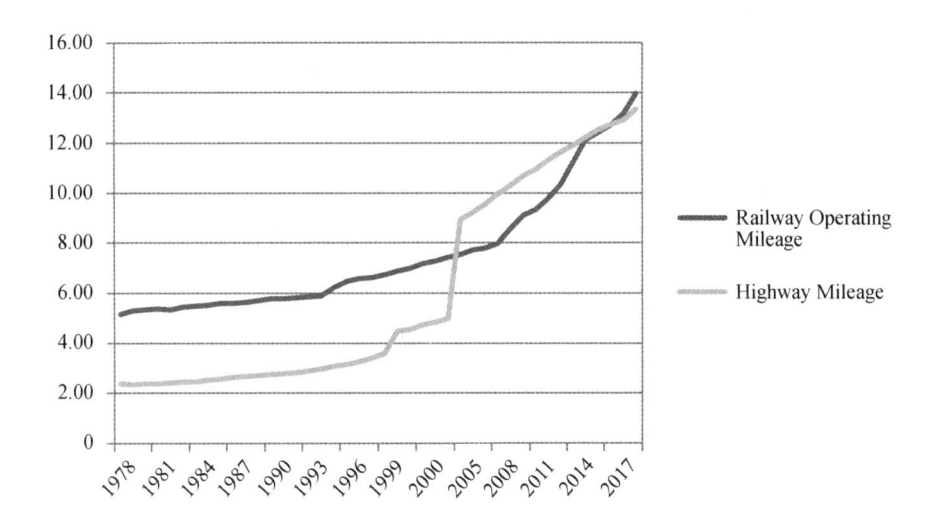

Figure 7 China's railway (left axis) and highway (right axis) construction mileage (10,000 kilometers)

Data source: Wind database.

In addition to the above factors, governments at all levels have a strong sense of service for enterprise development. In particular, local governments in coastal areas are often able to flexibly cooperate with

---

① Lv Tie, He Jun, "When is Government Intervention Effective: An Investigation of Technology Catch-up of the Chinese High-Speed Railway Industry", *Journal of Management World*, No. 9, 2019.

enterprises to solve key obstacles faced by industrial development①; a great emphasis on education and large-scale investment, thereby industrial development and technological upgrading, which help attract a large number of highly skilled talents; overseas Chinese who have worked and studied in Europe and the United States "come back", so that enterprises can master the hidden knowledge necessary for technological development and industrialization through talent flow, etc. Such factors are also crucial for China's manufacturing industry to realize catch-up development.

3 More Extensive and In-depth China-Argentina Industrial and Digital Economic Cooperation

Against the background of the joint efforts of the Chinese and Argentine governments and the reconstruction of division of labor in the global supply chain, the two countries have broad prospects for cooperation in industrial capacity, infrastructure construction, and innovation and entrepreneurship.

Deepen industrial capacity cooperation in multiple fields and promote regional industrialization process. In the foreseeable future, due to the continued influence of political and economic factors and the COVID-19, the global supply chain will develop in the direction of regionalization closer to the end market. A large number of Chinese industrial enterprises in the middle of the global supply chain will accelerate the deployment of overseas capacity to meet the needs of the regional market. Argentina, a major country of MERCOSUR,

---

① Rodrik, Dani, *One Economics, Many Recipes*, Princeton University Press, 2006.

faced with problems of foreign investment outflows in recent years, has broad prospects for accepting Chinese industrial direct investment. The governments of China and Argentina should work to enhance the Argentineans' trust in Chinese investors and jointly improve the environment for China's direct investment in Argentina; at the same time, they should actively support the Cooperation Plan with China for Argentine products and jointly seek cooperation projects in third-party markets for companies of the two countries, so as to give full play to the potential of the two countries' diversified cooperation on industrial capacity.

Improve the carrying capacity of resource-efficient and environmentally friendly infrastructure. The structure of infrastructure directly affects a country's economic structure and development level. One of the important advantages of emerging countries in infrastructure construction is that they can refer to the experience and lessons of countries with advanced development in technology route selection and directly apply them to the applicable infrastructure route suitable for their own conditions. The infrastructure construction projects that Chinese companies participate in Argentina are not the simple reuse of early mature technologies in traditional infrastructures, but the use of the latest applicable technologies in accordance with local conditions to develop more resource-efficient and environmentally friendly sustainable infrastructure. As of 2019, the Argentine government had approved more than 140 renewable energy investment projects, of which 40% are invested and constructed by China. The first photovoltaic power station in Argentina was constructed by a Chinese company, using China's advanced photovoltaic power generation technology and experience domestically accumulated in construction at high altitudes. In the future, China and Argentina should strengthen financial support for Argentina's infrastructure construction through the Asian Infrastructure Investment Bank and other channels, promote the high-efficient synergy of China's infrastructure construction capabilities and the needs of Argentina's infrastructure improvement, so as to promote the structural upgrade of Argentina's infrastructure and improve its internal growth momentum.

Build future-oriented digital infrastructure and a digital economy partnership. The development of the digital economy depends not only on the construction of digital infrastructure, but also on improving the inclusiveness of digital infrastructure and promoting the universal interconnection of the vast population and industries, thereby releasing the universal driving effect of digital infrastructure on economic development. China has become a global leader in the field of digital infrastructure and digital economy. It has the ability to support Argentina in building affordable and high-quality digital infrastructure to bridge the digital divide; it also has best practices in e-commerce and digital economy development that Argentina can learn from, as well as the ultra-large-scale e-commerce domestic market opened to Argentina, which can effectively promote the development of e-commerce and related industries in Argentina. Specifically, in terms of digital infrastructure construction, the Argentine government has always taken an open and positive attitude towards the cooperation between companies of the two countries in 5G network construction. The three major Argentine communications operators have also jointly carried out 5G network tests with Huawei, which has created favorable conditions for Argentina to build an inclusive network with high cost-effectiveness and high coverage by using Chinese communications technology. In terms of cross-border e-commerce development, based on the Memorandum of Understanding on E-commerce Cooperation signed between China and Argentina in December 2018, the two governments will actively strengthen policy communication and coordination, and promote bilateral trade of high-quality characteristic products through e-commerce. China's huge e-commerce market scale and a rising online consumer purchasing rate will promote the effective synergy of Argentine high-quality products, SMEs that lack marketing channels and the Chinese consumer market, giving full play to the driving effect of digital infrastructure on the inclusive development and overall development of the Argentine digital economy.

Forge closer innovation and entrepreneurship cooperation ties. In the context of the new round of global scientific and technological revolution and industrial revolution, collaborative innovation of science and technology is the long-term foundation for promoting sustainable development of industrial cooperation between China and Argentina and further complementing scientific and technological capabilities and industrial capabilities of the two countries. In recent years, in the field of aerospace, basic scientific research cooperation and industrial innovation investment cooperation between the two countries have become increasingly close. Chinese companies provide support for Argentine high-tech entrepreneurship such as satellite remote sensing through various means such as technical support and venture capital. Satellogic selected China's Long March carrier rockets to launch remote sensing satellites, and jointly solved many key technical issues in satellite launching together with Chinese scientific researchers. In addition, Tencent is also the lead investor in Satellogic's multiple rounds of investment. In the field of digital economy and other emerging industries, China and Argentina, as regional and even global powers, should carry out more extensive cooperation in the exploration of application scenarios and the formulation of application standards of emerging technologies (such as 5G), so as to defend common interests of emerging economies in global frontier industries.

Economic Globalization: Seeking for New Opportunities and Prospects[*]

The world today is facing major changes unseen in a century, and economic globalization is also undergoing profound changes as a result. Under the impact of the COVID-19, economic globalization is facing unprecedented challenges. How to understand the general development trend of economic globalization and seek for new opportunities and prospects in economic globalization has become a major issue facing all countries in the world, including China and Argentina.

1 The Development Trend of Economic Globalization is Irreversible

In April 2018, Chinese President Xi Jinping delivered a keynote speech at the opening ceremony of the Boao Forum for Asia Annual Conference and noted, "A comprehensive study of world development trajectories shows that economic globalization is an irreversible trend

---

[*] Xu Xiujun, Senior Research Fellow, Institute of World Economics and Politics, Chinese Academy of Social Sciences.

of our times."① Generally speaking, economic globalization refers to the process of increasing human economic interdependence. From the physical perspective, with the deepening of the division of labor and the expansion of the market, the scale and speed of cross-border flow of goods and services, as well as capital, labor, and technology, have increased and accelerated; from the institutional perspective, the original "local" rules have been more and more universally respected or adaptable on a global scale; meanwhile, the operation of the world is highly sensitive to and dependent on non-neutral international rules. From the ideational perspective, with the help of the media revolution, especially the information technology revolution, the values and ideologies of different people, ethnic groups, and countries have shown a trend of convergence and differentiation simultaneously during exchanges. ②

After the formation of the global division of labor, capital, labor and commodities have flowed to countries and regions with the highest utilization efficiency globally. On the whole, economic globalization has expanded the allocation of resources from the country level to the global scale, which improves the efficiency of resource allocation. More importantly, economic globalization, based on the international division of labor and market economy, transmits economic vitality, production efficiency and development opportunities to all countries in the world, greatly promotes the development of productivity and the growth of the world economy, especially providing a rare historical

---

① Xi Jinping, "Openness for Greater Prosperity, Innovation for a Better Future — Keynote Speech at the Opening of the Boao Forum for Asia Annual Conference", *Peace*, No. 127, June 2018, p. 6.

② Zhang Yuyan et al., *Globalization and China's Development*, Beijing: Social Sciences Academic Press (China), 2007, p. 55.

opportunity for developing countries to catch up with developed countries, by activating their potential. In his speech at the UN Office at Geneva, President Xi Jinping noted, " Economic globalization, a surging historical trend, has greatly facilitated trade, investment, flow of people and technological advances. Since the turn of the century, under the auspices of the UN and riding on the waves of economic globalization, the international community has set the Millennium Development Goals and the 2030 Agenda for Sustainable Development. Thanks to these initiatives, 1.1 billion people have been lifted out of poverty, 1.9 billion people now have access to safe drinking water, 3.5 billion people have gained access to the Internet, and the goal has been set to eradicate extreme poverty by 2030. "① All this demonstrates that economic globalization is in the common interest of all countries in the world and it is moving in the right direction.

Fundamentally speaking, economic globalization is an objective requirement for the development of social productivity and an inevitable result of scientific and technological progress. According to the dialectical analysis of productivity and production relations, economic base and superstructure, economic globalization can be regarded as the inevitable result of the development of human history to a certain stage. The development of world history has partly been the result of the movement of productive forces themselves represented by the industrial revolution. With the development of productivity, the world market was established, and the global economy has been

---

① Xi Jinping, "Work Together to Build a Community of Shared Future for Mankind — Speech at the United Nations Office at Geneva", *Beijing Review*, No. 7, February 16, 2017, p. 13.

increasingly and closely linked. Economic globalization depends on the development of social productive forces, and the development of productive forces has been closely related to technological progress. Science and technology are productivities and revolutionary forces that have promoted historical development. Throughout the history of world economic development, mankind has experienced the agricultural revolution, the industrial revolution and the information revolution successively. Historical experience has shown that each and every industrial technological revolution has a huge and profound impact on human production and life, and can significantly change the world's development pattern. This is even more true at the current stage. In particular, the rapid development of information technology represented by the Internet has accelerated economic globalization in new areas and forms, and brought people from all over the world together closer.

2 The Epidemic Has Severely Impacted the Process of Economic Globalization

Under the impact of the pandemic, the world economy has experienced its worst situation since the Great Depression in the 1930s. In January 2021, the International Monetary Fund (IMF) estimated data shows that the world economy would shrink by 3.5% in 2020, a decrease of 6.3 percentage from 2019. ①The pandemic not only caused a recession in the world economy, but also greatly impacted the economic exchanges of various countries. As a result, economic globalization faced major challenges. The impact of the pandemic on

---

① IMF, World Economic Outlook, January 2021.

economic globalization is mainly reflected on the global supply chain, industrial chain, service chain and value chain. After the outbreak of the pandemic, the cross-border flow of factors such as goods, services, and personnel was blocked by the epidemic prevention and control measures of various countries, which objectively caused the "decoupling" of the world economy. The sharp decline in global demand inevitably leads to a sharp decline in trade.

Affected by factors such as the increasing inward consideration of some countries' trade policies and the sudden epidemic, world trade was hit hard again in 2020. According to the United Nations Conference on Trade and Development (UNCTAD), world trade recorded a drop in value of about 9 percent in 2020, with trade in goods declining by about 6 percent and trade in services decreasing by about 16.5 percent; the effect of COVID-19 on global trade was most severe during the first half of 2020 with a drop in value of about 15 percent. ①Meanwhile, trade in electronic products and automobiles with a long industrial chain may decline even more drastically. In addition to the rupture of the industrial chain caused by the pandemic, some countries have also called for a comprehensive "decoupling" from other countries and the whole industrial chain in general, which has even been transformed into policy measures to accelerate the "decoupling" of the global industrial chain.

At the same time, the pandemic has plunged international direct investment, which has continued to grow weak, into a more serious predicament. After the international financial crisis in 2008, global foreign direct investment (FDI) fell sharply, and the growth of which lacked momentum. UNCTAD data shows that the average annual

---

① UNCTAD, *Global Trade Update*, February 2021.

growth rate of global FDI inflows reached 20.2% in the post crisis decade, while in the second decade, the average annual growth rate of global FDI inflows was −0.3%. After experiencing a strong recovery in 2015 due to the substantial increase in global cross-border mergers and acquisitions, global FDI has declined for three consecutive years since 2016, and the rate of decline in 2020 hit a new high since 2002. According to estimates from Investment Trends Monitor published by UNCTAD in January 2021, global foreign direct investment collapsed in 2020, falling by 42% to an estimated USD 859 billion, from USD 1.5 trillion in 2019; FDI finished 2020 more than 30% below the trough after the global financial crisis in 2009. ①

In the short term, a certain degree of "decoupling" in the global economy would be unavoidable. After experiencing the pandemic, all countries have become more vigilant about the economy's excessive dependence on the outside world, which may cause the prevalence of "decoupling" policies. Some people even believe that the pandemic provides a test for the "decoupling" of the global economy. Some economically dependent countries have begun to reflect on their industrial policies to reduce their excessive dependence on other countries. These circumstances may lead to a decline in global economic and trade interdependence and a break in the global industrial chain in the future. But in the long run, new business forms and models, and new industries that have accelerated economic growth during the pandemic will shape new growth momentum for economic globalization.

---

① UNCTAD, *Investment Trends Monitor*, No. 38, January 24, 2021.

3 Seeking for New Opportunities in the Challenge of De-globalization

In recent years, the accelerated application of digital technologies such as internet technologies, artificial intelligence, 5G, and big data have rapidly promoted the development of related industries. The normalization of epidemic prevention and control forcefully accelerated the growth of new business formats and models, and new industries in various countries. Relying on these new technologies, global supply chains, industrial chains, service chains, and value chains will establish closer ties during the reconstruction, so as to promote the development of economic globalization in a new form at a higher level. Digital economy will create new development opportunities for economic globalization driven by the pandemic.

As a new economic form, digital economy includes both the economy that takes data or digitized knowledge and information as key factors of production, and the economy that takes cloud computing, big data, internet of things, artificial intelligence, blockchain and other digital technologies as means. In recent years, the global digital economy has developed very rapidly. In 2019, the value added of digital economy in 47 countries around the world reached USD 31.8 trillion, accounting for 41.5% of GDP, and industrial digitalization accounted for 84.3% of the digital economy, becoming the leading force driving the development of the global digital economy. ① Since the COVID-19 outbreak in 2020, the development of the global digital economy has greatly accelerated. According to an OECD report, in

---

① CAICT, *A New Vision of the Global Digital Economy (2020) —New Drive for Sustainable Development under Great Changes*, October 2020.

the context of the pandemic, significant progresses have been made in all aspects of digital transformation, and epidemic prevention and control measures taken by all countries have further stimulated demand for broadband communications services. In OECD member states, an estimated 1.3 billion people work and study at home, and on the internet value chain, flow volumes of all participants have increased by as much as 60% from the pre-outbreak level. ① The widespread use of digital technology has greatly facilitated the digital transformation of industries, and the long-term influence of the epidemic on digital transformation also begins to emerge. According to the prediction of the International Data Corporation (IDC), 65% of global GDP will be driven by digitalization in 2022, from 2020 to 2023, investment directly derived from digital transformation will grow at a compound annual growth rate (CAGR) of 15.5%, with the total scale expected to be exceed USD 6.8 trillion. ②IDC also predicted that the overall revenue of global hardware, software and services market related to big data will reach USD 187.84 billion in 2020, an increase of 3.1% over the previous year. ③ Big data technology and services-related revenues will grow at a five-year CAGR of 15.6% in 2019 – 2024. ④

Led by some emerging economies such as China, the global

---

① OECD, *OECD Digital Economy Outlook 2020*, OECD Publishing, November 27, 2020.

② Shawn Fitzgerald, et al., *IDC Future Scape: Worldwide Digital Transformation 2021 Predictions*, October 2020.

③ IDC, *Worldwide Big Data and Analytics Spending Guide*, August 2020.

④ Chandana Gopal, et al., *Worldwide Big Data and Analytics Software Forecast, 2020 – 2024*, August 2020.

digital economy has been growing rapidly. At present, the overall level of China's digital economy ranks second in the world, digital industrialization has maintained rapid growth, industrial digitization has advanced in an all-round way, and the environment for the development of the digital economy has become better day by day. ① Especially after the outbreak of the COVID-19 in 2020, the digital economy played an important role in promoting the resumption of work and production and economic stability. According to the National Bureau of Statistics, the added value registered by information transmission, software and information technology services grew by 16.9% in 2020, 14.8 percentage points higher than that of the tertiary industry, and online retail sales reached 11.7601 billion yuan, up 10.9% from the previous year. ② In 2020, the digital economy accounted for nearly 40% of China's GDP and contributed nearly 70% to GDP growth.

Against the backdrop of the epidemic outbreak, many Asian countries have introduced new measures to promote the transformation of the digital economy, covering digital infrastructure construction, digital industrialization, industrial digital transformation, digital governance, and international digital cooperation. In terms of digital infrastructure construction, 5G has become a new highlight. In terms of the development of digital industrialization, information technology has played an important role in epidemic prevention and control and economic recovery. Big data and the Internet of Things have played a

---

① Yin Libo, *A Report on the Development of the Digital Economy (2019 – 2020)*, Publishing Housing of Electronics Industry, 2020, p. 125.
② The Research Center for National Industrial Information Security and Development, *Analysis of Digital Economy Situation in 2020 – 2021*, January 2021.

bigger supporting role, and the development of artificial intelligence has also entered a fast track. In terms of industrial digital transformation, the digital economy and the real economy are undergoing deeply integrated development, and such sectors as digital agriculture, digital cultural industry, "internet + medical and health", and "internet + tourism" are flourishing. In terms of digital governance, steady progress has been made in joint prevention and control of digital public security, standardized management of digital government affairs, intelligent upgrading of urban facilities, and competition in the digital market. In terms of international digital cooperation, some regional and international economic and trade cooperation covering digital economy cooperation has made new progress. At the G20 Special Meeting of Digital Economy Ministers in April 2020, participants reached a consensus on the use of digital technology to accelerate research on the novel coronavirus, enhance business flexibility and create job opportunities.

In short, the epidemic has made all countries more fully aware of the value of the digital economy and thus promoted its faster development. In the post-epidemic era, the digital economy will become a key force after agricultural economy, industrial economy and information economy that can influence the world economy and international relations, and create more space for economic globalization.

4 Jointly Promoting the Continuous Advancement of Economic Globalization

The various global problems which have emerged along with economic globalization are not inevitable products of this very process, but only a profound reflection of the current lack of effective governance of economic globalization. Therefore, economic globalization cannot be simply blamed for the problems plaguing the world, so as various protectionism and unilateralism of "anti-globalization". Currently, global problems and challenges are increasing, no country can be left alone, and the power of any single country cannot properly handle and respond to these issues. Therefore, all countries should continue to strengthen international economic coordination and cooperation, and jointly explore new solutions to promote the process of economic globalization.

First, insist on multilateralism and free trade to cope with the lack of driving force of globalization. Currently, economic globalization is facing huge obstacles precisely because the multilateral trading system and regional trade arrangements have failed to play an effective role in driving economic globalization. To this end, countries around the world should uphold the rules of the World Trade Organization, support an open, transparent, inclusive and non-discriminatory multilateral trading system, and build an open world economy. Making trade the basic driving force of economic globalization means that countries around the world should not only become supporters and defenders of the current multilateral trading system, but also promote the realization of equal rights, equal opportunities and equal rules for all countries in the formulation of international trade rules and global system construction. As Klaus Schwab, founder and executive chairman of the World Economic Forum, said, free trade remains the strongest driving force of global economic development and social progress, and it is the responsibility of world leaders today to both confront trade protectionism and to make trade a source of inclusive growth. Faced with the dilemma of insufficient driving force of economic globalization, China has repeatedly promised that "China will only become more and more open wider", and has made efforts to promote the formation of the new development paradigm, the global significance of which will be huge and far-reaching.

Second, participate in global economic governance and address the global governance deficit actively. In an era of unprecedented interdependence, mankind is facing increasingly urgent global problems. Strengthening global economic governance is one of the remedies to solve the problems of market failure and global governance deficit caused by economic globalization. In the new historical stage, global economic governance should be based on equality, oriented to openness, driven by cooperation and aiming at sharing. This is the fundamental way to promote the construction of an open, inclusive, balanced and win-win economic globalization. To this end, the world's leading countries should promote the functions of G20 and other international economic cooperation mechanisms, actively participate in the reform of the World Trade Organization, promote the formulation of rules for economic governance in emerging areas, and promote the improvement of a more just and reasonable global economic governance system.

Third, promote the construction of the Belt and Road Initiative, and continue to strengthen the solid foundation of economic globalization. The goal of China's Belt and Road Initiative is to promote mutual benefit and win-win situation, and its starting point and anchor point is the common prosperity of all participating countries. In current situation, the significance of the Belt and Road construction for economic globalization is that it is conducive to promoting economic globalization in the direction of inclusiveness.

In the face of the test posed by the epidemic, the Belt and Road Initiative has shown strong resilience and vitality, with relevant projects continuing to advance, cooperation yielding many fruits, and trade and investment keeping growth against headwinds. According to the data from the Ministry of Commerce, the volume of trade in goods between China and countries along the Belt and Road in 2020 reached USD 1.35 trillion, up 0.7% from the previous year; the non-financial direct investment of Chinese enterprises into 58 countries along the Belt and Road reached USD 17.79 billion in 2020, up 18.3% from a year earlier, accounting for 16.2% of their total amount of such investment during the same period, an increase of 2.6 percentage points year-on-year. Since the outbreak of the epidemic, various kinds of online transactions are on the rise, the degree of integration between online and offline is deepening, and the real economy and virtual economy promote each other, which all make the Belt and Road more dynamic. As of January 2021, China has signed more than 200 cooperation documents on the joint construction of the initiative with more than 130 countries and 31 international organizations. The achievements of the Belt and Road cooperation show that promoting interconnection and adhering to openness and inclusiveness are the only ways to cope with global crises and achieve long-term development, in order to fundamentally promote the common development and prosperity of human society.

Economic and Social Development in the Post COVID-19 Pandemic Era*

1 Winning the Battle Against COVID-19

The COVID-19 epidemic is the most serious global pandemic in the last century and the fastest spreading, most extensive, and most challenging public health emergency that China has encountered since the founding of the People's Republic of China in 1949. The CPC Central Committee and the State Council attached great importance to decease the spread of the epidemic, made the lockdown decision and practiced strict social distancing. The strategy of overall command, comprehensive arrangement, and three-dimensional prevention and control formed quickly both from central authorities to localities, which effectively curbed the extensive spread of epidemic and powerfully hindered the transmission of the virus, thus protecting people's lives and health to the greatest extent. China managed to contain the rapid spread of the virus in just over a month. In about two months, the daily increase in domestic coronavirus cases fell to single

---

* Sun Zhaoyang, Associate Professor and Associate Dean of School of Global Education and Development, University of Chinese Academy of Social Sciences.

digit. Meanwhile, a decisive victory was secured in once the hardest-hit Chinese city of Wuhan and province of Hubei in just about three months. Besides, the country has effectively contained regional clustered outbreaks or sporadic outbreaks of scattered infections, with a total of 102,700 confirmed cases and 97,400 cured cases by the end of March.

The CPC Central Committee quickly set up the Central Leading Group for novel coronavirus Prevention and Control to deal with the epidemic, and sent the Central Leading Group to build the Joint Prevention and Control Mechanism of the State Council. It proposed the epidemic prevention and control requirements of "early detection, reporting, quarantine and treatment", as well as the treatment principle in which "all confirmed patients must be hospitalized without delay, and severe cases must be sent to designated hospitals with sufficient medical resources", thus raising admission and cure rates and lowering infection and fatality rates. Every patient shall be treated with full dedication, with no one being left behind. And all costs for treating COVID-19 patients were covered by the government, thus maximizing the cure rates and minimizing the fatality rates. China first developed the nucleic acid testing kit, accelerated effective drug screening and vaccine R&D, and officially launched domestically-developed COVID-19 vaccines earlier 2021, with more than 100 million people vaccinated nationwide, taking the lead in getting the outbreak under control overall.

Party committees and governments at all levels, all departments and units, and the whole nation actively responded to the central epidemic prevention and control policy. High mobilization of socialism capacity played an important role. China mobilized the whole nation and carried out a campaign to save lives on an unprecedented scale, building the Huoshenshan Hospital in 10 days, the Leishenshan Hospital in 12 days, and 16 temporary treatment centers in just over 10 days. Moreover, over 600 collective quarantine places were opened within a short period. 346 national medical aid teams, more than 40,000 medical personnel, and 19 provinces, autonomous regions and municipalities were paired with Wuhan, realizing the remarkable shift from tension supply to dynamic balance in terms of the medical resources and supplies in the shortest possible time. More than 4.6 million grassroots Party organizations were fully committed to the epidemic control, and more than 4 million community workers were on duty day and night in 650,000 urban and rural communities nationwide. Various private enterprises, private hospitals, charities, elderly care centers and welfare homes actively made their own contributions. CPC members and officials took the lead in the fight; members of the People's Liberation Army, the Chinese Armed Police Force, and the public security police fought bravely in the fight; scientific researchers worked hard for breakthroughs; millions of couriers braved the epidemic; 1.8 million sanitation workers worked from dawn to dusk; and tens of millions of volunteers and ordinary people made indelible contributions to win the epidemic.

2 Promoting Rapid Economic Recovery and Orderly Development

After the global outbreak of the epidemic, the international trade and supply chains are severely hit. Due to the strict epidemic prevention and control measures, China's GDP growth rate in the first quarter of 2020 only witnessed the negative growth of -6.8%. On top of safeguarding people's health and safety and containing the spread of the epidemic, the Central Committee, based on China's realities, scientifically maintained a desired balance between various macro policies and strengthened their functions. On the basis of what we had done to ensure stability on six key fronts (employment, financial operations, foreign trade, foreign investment, domestic investment, and expectations), we carried out the task of maintaining security in six key areas (ensure security in job, basic living needs, operations of market entities, food and energy security, stable industrial and supply chains, and the normal functioning of primary-level governments). Governments at all levels resumed operation in a targeted and orderly manner, and strove to promote agricultural production, so that economic operation continued to recover steadily and the internal impetus, balance and sustainability of economic development were further enhanced. Our economy was the first to achieve positive growth in the third quarter in the world, with GDP reaching 101. 6 trillion yuan in 2020 and an annual growth rate of 2. 3%.

Policies were introduced to alleviate difficulties facing enterprises so as to promote their work and production resumption, thus boosting rapid economic recovery. Time-limited large-scale tax and fee cuts were implemented, introducing 7 batches of 28 tax and fee cut policies, in which temporary reduction and exemption were administered in VAT, corporate income tax, social insurance, provident fund, logistics costs, housing rent, electricity and gas credit fees, etc. , lifting the burden on market entities by more than 2. 6 trillion yuan for the year. Government adopted new approaches in implementing macro policies. The central government established a mechanism to directly allocate two trillion yuan of new funding to prefecture-and county-level governments, while provincial-level governments also increased their funding allocations to governments at these levels. The monetary support measures launched amounted to more than 9 trillion yuan, including the reduction of deposit reserve ratios, medium-term lending facility, open market operations, re-lending and re-discounting, and new monetary policy instruments that could directly stimulate the real economy. Government implemented support instrument for deferred repayment of inclusive loans for micro and small-sized enterprises and the support plan for inclusive unsecured loans for micro and small-sized enterprises so as to lower the financing costs for enterprises. The banking industry has cumulatively implemented deferred repayment of the principal of loans with interest for 7.3 trillion yuan in 2020, and cumulatively issued 3.9 trillion yuan of credit loans for inclusive micro and small-sized enterprises. This has continuously injected impetus into enterprises and helped them solve financing and operation difficulties and enhance their vitality.

Government will firmly implement the strategy of expanding domestic demand and give full play to the role of the domestic market. China boasts massive internal market, with per capita consumption of 36,200 yuan for urban residents and 14,900 yuan for rural residents by the end of 2019. The epidemic came as a terrible blow on the international industrial chain and market, which made the recovery and potential of the domestic market crucial for economic resurgence. China has been committed to enhancing the basic role of consumption, actively supported the accelerated development of new consumption with new forms and new models, and boost the cultivation and construction of international consumption center cities. Besides, we orderly promoted cultural and tourism consumption as well as information consumption pilot programs, boosted consumption of services like elderly care and childcare. We stabilized and expanded the consumption of major durables like automobiles, boosted food and beverage consumption, and further released rural consumption potential. Annual total retail sales of social consumer goods in 2020 reached 39.2 trillion yuan, and the national online retail sales reached 11.8 trillion yuan, an increase of 10.9%, of which the online retail sales of physical goods grew by 14.8%, accounting for 24.9% of the total retail sales of social consumer goods.

Give play to the pivotal role of investment. Opinions on Promoting High-quality Development of Infrastructure and Opinions on Promoting Accelerated Development of Municipal (Suburban) Railways in Urban Areas were issued, which proposed that government would invest more in new infrastructure and new urbanization initiatives as well as major projects, such as transportation, water conservancy etc. What's more, government should adjust and optimize the structure of the central budget investment plan to shift the focus on supporting public health and other shortcomings and weaknesses caused by the epidemic, and strengthen the construction of major railroads, highways, waterway, airports, water conservancy projects, major science and technology and energy infrastructure, renovation of old communities in cities and towns, etc. In 2020, the total fixed asset investment (excluding peasant households) reached 52.7 trillion, with a growth rate of 2.9%. And the total capital formation contributed up to 2.2% to the GDP growth rate, greatly facilitating the resumption of economic growth.

3 New Victories in the Fight Against Poverty and the Building of a Moderately Prosperous Society in All Respects

Faced with the adverse situation of the epidemic, the battle against poverty has achieved a comprehensive victory. In response to the unfavorable impact of the epidemic and floods on the fight against poverty, priority was given to supporting the poor workers in landing jobs, further providing jobs instead of giving grants through multiple channels, making great efforts to reduce poverty through the development of local industries and employment and promotion of consumer spending on products from poor areas. Besides, coordination between production and sales as well as technological assistance should be enhanced. And subsistence allowances should be provided for these most vulnerable groups. Policies and measures have been introduced to ensure that follow-up support will be given to the resettled population. Unsafe housing occupied by 7.9 million households, or a total of 25.68 million poor people, has been renovated, 35,000 centralized communities and 2.66 million units of housing for resettlement have been built, and more than 9.6 million people have emerged from poor, isolated, and backward places and moved into new homes. Great endeavors have been made to cement gains from Two Assurances and Three Guarantees (this refers to assurances of adequate food and clothing, and guarantees of access to compulsory education, basic medical services and safe housing for impoverished rural residents). Medical expenses of the poor have been effectively reduced due to basic medical insurance, serious illness insurance, and medical assistance. All of the 98.99 million rural poor, as well as the 832 counties and 128,000 villages classified as poor, had emerged from poverty, and regional poverty was eliminated. China realized its poverty reduction goal from the UN 2030 Agenda for Sustainable Development 10 years ahead of schedule.

Give priority to employment. Residents' income has steadily

increased. In 2019, employed population in China reached 775 million, of which 74.9% were employed in non-agricultural industries and 57.1% in urban areas. Lockdown during the epidemic made the employment for these groups grim, resulting in income and livelihood difficulties. Employment is pivotal to people's wellbeing. Efforts to protect market entities are also intended to stabilize employment and maintain living standards. Government therefore strengthened support for enterprises, lightening their burden and helping them to keep their payrolls stable and create more jobs. Government provided support and assistance to market entities including key industries, to MSMEs, and to self-employed individuals affected by the epidemic. Government also worked to increase employment by expanding effective investment. Startups and innovation were encouraged as a way of creating job opportunities. The average daily increase in market entities for the year was 41,000, including 13,000 enterprises. All level governments supported flexible employment through diversified channels, scaled up recruitment in individually-owned businesses, SOEs, public institutions, and community-level programs, and enlarged graduate education enrollment, military recruitment, and internship, encouraged college graduates to enter market-based employment, coordinated efforts to ensure employment for key groups such as demobilized military personnel and migrant workers. 11.86 million new jobs were created in urban areas in 2020, with 5.2% of unemployment rate, which proved that the employment situation was basically stable. The per capita disposable income of residents was 32,189 yuan, an increase of 4.7% over the previous year, of which the income of urban and rural residents was 43,834 yuan and 17,131 yuan respectively, with growth rates of 3.5% and 7.2%.

Income growth against the backdrop of the epidemic was even more remarkable.

Further improve the social security system. The basic old-age insurance for urban workers covered 456 million people, and basic old-age insurance for rural and non-working urban residents covered 542 million people, with the accumulative balance over 6.28 trillion yuan. The proportion of enterprise workers' basic pension funds under central government allocation was increased from 3.5% to 4.0%, realizing provincial-level collection and payout. Retirees' basic pensions were increased steadily. Workers' compensation benefits were paid out to 1.85 million employees who had suffered work-related injuries and their dependents. It is necessary to expand the scope of unemployment insurance, provide temporary unemployment subsidies, and extend such subsidies to more unemployed migrant workers on a time-limited basis. In 2020, 13.37 million unemployed people received unemployment benefits from varying insurance schemes. A total of 104.2 billion yuan from unemployment insurance funds was refunded in order to help 6.08 million enterprises maintain stable employment, benefiting 156 million employees. The policy on extending the scope of social assistance was introduced, which promptly increased social security assistance and benefit payments in step with price increases, and stepped up assistance to people who fell into poverty due to COVID-19 and to uninsured workers who had lost their jobs, making sure that assistance could reach all those in need. Subsistence allowances were extended and basic assistance to persons living in extreme poverty was provided to approximately six million people affected by the epidemic, and more than eight million applications for temporary assistance were approved. Government will continue the nursing care subsidies for people with disabilities, a system that has benefited 11.53 million poor disabled people and 14.33 million with severe disabilities in need of nursing, as well as providing more than 4,400 service facilities for disabled persons.

4 Build a Modern Socialist Country in All Respects

The year 2021 coincides with the first year of the 14th Five-year Plan period. The international epidemic situation is not optimistic, with constant flare-ups of international trade friction and unilateralism. China's economic and social development aims at building the new development pattern in which domestic and foreign markets boost each other, with the domestic market as the mainstay. First, raise the capacity for pursuing scientific and technological innovation, and improve our strategic scientific and technological strength. The development should focus on construction of new infrastructure. Scientific and technological innovation should be accelerated in artificial intelligence, quantum technology, brain science, biological breeding and other fields. We will organize the implementation of integrated innovation demonstration projects in enterprises with different sizes, encourage large enterprises to share resources, scenarios, applications, and innovation demands with small and medium enterprises, and create an innovative and entrepreneurial ecosystem that is integrated with industrial and supply chains. It will improve financial support for innovation and direct more investment into basic research, R&D, and the commercialization of new advances. By employing such mechanisms for preferential tax treatment, it will encourage enterprises to increase R&D spending and improve financial support for innovation and direct more investment into basic research, R&D, and the commercialization of new advances.

Second, focus on the revitalization and development of the real economy and improve the core competitiveness of industry. The real economy is the main driver of productivity growth. China needs to enhance the core competitiveness of the manufacturing industry, promote the localization and industrialization of key technologies in major technical equipment, high-end new materials, robotics and intelligent manufacturing. Efforts are required to expand the upgrading and renewal of manufacturing equipment and technological transformation, and promote the high-end, intelligent and green transformation of traditional industries, optimize and upgrade their entire industrial chains. Implementation of preferential tax concessions was conducted for enterprises in the advanced manufacturing industries; the proportion of manufacturing loans increased, and investment in manufacturing equipment upgrading and technological transformation expanded. Efforts need to be made to accelerate the growth of new energy industries and other industries, promote the healthy and orderly development of new energy vehicles, and accelerate the building of intelligent automobile infrastructure, industrial ecology and other support systems. Besides, it is critical to promote the bio-economy, promote the development of biotechnology integration, and accelerate the development and industrialization of urgently needed clinical drugs and high-end medical equipment.

Third, advance the high-quality construction of the Belt and Road Initiative, and pursue a new system of open economy of higher standards. It is essential to uphold the principles of extensive consultation, joint contribution, and shared benefits, pursue open, green, clean philosophy, and advance practical cooperation. Government should deepen the integration into the planning of key countries and regions, strengthen cooperation in production capacity, and promote positive progress of major connectivity projects such as railroads, ports and energy. Moreover, government should continue to deepen cooperation with international organizations in terms of BRI development, and be well prepared in risk prevention and response, actively participate in global economic governance, firmly uphold the multilateral trading system, promote the G20 to play a role in international economic cooperation, and facilitate the reform of the WTO and the international financial system.

Fourth, with a strong sense of responsibility as a major country, China has worked to contribute its part to the international epidemic prevention and control. In an open, transparent, and responsible manner and in accordance with the law, China gave timely notification to the international community of the onset of a new coronavirus, publicized key information including the genome sequencing of the virus, and published diagnosis and therapeutic solutions as well as prevention and control protocols so as to support WHO's crucial leadership role in this endeavor. China has carried out its largest emergency humanitarian action since the founding of the People's Republic of China in 1949, providing support for the Global Humanitarian Response Plan of the WTO and the UN. China sent 36 medical expert teams to 34 countries. Besides, it provided assistance to 150 countries and 13 international organizations. Giving full play to our strengths as the world's largest supplier of epidemic prevention materials, over the course of the year we provided more than 200 countries with over 220 billion masks, 2.3 billion protective suits, and 1 billion testing kits. More than 102 million doses of COVID-19 vaccines had been administered in

China by March 27, 2021, making a solid stride towards herd immunity.

5 Strengthen Multi-level Cooperation with Argentina

Argentina is the third largest economy in Latin America and an important developing country with rich natural resources, high human capital, open foreign policy and diversified industrial system. Also, it is an important trade partner of China in Latin America. The two sides are complementary to each other in the import and export business of mechanical and electrical products, high-tech products, communication products, soybeans, crude oil, meat and other commodities. In the current international trade environment, developing countries need to achieve greater cooperation in order to break through the trade barriers set by developed countries. In 2020, trade between China and countries along the Belt and Road stood at 1.35 trillion dollars, an increase of 0.7% to 2019, accounting for 29.1% in the total foreign trade volume. China is willing and able to expand the scope of trade with Argentina, continue to promote innovative trade development, optimize the layout of domestic and international markets, commodity structure and trade patterns, improve the quality of exports, and strengthen cooperation with Argentina in food, resources, energy, industry and infrastructure, and increase imports of high-quality products.

Strengthen the supply of vaccines to Argentina. According to data from the Ministry of Industry and Information Technology, China has approved the marketing of four COVID-19 vaccines to be marketed, with a daily production of about 5 million doses. Meanwhile, significant progress has been made in other vaccines, which will further increase China's vaccine production capacity once they obtain approval for marketing. This will enhance vaccine R&D and global prevention and control. We will support the WHO in mobilizing and consolidating resources and distributing vaccines fairly and efficiently so as to assist countries and regions less prepared for the pandemic. As the largest supplier of the anti-pandemic materials, China will promote the building of a global community of health for all. China and Argentina can strengthen cooperation in vaccine manufacturing, transportation and vaccination, establish the fast track in shipping, entry and exit customs and taxation, and promote universal vaccination as soon as possible in a mutually beneficial manner, and promote the building of herd immunity.

Social Science Research and Its Role: A Perspective of Argentina[*]

1 Evolution and Development of Social Sciences in Argentina

Social studies on Argentina's situation go back decades. At the end of the 19th century, the main social imaginary of discussion in bourgeois circles and their organic intellectuals was the tension between civilization and barbarism — on the one hand, civilized, evolved and developed countries and societies; on the other hand, barbaric, backward, ignorant peoples and countries.

---

[*] The researchers of Argentine experts team are Fortunato Mallimaci, Senior Researcher of the National Scientific and Technical Research Council of Argentina (CONICET) & Professor of the University of Buenos Aires; Mario Pecheny, Principal Investigator of the National Scientific and Technical Research Council of Argentina (CONICET) & Professor of the University of Buenos Aires; Carolina Mera, Principal Investigator of the National Scientific and Technical Research Council of Argentina (CONICET) & Professor of the University of Buenos Aires; Victor Ramiro Fernandez, Independent Researcher of the National Scientific and Technical Research Council of Argentina (CONICET) & Professor of the National University of the Litoral; Cristian Lorenzo, Adjunct Researcher of the National Scientific and Technical Research Council of Argentina (CONICET) & Professor of the National University of Tierra del Fuego.

The largest production of knowledge about society was in the hands of lawyers and physicians who accounted for the "anomalies" in Argentine society. Predominant ideologies were Social Darwinism and Positivism. Between 1880 and 1930 about five million foreign migrants arrived in the country, especially from Europe and the Mediterranean, and the threat of the migrant "other" created new tensions and repressions. The country became rapidly urbanized and by the time of the First World War most of the population lived in cities.

For the first time by the mass and popular vote implemented at that time, in 1916 the Radical Civic Union was elected to govern the country and increased citizenship and rights. At the same time, the emerging labour movement (all its different wings, i. e., anarchists, socialists and Catholics) was concerned with studying the cost of food and housing in relation to low wages. This was the beginning of a long history of attention to and concern about the price of food in the domestic market that continues to these days. It must be noted that those same goods, meat and cereals, are the main exports of large agricultural-livestock producers and the main source of foreign exchange income for the country. Thus, food production has always been at the centre of political and social concerns and disputes.

In 1930 a military coup put an end to the first popular government experience and the militarization of Argentine society began. This coup and the global economic crisis of 1930 and 1943 destabilized the state and the liberal export-led growth model, making room for another industrialization model based on import substitution and lukewarm government regulations. Government regulators for prices and local production (meat, grain, oil, coal and others) are created and begin to conduct studies on these issues. The limitation and control of the labour and popular movement is coupled with the elimination of the male popular vote. By that time the model based on popular impoverishment, liberal conservatism and English imperial domination became the target of social criticism from various social and religious organizations outside the state's orbit.

The second democratic experience in Argentina ran between 1946 and 1955, when the Peronist government assumed power by popular vote, with the strong support from mobilized sectors of the labour and social movement. The country is industrialized and diversified, with unionization expanding to almost the entire working and rural world. Social studies organizations are created within the state to deal with issues such as education, habitat, infrastructure, population censuses, workers' organizations, health, military manufacturing, state-owned and privately-owned industrial companies, etc., that expand the available social knowledge about conflicts and needs in these sectors.

This new benefactor state model supports the expansion of social rights along with new studies on Argentine society. 1954 will be the year with the most equitable distribution of wealth during the entire 20th century. What's more, the link with Latin America expands based on a proposal of political sovereignty, economic independence and social justice and a non-aligned third position, where anti-imperialism causes workers to mobilize against the new colonialisms. However, in 1955 the dominant sectors of the country, together with business people, the military and catholic groups, overthrew this second mass democratic experience.

In the 1960s, a number of civil-military dictatorships and civil governments, while seeking to discipline working-class and popular sectors, expanded and created new spaces at public universities for the development of Social Sciences in disciplines such as history, anthropology, sociology, education, economics, urbanism, psychology, social work and habitat, that also energized the old Schools of Philosophy and Literature and Law and Social Sciences.

During these years the Argentine Social Sciences maintained a broad dialogue with the Social Sciences all over the rest of Latin America, revitalized first by developmentalist theories, then theories of an unequal exchange between developed and undeveloped countries, and later by theories insisting on dependency relations with the big capitalist countries. The social and political effervescence of the 1960s and subsequent radicality of the 1970s in these working-class, popular, academic, student and religious spheres questioned this capitalist domination and promoted transformation programs based on different socialist and popular nationalist experiences.

In 1976 a new coup by business, religious and military sectors put an end to these experiences and carried out a systematic plan to eliminate all forms of social protest and resistance. Thousands of arrested-missing persons, thousands of exiles and thousands of political prisoners would be required to implement the greatest urban impoverishment, de-industrialization, indebtedness and change of productive matrix ever suffered by the Argentine society. Universities would be intervened by the military power and social science disciplines would be reduced to their minimum expression. The term "subversive" would be used to legitimize this repression. The field of critical social sciences in Argentina was decimated by political/ military repression.

Since 1983 Argentina has lived the longest democratic period in its history. Beginning in the 1980s the Social Sciences have slowly recovered academic and scientific spaces in relation to teaching and production of critical knowledge at universities and CONICET.

Thanks to the return to democracy, degree programs for various social sciences disciplines reopened at public universities and research centres in the major urban centres of the country, which had stopped or reduced their activities during the last military dictatorship, and new degree programs in social sciences were also created.

This institutional expansion of Social Sciences intensified in the 2000s with the creation of new undergraduate, master's and doctoral degree programs in newly created universities in different locations in the province of Buenos Aires and in all Argentina. Simultaneously CONICET created new spaces for social and human sciences, with the result that today in 2021, Social Science is one of the four areas that make up CONICET (the others being Agricultural Sciences, Engineering and Materials; Biological and Health Sciences; and Exact and Natural Sciences), each area having the same number of researchers and fellows. In sum, during the last 20 years there has been an important expansion, diversification and institutionalization of undergraduate and graduate programs at social science research centres and universities across the country as well as an expansion of the generational base of researchers and teachers.

Last but not least, it must be noted that the progressive expansion of citizens' rights that began in 1980 has not yet succeeded in reversing the unequal distribution of wealth that originated during the previous dictatorship. Different modernizing or neoliberal or deregulated market or sustainable development projects are vying for hegemony in the democratic vote, with the active participation of the media, that emerge as a new significant actor. Currently almost half of the people in our country are in poverty, with almost all of them being cases of persisting urban poverty (official Government data). Social Sciences in Argentina are not alien to these processes and these issues are central to the reflection on the past, present and future of our country.

2. Current Status and Challenges of Social Sciences in Argentina

At present, Social Sciences in Argentina are remarkable for the high-level training of professionals, scientific production of excellence and wide insertion in international Latin American networks. The social sciences programs of public universities provide a solid conceptual, methodological and historical training. Students are trained based on a dialogue between disciplines. Research is conducted at universities and research centres throughout the country. At the same time, there is a fluid dialogue between the Social Sciences, the civil society and governmental agencies. In fact, many professionals employed by agencies at different (national, provincial, municipal) government levels have pursued an undergraduate and graduate education in social sciences.

2.1 Theories, methods and fields of social sciences research

In Argentina, among Social Sciences, various orthodox and heterogeneous theoretical traditions co-exist according to subdisciplines. Since the 1950s the following analytical approaches have prevailed: structural-functionalism and developmentalism, European and Latin American historical materialism, interpretative currents and cultural studies, all of them interpreted and redefined according to the political, social and cultural realities of Argentina and Latin America.

At the methodological level, quantitative survey methods co-exist in tension with and supplemented by qualitative methods such as life stories, interviews, social ethnography, participant observation and case studies and active triangulation for validation. There are methodological pluralism and critical-reflective approaches.

The most sought-after fields of study are economic and social development, poverty, inequality, social classes, collective action, political parties and political life, education, health, environment, religion, the media, international relations, immigration and cultural identities, rural studies and political economy.

2.2 Challenges for social sciences in Argentina in the post-epidemic era

Semi-peripheral countries such as Argentina face a challenging time in considering their insertion in the world economy, intensified by the the ongoing spread of the COVID-19.

2.2.1 Development Challenges

The persistence of the internal crisis, now intensified by the devastating effects of the pandemic, not only requires short-term responses; it also opens up important opportunities and challenges to put on the agenda the discussion of the role of industrial and technological policy. The urgency of these policy issues, also revealed in face of a worldwide scenario of productive capital over-accumulation and excess liquidity, is not exclusive to Argentina. These process are accompanied (and to a certain extent reinforced) by a new phase of the technological revolution of Information and Communication Technologies (ICT) and Bio-technologies.

In this context Argentina faces the old dilemma of how and where to redefine the pattern of productive specialization needed to industrial upgrading. Although the starting point is an economically unfavorable situation, there are "economic advantages of backwardness" which have to do with the possibility of imitating and develop their own idiosyncratic solutions adopting "creatively" the new technologies and undertake a rapid industrialization process based on it. Nevertheless, there are limitations imposed by backwardness in the initial phases of emerging paradigms. While low scale and learning thresholds offer advantages to latecomers, the costs of imitation could be rather high in the absence of a science and technology infrastructure, which is taken for granted in mature industrialized countries. Whether developing countries develop these infrastructure thresholds or not depends on the national systems of innovation and on the nature of the new waves of technology pervading the system, as was suggested by Freeman (2002). Finally, the challenge facing these countries lies in the different institutional conditions that are required and must be built. When other countries have already consolidated their industry leadership, a different capability building path is required for new countries wishing to achieve the same goals.

The strategic dimension of industrialization refers to the design and promotion of a endogenous nucleus (Fajnzylber, 1984). The identification of the productive activities that could act as sectoral axes of this process is one of the fundamental elements to consider. The actual international situation, despite being devastating and uncertain, appears to open a historical window of opportunity for Argentina in certain differentiated sectors at the productive level that rely on "partially common" scientific and technological bases associated to TICs and biotechnology, with strong potential for complementarity.

Between mid-2000s and 2015, Argentina introduced or reinforced a set of instruments and institutions aimed at generating opportunities and technological capabilities in the manufacturing industry (Abeles, et al, 2017). With the 2016 – 2019 political administration, industrial and technological policy entered in an impasse in the context of a lower institutional and budgetary hierarchy. Despite their financing difficulties, this set of institutions and instruments are an important starting point for an industrial and technological policy oriented towards a selected set of sectors that pivot from the knowledge bases of biotechnology and ICTs.

2.2.2 Globalization Challenges

The crisis of the 1970s gave rise to profound transformations in both the financial and productive sectors that led to what we know today as economic globalization. With the rise of neoliberalism, a process of liberalization began in the financial sphere that would deepen throughout the decade, first in the central countries and then spread to the rest of the world (Basualdo et. al., 2016). This process was reflected at the international level with the progressive dismantling of all obstacles and regulations to capital movements in line with the recommendations made by international financial institutions such as the IMF and the World Bank. Financial reforms were presented by these organizations as the indispensable way to eliminate existing imperfections in local markets and as the only way to obtain the necessary resources for countries to finance their economic development.

These changes in the financial sphere also have their analogous effect in the productive sphere, which can be seen by two profound transformations in the behavior of large industrial companies, which are closely linked to each other. First, there has been a growing process of internationalization of production processes in which large industrial companies gradually cease to operate with the logic of subsidiaries designed to supply local markets, and decided to start producing the components of their products where the cost of production is lower and assemble the goods in different places according to their different strategies. The second transformation is related to the fact that large industrial companies develop a new type of investment that rests on the articulation, at the global or regional level, of a network of contractors and subcontractors; and where there is a growing centralization of the administration of large firms that not only evaluates the possibilities of productive investments but also financial ones (Santarcángelo, 2019). This process was consolidated over the following decades, giving rise to an unprecedented phenomenon of productive, regional and global integration, in which the world's financial sectors are closely linked.

2.2.3 Epidemic Challenges

The Social Sciences Commission of the Coronavirus COVID-19 Unit (MINCYT-CONICET-AGENCIA) carried out a national survey in March 2020, in which more than 800 social researchers from all over the country collected information with key informants present in the most vulnerable territories and groups, and wrote reports based on a questionnaire and instructions designed by the members of the Commission. The organization of the survey had the support of the Council of Deans of Faculties of Social and Human Sciences (CODESOC), the National Association of Faculties of Humanities and Education (ANFHE), CONICET and the National Inter-university Council (CIN).

The first report submitted to the MINCYT and through him to the President of the Nation and the ministers was based on information provided by 1,487 territorial referents, who were consulted as key informants on the situations detected in their thematic areas and performance venues. Specifically, it indicates the difficulties faced by the population in complying with the preventive measures, the problems derived from their compliance, and the expectations regarding a possible extension of the pandemic. Likewise, it defines and analyzes critical problems in the COVID-19 policy that allow a comprehensive diagnosis of the current and future key issues that demand priority state intervention.

From both a social science and public health perspective, the most important social and political issue is the deepening of historical and structural inequalities and injustices. Furthermore, another key aspect is the health system: issues of social and regional inequalities, accessibility to prevention, care and treatment, production and provision of vaccines and drugs, as well as issues of governance and articulation at the local, provincial, national, regional and global levels.

3 New Topics in Social Sciences in Argentina

3.1 General axes of research on economy of industrial organization

3.1.1 Diagnosis and characterization of the world production and technological scenario

It includes the relationship between ICTs and Biotech. The relevance and pertinence of the concept of paradigm and its link with the long waves of capital accumulation.

An extensive literature has studied how technological revolutions have historically been associated with long cycles (or long waves) of accumulation processes (Kondratieff, 1925; Mandel, 1981). Even if there is an important debate regarding the possibilities of relaunching the world economy, on the analysis of continuities and discontinuities of the technological base of ICT, biotechnology and older paradigms, the identification of old and new key inputs and their localization, the creation/displacement/coexistence of infrastructures (such as 4G, 5G) and institutions supporting them, and notably the national location of leading actors, are at the core of the opportunities and challenges for Global South.

3.1.2 Science, technology and State

It refers to industrial / innovation policy approaches to structural change in semi-peripheral countries, challenges and constraints of the new global scenario.

Mobilizing these resources and capabilities is not an easy task. It requires a vision of industrial policy articulating the development of the scientific and technological system with the promotion of productive capacities in a common strategic nucleus. Public intervention should not be seen as an external factor resulting from the "good planner". Because actors are, at least in part, the result of the process of change itself, it is not possible to assume the existence of a bourgeoisie with a vocation for transformation or a developmental state. A project of this nature demands the definition of an endogenous nucleus as the mobilizing axis of existing resources and capacities and deliberate command over social groups with contradictory interests.

3.2 From biopharmaceuticals import substitution to (regional) exporter

The pandemic requires urgent responses to a multiplicity of

health demands, stressing out both scientific and technological policy and industrial policy. The development achieved in the last thirty years shows that the country has attained the minimal threshold of (bio) technological capabilities necessary to adopt a catching up strategy based on an imitative approach of biotech drugs (Lavarello, Gutman and Sztulwark, 2018). A small though relevant number of Argentinian companies have reached the capabilities required for the development of complex biotech active pharmaceutical ingredients (API), for therapeutic drug manufacturing (among them, monoclonal antibodies), and for DNA and RNA based vaccines, in close articulation with national scientific institutions, and with varying degrees of integration into international R&D and production networks.

The fact that Argentina has been chosen for its biotechnological capabilities to produce at the regional level the active substance developed by one of the five multinational companies that lead the competition for the COVID-19 vaccine is a good example of the internal potential that exists in this field. However, scalation towards the manufacturing phase (including fill and finish) collide with the restrictions that arise from the disarticulation between science and technology policies, on the one hand, and industrial policy, on the other hand. This situation shows the need to accelerate the generation of technological and productive capacities in these fields to move towards a greater integration of an industrial health complex at the national level; and to explore new paths of specialization looking towards the integration in the international market. This area of research opens a wide range of South-South collaboration opportunities with China and other countries (ex: LAC countries, India and Rusia) in areas such as scalation of therapeutical drugs and vaccines, and industrial projects looking for the convergence between biotech and 4.0 technologies.

3.3 Opportunities for insertion as a provider of agricultural biotechnology at a regional and global level

Argentina is a great adopter of the great innovations of global agrobiotechnology. From the rapid adoption of mostly imported technology packages (although with certain national capacities in the non-core segments of these new technologies), it built a strong capacity to produce primary goods or agricultural-based products with some degree of industrial transformation. Despite this nature of adopter and the distance with respect to the knowledge production systems of developed countries (Sztulwark and Girard, 2020), the country has a scientific base capable of producing biotechnological events of global relevance, including in the most disruptive segment associated with recent advances in gene editing. The country also has an expanded market (in the Mercosur area) to advance in a significant process of innovation substitution. But this innovative potential cannot be unfolded without an industrial policy that manages to deploy and orient the national-based entrepreneurial capacity towards the minimum productive threshold necessary to face the competition of the global giants in this sector.

Sharing the knowledge base with the applications of biotechnology in health, this sector shows great potential for an expanded internal market and for South-South technological collaboration with China. The presence in the country of one of the main Chinese players in the development of seeds and in the grain trade, accompanied by the need to promote new national public-private actors makes the study of the modalities of strategic alliances

South-South a main topic of interest for policy-oriented research.

3.4 Farm machinery as a diffusion vector of ICTs in agriculture

The agricultural machinery industry is among the industries with the greatest potential for spreading the so-called "Agriculture 4.0" internationally. At the moment, the diffusion of "Agriculture 4.0" is limited internationally, with greater adoption in the United States and Europe, and applications are expected to grow rapidly in other countries such as China. One of the main challenges for its dissemination is the development of communication networks and the adoption of standards that ensure interoperability, compatibility and communication between devices.

This scenario finds Argentina at crucial moment for the positioning of the local industry. This industry has been historically characterized by metalworking technological trajectories with potential to compete internationally in various niches (Lavarello and Goldstein, 2011). This potential of international insertion as a regional (or global) producer has not been achieved yet and the industry suffers a persistent trade deficit. At the same time, China is advancing in a strategy of articulation of its telecommunications companies and the agro-industrial chains. These initiatives are accompanied by support for the accelerated generation of "Industry 4.0" capabilities in companies, through the creation of start-ups in "Agriculture 4.0".

There are several areas of common research in this subject. In particular, the analysis of the coexistence of 5G and other communication networks in agriculture; the possibility of South-South technology transfer between both countries and a shared strategy in the adoption of electronic interoperability standards between machines and implements (eg: ISOBUS).

3.5 Human and social dimension of climate change, environmental protection, sustainable development and natural resources

Climate change, environmental protection and sustainable development are topics closely intertwined in a global context of environmental change that challenges the future of different countries and regions in the world (Lorenzo, 2020). Climate change is one of the biggest challenges of our times, evidenced through the nexus between climate science, politics and economics. In the context of the United Nations Framework Convention on Climate Change (UNFCCC) and the Paris Agreement, we seek common views and long-term cooperation in policies regarding mitigation, adaptation, financing, technology and capacity building, as well as the dynamics of participation in groups of negotiation (Klöck, 2020; Bueno Rubial, Siegele, 2020). This interest is accentuated by the climate emergency, as well as by the need to guarantee that all the elements of the Paris Agreement are equitably represented in the Global Stocktake (Winkler, 2020). At the same time, this cooperation can be strengthened in the G20, aspiring to greater ambition and climate leadership from our countries in this area (Hughes, de Jong, Thorne, 2020). The legacy of the Argentine Presidency in terms of adaptation can be strengthened through permanent work programs that link the research-policy interface. It is also of interest to develop more comparative studies on climate mitigation and adaptation policies at the national and subnational level.

Climate change, environmental protection and the rational use of natural resources can be examined in the Last Continent, where the human footprint has extensively affected different biodiversity areas (Leihy et al., 2020) and raises concerns about the role of this region for the global ecosystem. Because of the latter, an increase in Antarctic cooperation is key to strengthen the resilience of the Antarctic Treaty System, in which Argentina and China are active members. Over the last decades, new challenges and dilemmas emerged. More specifically, the impacts of climate change on the Antarctic is by far one of the major concerns, evidenced through the accelerated Antarctic ice sheet loss, as well as changes in the temperature and precipitations (Chown & Brooks, 2019). It is also worth addressing challenges related to the conservation of Antarctic marine living resources, protected areas in the Antarctic, as well as the implications of COVID-19, paying special attention to the short and long term impacts on science, decision-making and commercial activities in the region. Although the Antarctic Region has been mainly studied by scientists with backgrounds in different natural sciences, it offers a unique opportunity for conducting research in Social Sciences (Chaturvedi, 2016).

4 Viability of Argentine-Chinese cooperation in social sciences

The path followed by all peripheral countries was not the same in the last fifty years. On the one hand, we have the case of Southeast Asia and China, which, based on a strong intervention of the state as the driver of the development process, with strong participation and decision-making capacity in key sectors and underpinned by a very successful process of science and technology generation, managed to consolidate highly virtuous development models that have led China to occupy an elite position among the world's countries.

On the other hand, most Latin American countries abandoned their import substitution industrialization model and began to apply neoliberal policies in the mid-1970s. Initially under the rule of military dictatorships, these same policies were later consolidated by democratic governments that deepened the path of economic liberalization, market deregulation and privatization, which led to deep economic and social crises at the beginning of the 21st century. The reversal of the manufacturing matrix destroyed the capacity to add value and deepened the process of productive specialization based on natural resources. This resulted in a weak accumulation nucleus, increasingly transnationalized and subordinated to external demand, with scarce capacity to retain the surplus in national spaces and in their producing territories.

This different development strategy on the part of these two regions has had several consequences, and among the most important is their differential participation in global value chains (GVCs). While the participation of Latin America and Argentina in particular is absolutely marginal, China's participation is enormously significant and in several of them they have a strong participation and even govern them. This created a great window of opportunity for Argentina, given the strong complementarity between both economies. The bilateral exchange between Argentina and China grew from USD 3.2 billion in 2003 to USD 15.5 billion in 2019. Although Argentina's trade deficit with China grew steadily since 2008, in 2019 the sharp increase of exports reduced the deficit to USD 2.9 billion (the lowest since 2010). Exports reached a historical record of USD 6.4 billion, representing a 64% increase compared to 2018 (UN Comtrade, 2021).

Regarding the composition, the productive complementarity favored the deepening of the exchanges, generating an inter-industrial trade (industrial manufactures for primary products and derivatives). In this configuration, Argentine exports to China are concentrated in soybeans, frozen beef, seafood, poultry, soybean oil and peanut oil, which accounted for 64 percent of the total sold to this partner in 2019. In 2020, bovine meat became the main export product, surpassing soybeans, as a result of the agreements signed in 2018.

The financial instruments that China deploys in Argentina are multiple. Regarding loans, between 2007 and 2018 the approximate amount agreed by Argentina with China in this concept amounts to 16.9 billion dollars (Gallagher and Myers, 2019). Some of the committed projects are: (1) the development of the solar plant in Cauchari (Jujuy province) with a participation of Chinese capital for 331 million dollars (operated by China Exim Bank) agreed in 2017; (2) the modernization of the Argentine railway system, through agreements agreed in 2010, 2014 and 2018 for a total of 13.2 billion dollars (Gallagher and Myers, 2019); and (3) the construction of the "Condor Cliff" and "La Barrancosa" hydroelectric plants in the province of Santa Cruz for an estimated amount of 4.7 billion dollars by China Development Bank (CDB), Industrial and Commercial Bank Corporation (ICBC) and Bank of China (Rius, 2017; Marchio, 2019).

The strengthening of China's investments in infrastructure from projects that contemplate spatial articulations and connectivity between Latin America and China, would allow strengthening the scope of South-South economic relations in line with the re-profiling that is taking place on the global geoeconomic and geopolitical scene.

The link between Social Sciences in Argentina and their Chinese peers is a unique opportunity to reflect on the epistemological and geopolitical postulates involved in the global and national production and legitimization of social knowledge. In particular, Argentine social sciences need access to the diverse Chinese thought in social sciences without the epistemological and theoretical mediations of the European and Anglo-Saxon academies. Deeper relations between Argentina / Latin America and China in the field of Social Sciences will help decentralize the epistemological positions from where the so-called global processes are thought, identified and conceptualized.

We believe that an intercultural dialogue enables the production of plural epistemologies nourished by multiple sources of knowledge. This implies moving from a subject-object epistemology to a subject-subject epistemology where both researchers and studied groups produce situated, related and historicized knowledge. This epistemology is based on a known subject that recognizes the other as equal when it comes to producing ideas and concepts about the social world, thus assessing the identical ability to know possessed by different people of and in cognitive interaction.

Hence, we conceive the production of knowledge about social life as a co-production between academic research and the reflexivity of the social actors themselves. We think that there is a complementarity, although not devoid of tensions and negotiations, between the ways in which scientific knowledge is created in universities and academic centres and the ways common sense and people's beliefs are created in society.

5 Orientation and selection of topics for Argentine-Chinese cooperation in social sciences

To strengthen the academic and scientific links between Argentina and China in the area of social sciences, it is key to promote mobility of students, teachers and researchers between both countries. Scientific and academic mobility facilitates intercultural knowledge and allows building bonds of friendship and mutual trust that are instrumental in building lasting social and institutional ties. We propose different modes for exchange and joint work between Argentina and China.

5.1 Study and research

Study and research stays lasting from six months to one year in Argentine and Chinese universities and research centres to attend courses, carry out empirical and bibliographic research, participate in research projects, deliver lectures & courses and mentor undergraduate and postgraduate students. Stays may include Spanish and Chinese language courses in each country.

5.2 "Summer schools"

It provides an introduction to Argentine and Latin American social sciences for Chinese students, teachers and researchers (organized by MinCyT/CONICET) in Argentina, and "summer schools" in China for Argentine and Latin American students, teachers and researchers on topics relevant to both countries/regions.

5.3 "Permanent Observatory of Latin American-Chinese Relations"

It made up of Argentine and Chinese researchers and teachers in coordination with other government agencies. This "think-tank" was created to produce relevant knowledge for the academic agenda and the design of public policies on issues related to Argentine/Latin American and Chinese relations.

5.4 Joint and comparative research project on common topics

(1) Argentina and Latin America under the rise of China and the Belt and Road Initiative: Challenges and proposals for a constructive integration.

- Analyze the integration strategy that both countries have had in the GVCs and the role that the state has played (not only through state-owned companies) for the achieved integration.
- Explore, identify and develop policy suggestions for the promotion of specific productive sectors in different territories in Argentina in order to achieve a virtuous integration.
- Industrialization process, techno-economic paradigm and endogenous nucleus: Moving towards High-quality Development in Argentina.

(2) Development and mutual learning between Argentina and China.

- Explore conditions, capabilities and potentials in Argentina for investments in sectors linked to renewable energy, telecommunications, R&D, and also in productive sectors with strong impact in export growth and job creation. In order to obtain a comprehensive picture of Chinese investments, this axis also proposes to survey, systematize and map all investments in Argentina, by sector and province, and by enterprise.
- Examine China's promotion and integration strategy in the sectors of renewable energy, telecommunications, and R&D in order to obtain viable development strategies and possible dynamics of interaction between both countries.
- Identify and analyze productive sectors promotion and

territorial development policies in China as a mechanism for sharing experiences and enhancing mutual knowledge.

(3) Argentine-Chinese cooperation on climate and environment.

- Climate change multilateral cooperation: UNFCCC and the Paris Agreement national contributions, long-term goals and cycles of ambition. G20 leadership in climate action. Action and means of implementation in the negotiation processes, including groupings and alliances.

- Climate change policies: pathways and scenarios of transition, in particular through renewable energies. Adaptation related policies: communities and ecosystem-based adaptation; national, subnational and regional National Adaptation Programs (NAPs). Gender considerations in NAPs. Monitoring, evaluation and learning (MEL) systems. Climate considerations in financial systems.

- International tourism relations: International tourism policies (bilateral, regional, international organizations). Exchanges related to tourism: social (tourists), cultural-symbolic (soft power and country brand strategies), environmental (climate change), health (COVID-19).

- Antarctic governance: protection of Antarctic marine living resources. Implications of the COVID-19 for Antarctic environmental protection and conservation. Tourism in Antarctica. Implications of climate change for Antarctica.

(4) Argentine-Chinese cooperation on social studies.

Academic institutions in general, and the Social Sciences in particular, have to take the responsibility of studying and reflecting upon the experiences of our two countries, thus contributing with informed recommendations for understanding and managing contemporary social issues, such as new mobility and circulation of human beings, environmental challenges, new forms of social and affective relations, new cultural consumptions and the development of tourism as novel aspects in the intercultural dialogues in the new era. We understand that these issues deserve to be thoroughly researched in order to understand the development of contemporary societies and their mutual relations. Therefore, we consider it imperative to carry on comparative studies on these topics and share our research with our distinguished colleagues in China: Migration processes and migrant identities; New configurations of family, gender and family roles; Women's role in politics, business, the State, family care. Strategies and policies for the inclusion of women and trans people; Beliefs, religions and their social role: social assistance and volunteer work, inter-religious dialogues, values and propositions for the State; Intercultural dialogues and practices: foreign language learning, Chinese martial arts in China and Argentina, dance (tango in China), traditional foods and local fusions; Cultural industries and tourism as areas for economic development in their relations with new consumption practices and circulation platforms.

Taking into consideration the dimensions of the multiple inequalities involved (economic, environmental, cultural and sociopolitical), and the social categories among which COVID-19 is having a deepening effect (class, gender, age, ethnicity, citizenship, religion), research should focus on the following aspects. Impact of the pandemic on social inequalities; Demographic challenges; Impact of the pandemic on the organization of the health systems; Impact of the pandemic on care beliefs and practices, including care economy: family, social policy, market forces and community solidarity, employment and work; Impact of the pandemic on affective relationships; Economic hardship and inequalities; Gender relations, including gender violence; Impact of the pandemic on the digital economy (e-commerce, digital money, electronic means of payment, digital currencies) and virtual-work / virtual-medicine; Impact of the pandemic on the uses of urban space: transformations of movements and flows; Impact on cities and migration.

Argentina and Latin America under the Rise of China and the Belt and Road Initiative: Challenges and Proposals for a Constructive Integration[*]

1 The Crisis of Hegemony, the Rise of China, and the Multipolar Project of Global Articulation under the Belt and Road Initiative

The COVID-19 pandemic accelerated a set of trends in the contemporary global historical-spatial transition, setting a new moment of change and reconfiguration of the international relations that were already underway. Among these transitions, it is worth mentioning both the relative rise of China and the Asia Pacific and the relative decline of the US and the West; the increase of political-strategic contradictions that fuel already existing conflicts over

---

[*] The researchers of Argentine experts team are Victor Ramiro Fernandez, Independent Researcher of the National Scientific and Technical Research Council of Argentina (CONICET) & Professor of the National University of the Litoral; Juliana Gonzalez Jauregui, Researcher of the Latin American Faculty of Social Sciences (Facultad Latinoamericana de Ciencias Sociales, FLACSO); Gabriel Merino, Researcher of the National Scientific and Technical Research Council of Argentina (CONICET) & Professor of the National University of La Plata.

multiple fronts and territories, threatening global stability; the crisis of the US hegemony and its consequent "global disorder"; the economic crisis, characterized by structural features, but with particular consequences for core parts of the global capitalism and its areas of influence, and expressed in the exacerbated financing process; the transformations of articulated production relations to a new technological paradigm; and important dilemmas regarding the strategic paths that Global South countries have to design if they aim to move forward to development.

The dynamic global accumulation center has moved from the West to the Asia Pacific, producing a geo-economic transformation with China as the main driving force. In contrast to the Global North, China recorded economic growth rates that averaged 10% annually between 1978 and 2010 and, since then, ranged from 6% to 7% annually, to 2019. In 2020, as a result of the global crisis of the COVID-19 pandemic, China grew by only 2.3%, but at the same time, China was the only large economy in the world that recorded positive rates.

China has acquired a central role in global trade, investment, and financing. In 2013, it became the largest exporting country, while in 2014, it surpassed the US as the largest state economy measured in GDP at PPP (which has not happened since 1872). In 2020, it became the European Union's main trading partner rather than the US. At the same time, since 2011 it has positioned itself as the world's leading importer of goods and, in that context, as the world's first global consumer of energy, various minerals, and foodstuffs.

Regarding investment flows, it is the first recipient and the second issuer on a global scale, with a cumulative stock of foreign investment exceeding USD 900 billion, and an increasingly relevant role in developing countries. Its efforts to respond to the 2008 – 2009 international financial crisis, along with associated industrial policies, led to a credit boom, which drove an even more significant positioning of Chinese products in the international markets. In 2009, China turned from net debtor to net creditor; financing for development took a central role within its national modernization goals.

Moreover, in 2019 Chinese industrial GDP was USD 4 trillion (28.4%), equal to the sum of the US, Germany, and Japan. But China is no longer just the world's largest factory as a Global North industrial semi-periphery, as it now competes in design, high finance, state-of-the-art technology, and strategic management functions. In this sense, it has emerged as the main country in patent applications, leads some cutting-edge technologies of the so-called "Fourth Industrial Revolution" and is ahead together with other Asian Pacific countries in the energy transition.

The ascent of China and the Asia Pacific region in the global sphere, or the re-emergence and strengthening of other power poles, reflects a critical change in the world power map and progress towards a multipolar reality. New dilemmas and opportunities arise in the semi-peripheries and peripheries that are part of the Global South. Thus, new initiatives emerge to democratize the access to wealth and the participation in global decisions, as well as new proposals, arise for the articulation of national and regional development, disputing the center-periphery relations established among the Global North and the Global South, the traditional hierarchies of the interstate system, and the economic dynamics based on an unequal international division of labor.

As a result of crystallized unipolar neoliberal globalization in the framework of the Washington Consensus and the financing of capitalism that affects both the production and labor sectors, and the civilizing dilemmas posed by dominant development models, other visions, and forms of globalization are emerging. There is a growing demand to reform the existing multilateral institutions, jointly with the creation of new regional and global multilateral institutions, that express these new realities of the southern countries, such as BRICS and its NDB, the SCO, UNASUR, etc. Among them, for its scale and characteristics, China's Belt and Road Initiative (BRI) stands out. BRI was launched in 2013 by Beijing, with the support of Russia, Central Asian countries, and other Eurasian countries; progressively, states from different regions of the world joined the initiative. At present, it includes more than 70 countries, representing more than 4,000 million inhabitants, 75% of the world's known energy reserves, and more than 55% of the world's GDP at PPA.

To understand the context of the hegemonic transition of global power, it is worth considering the long-term vision that defines Chinese policies, and the process initiated since the 1949 revolution that ended neocolonial dominance by the great powers. The current goal of achieving the "Chinese Dream", i.e., "the return to historical normality", is based on the aim of regaining a central place in the international system—China's position in the global economy and civilization until the 18th century—and, thus, become a leader in globalization, technological change, and the knowledge society by 2049. These objectives were defined at the 18th National Congress of the Chinese Communist Party and coincide with the 2009 – 2011 turn in its domestic and foreign policy after the 2008 – 2009 international financial crisis, which erupted into the Global North. Since its foundation, the PRC has pursued a divergent development path that differs from those historically followed by other powers, founded on "socialism with Chinese characteristics" as a specific mode of production.

The BRI is part of those broad objectives and gave renewed impetus to the "Going Out" policy. These policies are not only central to the national socialist modernization strategy and its consequent projection abroad but are relevant axes when analyzing China's link with Latin American countries. In contrast to the paths taken by China and the Asia Pacific, Latin America (LA) under the rule of the Washington Consensus suffered a significant relative set back since the late 1970s, a major peripheralization process that was difficult to reverse despite changes at the beginning of the 21st century.

2 Latin America and Argentina's Relations with China, and the Extension of the BRI to the Region

In LA, 21 countries① have already joined the BRI. This advance in levels of associativity and cooperation is in tune with China's growing relevance in the region. The volume of trade between China and LA rose from USD 17 billion in 2002 to USD 315 billion in 2019; estimations calculate that bilateral trade could reach USD 500 billion by 2025. In this framework, it is worth noting that China has become South America's leading trading partner.

Furthermore, LA became a major recipient of Chinese Foreign Direct Investment (FDI): between 2005 and 2019, Chinese FDI in

---

① In South America: Uruguay, Ecuador, Venezuela, Chile, Bolivia, Peru and Argentina.

LA accounted for USD 130 billion, that is to say nearly USD 10 billion annually. During the first ministerial meeting of the China-CELAC Forum, held in 2015 in Beijing, President Xi announced that from 2015 to 2025, Chinese companies would invest USD 250 billion in LA. As a result, the relative weighted share of Chinese investment as part of regional FDI went from 1.67% in 2003 to 6.30% in 2017.

In recent years, mergers and acquisitions (M&A) became the world's leading Chinese FDI channel; LA is far from an exception: it represented, before 2020, 62% of flows, and the countries with the largest participation in South America have been Argentina and Brazil, while Chile and Peru are becoming increasingly important. In 2020, M&A by Chinese companies worldwide recorded their fourth consecutive annual decline, which deepened with the pandemic. In the case of LA, not only did it not decrease but recovered from previous periods, surpassing those provided to Europe and North America, combined.

Chinese FDI in LA is distributed in various sectors, though those considered as strategic—infrastructure, energy, and raw materials extraction—stand out. Among these projects, there are large infrastructure projects which are core in terms of LA countries aim to move forward development and emulate those carried out in other regions within the framework of BRI, such as bridges, roads, tunnels, electric transmission networks, renewable energy parks, pipelines, dams, nuclear power plants, transcontinental railways, and even an inter-oceanic channel.

China's growing role in the region is also notable with the provision of loans to LA countries; this financing surpasses those granted during the last decade by the World Bank and the Inter-American Development Bank, combined. Since 2005, two policy banks, the China Development Bank (CDB) and the China Export-Import Bank (CHEXIM), have lent to countries in the region amounts that exceed USD 140 billion. Unlike other global financing providers, Chinese loans initially do not require macroeconomic conditionality clauses. Moreover, since 2009, the Chinese Central Bank has implemented an active swap-giving policy with the objective of both promoting the internationalization of the renminbi, and enhancing China's financial power.

Regarding China and LA relations, it is also worth mentioning the support given to the cooperation with the Community of Latin American and the Caribbean States (CELAC). While Chinese President Xi Jinping first expressed on his visit to Chile, Ecuador, and Peru in 2016, China's intention to integrate Latin American countries into the BRI. In 2017, LA was declared as a "natural extension" of the Initiative, specifically of the "21st Maritime Silk Road" by President Xi Jinping. However, CELAC, created in 2010 as part of the advancement of autonomist regionalism in Latin America, within the context of a shift towards South-South ties, lost relevance in recent years, highlighting the setbacks in terms of regional integration. At times, it appears to be China that is interested in linking with the region through CELAC and strengthening the institution, rather than the countries of the region themselves. Similarly, it should be noted that China has designed a strategy of engagement to LA, materialized in different ways of rapprochement during more than two decades. Indeed, it not only established both bilateral and regional strategic partnerships, and comprehensive strategic partnerships, with the countries of the region and CELAC, respectively, but also increased its high-level visits. Also, it signed Free Trade Agreements with Chile, Peru, and Costa Rica, and

Bilateral Investment Treaties with several countries in the region. Besides, it expanded its participation in regional and multilateral institutions, issued two "Policy Papers on Latin America", and created specific plans to promote the creation and deepening of a common agenda. By contrast, the region still lacks a joint strategy that addresses and plans its ties with China in the medium and long term.

In this sense, the problems of Latin America regional integration are a core obstacle to improving its countries' international insertion, strengthening their voice against other powers, reducing existing asymmetries, and achieving greater degrees of relative autonomy. Also, the fragmentation of LA in terms of regionalism restricts the advancement of development projects consistent with regional needs, as well as the building of the necessary scales to make production more complex, and the expansion of strategic state capabilities.

Concerning China and Argentina's economic relations, bilateral trade increased from USD 2 billion in 2000 to USD 16.3 billion in 2019, where Argentinean exports accounted for USD 7 billion and imports for USD 9 billion. China is Argentina's second trading partner after Brazil; in fact, it became its first trading partner during the most critical moments of the pandemic in 2020, while the trade between MERCOSUR partners fell, reflecting a process of deindustrialization and primary-export specialization of both South American countries in recent years. It is noteworthy that Argentina's trade balance with China registers a deficit since 2008, which fell considerably in 2019 but increased again in 2020, becoming the largest compared to those with other countries and regional blocs.

As for Chinese FDI in Argentina, those conducted in the soya complex cover all stages of the production chain. China's investment in the country also comprises the financial sector, the meat industry, the automotive sector, retail, fisheries, and telecommunications. Furthermore, Chinese companies invested in economic sectors considered strategic such as oil and natural gas, mining (copper and lithium, among other relevant minerals), logistics and transport infrastructure, and wind, hydroelectric and solar energies, while an agreement was signed for the construction of the fourth nuclear power plant in the country. A medium-term investment plan, amounting to approximately USD 30 billion, is currently being negotiated. In line with this, between 2020 and 2021, Argentina has signed several investment agreements with China in energy and transport infrastructure that emulate the projects that characterize the BRI.

Concerning financing, Argentina has received loans from the BDC, the CHEXIM, and the ICBC. These financing agreements mainly cover transport and logistics infrastructure projects and the energy sector. Besides, Argentina is an extra-regional member of the Asian Infrastructure Investment Bank and has signed several currency exchange agreements with China from 2009 onwards.

It should also be noted that Argentina and China became "strategic" partners in 2004, and turned into "comprehensive strategic" partners in 2014. Thus, the deepening of bilateral ties and its implications for Argentina's development model and its international insertion must be analyzed. From the perspective of South-South cooperation in a multipolar world and the win-win logic, Argentina's imminent accession to the BRI must consider certain prior objectives to reduce existing asymmetries, reverse the processes of "primarization" of the productive matrix, establish mutually beneficial economic exchanges.

3 The New Global Order and China's Belt and Road Initiative: Challenges for a Win-win Integration

The integration of Argentina and Latin America into the BRI and, in general, China's intention to further deepen its ties with LA and Argentina, faces the challenge of being part of a shift in the patterns of integration that characterized this scenario since the formation of its national states and the deployment of British hegemony first and the more recently US hegemony. This requires both at the academic level and in the public policies field to orient actions that from the Argentinean / Latin American point of view.

First, an integration from autonomy: this is an aspect with a long tradition in Latin American thought and represents an essential part for a process of coupling with feedback to the Asian stage and to that of China in particular. Among the multiple issues that it reaches, the most relevant is the formation of an endogenous and dynamic accumulation nucleus with macro-regional scope.

Second, integration from the strengthening of the own macro-regional integrations. The construction of this autonomy requires a macro-regional integration process, which includes the Latin American region as a whole and is not limited to an agreement for the exchange of investment and trade flows but has the challenge of building this accumulation pattern whose main vector is the integration of its (macro) regional productive chains. Likewise, this vector has two interrelated subvectors: the development of a joint process of industrialization and technological development to strengthen and qualify the global value chains.

Third, integration with/through industrialization: the first of these mentioned sub-vectors is represented by the industrialization process. Also being a neuralgic part of the structuralist thought of

Latin American development, it forms an inescapable pillar of all the dynamic centers that have been emerging and consolidating for the deployment of non-subaltern and "primarizing" patterns of accumulation that have been prevalent in the Global South international integration. This being a central aspect, its truncated character in LA and Argentina since the mid-1970s and particularly since the Washington Consensus, demands to regenerate an industrial strategy compatible with the new conditions of production and realization. This includes multiple offshoring processes and combined dynamics of decomposition and decentralization in multi-localized productive chains as well as the assimilation and autonomous generation of new technologies that enable upgrades in global chains.

Fourth, integration with technological development and strategic control of the industrialization process: under these new reproductive conditions, a more autonomous and globally and regional integrated industrialization that structures accumulation nucleus and its dynamics, demands the deployment, in strategic sectors, of coordinated learning and innovation processes (including industrialization of the primary sector).

Fifth, macro integration from federal/local/sub-regional integration. The macro-regional integration process as a condition for a feedback integration with China under the BRI, additionally requires the deployment of these combined processes of industrialization and learning, within the framework of decentralized productive networks in the whole of the national territory. Overcoming regional imbalances and integrating sub-national spaces into macro-regional linkages is a fundamental requirement so that the interrelationships within the Belt and Road do not become a consolidation of spatial imbalances and favor a nationally coordinated multi-scalar developmental process in which subnational spaces—particularly those peripheral ones—become protagonists.

Sixth, integration from/with the capacities of the State and the direction of the State: all the afore-mentioned aspects become viable to the extent that a process of state construction takes place aimed at reversing the structural weaknesses. That has affected both their infrastructural capacity to achieve a deeper and more coordinated socio-spatial penetration, as well as their managerial skills to condition and guide investment and learning processes. Macro-regional integration processes such as the BRI demand progress in the construction of state capacities that, overcoming these weaknesses, manages to develop an adequate scalar articulation (national, local regional) and from the functional point of view, control the progress of their currencies and the financial system to guide them to strengthen their strategic productive and technological processes.

By assuming the individual and articulated relevance of each of the six previous items for a successful China / Argentina / Latin America integration strategy, their inclusion within a complementary research agenda acquires a strategic character. This agenda could be relevant to provide inputs for policies and actions that allow LA / Argentina to develop those processes that Asia in general and China, in particular, are progressively leading, that is macro-regional integration, industrialization, development of knowledge and learning, scalar articulation and development of state capacities.

王镭，中国社会科学院国际合作局局长。于荷兰社会科学研究院（ISS）获公共政策与管理学硕士学位、中国社会科学院研究生院获经济学博士学位。现为中国人民对外友好协会理事、中国欧洲学会理事、中国社会科学院丝绸之路研究院执行院长。曾在荷兰蒂尔堡大学法律系、比利时鲁汶大学欧洲税收学院从事欧洲经济一体化背景下的欧洲税收协调、WTO税收相关规则的研究。研究领域涉及投资、贸易、税收问题。

Wang Lei is the Director-General of the Bureau of International Cooperation of the Chinese Academy of Social Sciences (CASS). He obtained his M. A. degree in Public Policy and Administration at the Netherlands Institute of Social Studies, and Ph. D. degree in Economics at the Graduate School of the Chinese Academy of Social Sciences. He is a Board Member of the Chinese Association of Friendship with Foreign Countries and a Board Member of the Chinese Association of European Studies as well as the Executive Director of the Silk Road Academy, CASS. He conducted research on European tax coordination in the context of European economic integration and the tax-related rules of WTO in the Faculty of Law under the Tilburg University of the Netherlands and in the European Tax College under the Leuven University of Belgium. The focus of his research is on China's external economic relations covering issues of investment, trade and taxation.